LIEDER

By the same author

DIETRICH FISCHER-DIESKAU: MASTERSINGER

THE THEATRE OF FRIEDRICH DÜRRENMATT

ZUSAMMEN (WITH J. MARJORY WHITTON)

SCHUBERT: A BIOGRAPHICAL STUDY OF HIS SONGS
(BY DIETRICH FISCHER-DIESKAU;
EDITED AND TRANSLATED BY KENNETH WHITTON)

LIEDER

An Introduction to German Song

Kenneth Whitton

FOREWORD BY DIETRICH FISCHER-DIESKAU

Julia MacRae

A DIVISION OF FRANKLIN WATTS

Copyright © 1984 Kenneth Whitton
All rights reserved
First published in Great Britain 1984 by
Julia MacRae Books
A division of Franklin Watts
12a Golden Square, London W1R 4BA
and in the United States of America by Franklin Watts Inc.
387 Park Avenue, New York 10016, N.Y.
and Franklin Watts, Australia
1 Campbell Street, Artarmon, N.S.W. 2064
Designed by Douglas Martin
Printed and bound in Great Britain by
Garden City Press, Letchworth

British Library Cataloguing in Publication Data
Whitton, Kenneth
Lieder
1. Songs, German – History and criticism.
I. Title
784.3'06   ML276.1
ISBN 0-86203-122-2 UK edition
ISBN 0-531-09759-5 US edition
Library of Congress Catalog Card No: 84–50908

FOR MARJORY, KIRSTY AND KENNETH

'If music and sweet poetry agree . . .'
(Richard Barnfield, 1574–1627)

CONTENTS

PART FOUR

LIEDER ON RECORD

APPENDICES

FOREWORD

THROUGHOUT his professional career, Kenneth S. Whitton has worked intensively on the literature of the German-speaking peoples and on the art of the German Lied. He is also a distinguished author. What better qualifications could one have for writing on that musical genre which, outside the German-speaking countries, is still neither fully known nor fully appreciated? This sublime congruity of poetry and music, which grants both elements equal rights and the same formative power, could only arise, flourish – and fade – in a particular place and at a particular time. The author's concern has been to explain this process and, in so doing, to acquaint the reader with a variety of little-known details.

This book by an expert on the subject is most warmly recommended to all those who treasure the German solo song with accompaniment as one of the germ cells of European music. It embraces its theme in a thorough and scholarly fashion, opening up new ways of understanding and appreciating the German Lied.

I wish the book a successful journey. There is not only a good deal of learning in it; one is also aware everywhere of enthusiasm and love.

DIETRICH FISCHER-DIESKAU, Berlin, August 1982

INTRODUCTION

WHETHER it comes from Bach or The Beatles, the international appeal of music is undeniable. Beethoven's Fifth Symphony, Tchaikovsky's First Piano Concerto, Chopin's Etudes and the great Verdi operas, or the music of George Gershwin, Cole Porter, Sammy Cahn or Stephen Sondheim can be heard daily from New York to Tokyo on radio and cassette, television or record.

The well-known symphonies, the popular works for piano and violin, the beloved operas, take the lion's share of the public interest, of course; but there are also many 'minor' roads which run alongside the great motorways of music and which are well worth a détour from time to time.

This book describes some of the pleasures to be found on one such détour: the world of the German Lied is not so strange or esoteric as some might think. These songs were composed, after all, by those same composers who wrote the symphonies and concertos: Mozart, Beethoven, Schubert, Schumann, Brahms, and many of the tunes are indeed already as well-known and well-loved as those from the better-known works: Schubert's 'Serenade' and 'Ave Maria', Mendelssohn's 'On Wings of Song' and Brahms' 'Cradle Song' are all 'Lieder' – even although they are now heard played on every imaginable combination of instruments from tea-shop quartets to brass bands.

I have tried to describe the paths that this art-form has taken, to suggest ways and means of becoming acquainted with the many less well-known, but still very beautiful songs and, above all, of overcoming the seeming barrier of the German language. The book is the result of many years' work with groups of all sorts: school, university, adult, who have convinced me of the joys to be gained by the non-specialist from these songs. I would like to thank them for the encouragement that I have received from them over these many years.

I would like to thank also the great Lieder singer Dietrich Fischer-Dieskau, for having given me so many insights into the performance of Lieder, and for his generous Foreword; Mr Derek Bell, the Music

Librarian of the City of Bradford Library, for his assistance with the music examples, and Julia MacRae, for having commissioned the work out of her own deep interest in German Lieder.

If the very last word of thanks goes to my wife, it is because her perceptive awareness of the German language and of German poetry has supported my own researches over so many years. Without her, there would have been no book; truly, 'Wir wandelten, wir zwei zusammen . . .'

KENNETH S. WHITTON

PART ONE

The Development of the German Lied

[1] DEFINITIONS

WHY LIEDER? To the German man-in-the-street, the words 'Die Lieder' are simply the plural form of the neuter noun 'Das Lied', the song, any type of musical form with words, although Mendelssohn certainly, and other composers, wrote countless *Lieder ohne Worte* (songs without words) while the famous German poet, Heinrich Heine, called a volume of his poems *Buch der Lieder* (book of songs).

In Anglo-Saxon countries, however, Lieder is a word taken over from the German language to describe a particular art-form which is the subject of this book. There are many such words in the English and American languages, taken over from other languages because they describe objects, peoples, states of mind and so on which we feel are peculiar to the area or country to which they belong. From French we have: a gaffe, a cri de coeur, a croissant; from German: Angst, the blitz, a rucksack, and from Italian: pizza, pistachio and of course all the musical terms, sonata, mezza voce, fortissimo, etc. Some of these can be translated, of course, but there is general agreement that they are *sui generis*. So too then with Lieder. It has become recognized that Lieder form a specific German art-form or genre, performed with its own particular mystique and celebrants. Lieder singers give *Liederabende*, evenings of Lieder, by different composers or sometimes by the same composer, as we shall see. It is by the way not 'Teutonic pedantry' to insist on spelling the word with a capital letter, since *all* German nouns commence with a capital.

What then *is* a Lied? Generalized definitions are always dangerous, but perhaps we might hazard the following: 'A Lied – or perhaps more accurately a *Kunstlied*, literally an "art-song" – is the musical setting of an original poem written in German'. The important point is that the poem existed *before* the music, a very important point, since I shall be demonstrating later how essential it is for both performer and audience to appreciate the full meaning of the poem in order that the performer might interpret, and the audience might understand the Lied to the full so that both might receive the deepest artistic experience possible.

3

A Lied is therefore not 'a song', or at any rate not *just* a song, but something more. Of course, many composers have written music to existing words – one thinks of the operatic composers who have written music to *libretti* (in Italian, books of words), supplied by their 'librettists', Sonnleithner for Beethoven (*Fidelio*), Boito for Verdi (*Falstaff* and *Otello*) with some help from Shakespeare, Hugo von Hofmannsthal for Richard Strauss, and there have been composers since the earliest times who have set poems to music. Some of these solo 'songs' had their own specialized, technical names: 'ayres' or 'songes' in John Dowland's 16th and 17th century England, or 'arie antiche' in the 17th century Italy of Caccini, Carissimi or Scarlatti, or the 'chansons' and 'mélodies' in the 19th and 20th century France of Fauré and Debussy.

But the German word *Lied* has been retained for that subtle psychological blend of word *and* music seen at its finest distillation in the music of the Austrian composer Franz Schubert (1797–1828), many of whose over six hundred extant Lieder form the major part of Lieder recitals all over the world. Schubert's Lieder ushered in the Golden Age of the Lied which effectively spanned the 19th century and came to an end with another Viennese composer, Hugo Wolf (1860–1903).

Many writers, singers and others have tried to encapsulate the genius of the Lied in words. The pre-war soprano Lotte Lehmann (who died, however, only in 1976) in her book *Eighteen Song Cycles* counselled budding Lieder singers thus:

> First there was the poem. That gave the inspiration for the song. Like a frame, music encloses the word picture – and now comes your interpretation, breathing life into this work of art, welding words and music with equal feeling into one whole, so that the poet sings and the composer becomes poet and two arts are born anew as one.

That is maybe a rather romantic, 'artistic' view of what a Lied is; the German philosopher G.W.F. Hegel (1770–1831) devoted quite a few pages of his Berlin *Lectures on Fine Art* to the Lied, and it is possible that no one has defined it better, since Hegel wrote that it was harmful 'to think that the nature of the text is of no importance to the composition.' 'Nothing musically excellent', he went on, 'can be conjured out of what is inherently flat, trivial, bald and absurd. The composer can add whatever seasoning and spices he likes, but roasted cat will never make a hare-pie'! This statement, we shall see, runs counter to the belief of many who claim either that some composers (Schubert *a fortiori*) can make the very greatest Lieder out of the poorest poems, or conversely, that to set a truly great poem to music is simply gilding the lily, a worthless occupation. Hugo Wolf was of the opinion indeed that Schubert could have made a Lied out of a 'cheese-label', while we know

4

that Darius Milhaud actually did set a nursery-gardener's price-list to music – in 1920!

Hegel saw astutely however that the really great Lieder go to the heart:

> A song, for example, may have as its words a poem which is a whole, containing a variety of shades of moods, perceptions and ideas, yet it usually has at bottom the ring of one and the same feeling pervading the whole, and therefore it strikes above all one chord of the heart. To hit this chord, and to reproduce it in notes, is the chief function of such song-melodies.

He saw too at that early stage that lyrical poems would be more effective:

> . . . particularly suitable for composition are deeply-felt shorter poems, especially those that are simple, laconic, profound in sentiment, which express with force and soul some mood and condition of the heart, or even those that are lighter and merrier . . .

But what distinguish Hegel as an early 'expert' on the Lied are his perceptive comments on the marriage of words and music. The best Lieder, he claimed, are a perfect amalgam of word and sound, the one enhancing the other to produce a superior synthesis (a good Hegelian word, by the way!). Hegel noted too that the words must not convey 'too difficult thoughts or profound philosophies', but should provide rather 'sketches' to which the composer can marry a suitably subtle accompaniment.

The problem of the balance of the text and the music in a Lied has caused endless heart-searching among German composers. They have even given the 'problem' a name: *Das Wort-Ton-Problem*, the problem of word and music. The various ages of music have 'solved' the problem in their very different ways, producing various types of Lieder. For the student of the Lied, whether he or she is a professional or amateur performer, a concert-goer or (just!) a record-collector, the fascination lies in the way in which the composer has treated his responsibilities towards the poet, and I am certain that the more the student or the listener knows about these responsibilities, the greater will be the enjoyment to be gained from this art-form.

It is also true that a knowledge of the language of the poem set is of inestimable value, and it would be pleasant to think that there may be some who, after reading this book, might feel – as the distinguished music critic Philip Hope-Wallace felt – that it would be worthwhile learning German just to be able to understand the many wonderful Lieder! The composer and the interpreter have to approach the song by way of the poem. Unlike a piano sonata, a quartet or a symphony, the music alone does not hold the secret of the work. The original poem, its language, structure, the organization of its rhyme-scheme, line-lengths and verse-patterns, are all of paramount importance, because they will determine the form of the music. Above all, the *sound* of the poem can often determine the nature of the setting. German can be a very soft, musical language – it can also give rise to harsh and what are often called 'guttural' sounds: *Ach – Bach – lachen*. It is a language of pure vowels, like Italian, which allows a composer to write a good top note for an 'o' or a 'u' sound, and strong consonants, which give a performer every opportunity of interpreting a word like *brechen* (= to break) in a strong, vigorous way, as he comes off the first two letters *br. . .* in the trilled Scottish manner.

Those who do not know the history of the German language or of German literature are often surprised to learn of the wealth of beautiful folk-music – romantic, sentimental music dealing with the basic emotions: love, nature, home – which German-speaking races possess. Germans and Austrians, like the Italians and the Welsh, are 'natural' singers whose culture has been dominated by lyric poetry and music since the earliest civilized times; like the Welsh, the Germans seem to be able to sit down and start to sing, without prior arrangement, it seems, naturally, in four-part harmony. (Such occasions are still called 'Liedertafeln', literally, 'song-tables'!) German soldiers even march to song, the sergeant-in-charge calling out the numbers of the songs as they appear in the *Kommissbuch* (a book of marching songs issued to each soldier!). So the tradition lies very deep indeed. It was, of course, made more fundamental by the regionalization of the German peoples – even in the 18th century, when Britain and France were each united under one Government, 'Germany' consisted of over three hundred little Kingdoms and princedoms, some, like Goethe's Weimar, with a population of just over seven thousand, while 'Germany' itself became a political unity, under the Emperor Wilhelm I and Otto von Bismarck, only on 18th January 1871. This meant that there was a much longer period of regional rather than national development – in language, customs, literature and so on – than in, say, Britain or France. Germans are still, on the whole, more aware of their regional origins than the British or the French, and they will fall readily and easily into their regional dialect when they meet an old friend from their native heath. Few 'Oxbridge' professors hailing from Somerset, Lancashire or Scotland would drop their 'Oxford' accent and fall into *their* regional 'dialect', I feel, as a German professor might do on meeting an old friend from his home district. This bond with the 'Heimat' (the homeland) accounts for a large number of the tuneful (albeit sentimental) folk-songs (*Volkslieder*) still heard in Germany today, and there are many *Kunstlieder* too of this type, settings of sentimental poems about local and regional sights and sounds. *Mutatis mutandis*, the same holds for Austria.

Of course, no one who knows modern Germany, the 'Bundesrepublik Deutschland', and its neighbour, the German Democratic Republic, the 'Deutsche Demokratische Republik', would deny that these *Volkslieder* play a much less important rôle in the nations' lives today than formerly. In the Western part, the influx of Anglo-American mores, in dress, literature and music, has tended to swamp the old 'German' traditions – many young Germans, brought up on The Beatles, The Rolling Stones, Punk Rock and the later manifestations of the 20th century Pop scene, find these old songs trite and sentimental – 'Opas Musik' (Granddad's music) they call it! In the Eastern part, many of the old Lieder are felt to belong to a dangerous past, a link with the ages of Prussian, and then Nazi, militarism and barbarism. (It is true, nevertheless, that some of the old *Volkslieder* are still heard in the GDR, albeit set now to new 'progressive' texts!)*

But no nation can entirely free itself from its traditions, and, just as the Welsh will always sing *Cwm Rhondda, Myfanwy* and *Cartref*, and the Scots *Westering Home, Loch Lomond* and *Auld Lang Syne*, so too we will always be able to hear the *Lorelei, Am Brunnen vor dem Tore* and *Hoch auf dem gelben Wagen* in German-speaking countries. Singing seems to be one of the most natural expressions of feeling which can move a listener by the simplicity of its directness and its ability to conjure up fond and deep-seated memories. As long as that remains true, the *Volkslied*, and its more sophisticated brother, the *Kunstlied*, will survive.

Although we shall have to look from time to time at the *Volkslied*, our main concern here in a chapter on 'Definitions' must be with the form and structure of the *Kunstlied*, the so-called 'art-song'. The 'art-song' itself is not of course peculiar to Germany – most Western countries have developed similar forms where composers of vocal music have set their countries' poems to music. Over the many years of trial and practice, a conventional design has evolved which allows us to suggest three main types of *Kunstlied*: the strophic, the modified strophic and the 'through-composed', a not too happy translation of the German word 'durchkomponiert'.

Most folk-songs in all languages are strophic, that is to say, the verses

---

* Yet another song tradition is represented, of course, by the so-called *Liedermacher* (lit. 'song-makers') in the 20th century. Following the example of Frank Wedekind (1864–1918) and Bertolt Brecht (1898–1956), ballad-singers of 'protest-songs' like Franz Josef Degenhardt (born 1931) and Wolf Biermann (born 1936) fill the largest halls in the Federal Republic with their guitar-accompanied Lieder or 'Songs'.

are all sung to the same melody, and, according to the composer's genius, the words of each stanza or 'strophe' fit – or do not fit – that melody. The Welsh air *All through the night* (*Ar hyd y nos*) would be a fairly typical example: a four-bar melody repeated (= AA), then a different central section (= B), and then the melody repeated (= A), the whole being represented as AABA.

The composer must then clearly try to find a melody which does not conflict too much with the varied sentiments of the poem – and we realise now what Hegel meant when he wrote that the composer's melody must hit 'one chord of the heart'. The strophic setting is not so concerned with representing all the subtle gradations of emotion contained in the poem, but rather with evoking the *general* sentiment – 'Love,' 'Night', 'Dreams' and so on. This is not to say, of course, that each stanza need necessarily be sung the same *way*, even although they are sung to the same *tune*. A great singer will 'interpret' a strophic song too by stressing this or that word, lightening or darkening the tone on this or that syllable – but, in essence, he or she will be concerned to evoke the general mood: peace, joy, exultation, despair. The form of the poem does not always dictate the structure of the music, that is the composer's choice, and quite often, of course, the composer simply makes a mistake, as we shall see. There are literally hundreds of settings of certain popular German poems, which give us the opportunity to spot these 'mistakes' and learn from them how to recognize the truly great settings. The strophic setting, then, is by far the most common form met; indeed, for the average listener, it is what is meant by 'a song' – in popular music particularly, to take *Ar hyd y nos* again, we have the standard form AABA, that is, two verses sung to a similar melody, a third verse with the same or a related melody, (perhaps in a different key or with a different structure), and then a return to the fourth verse in the original key. In instrumental music, this is called 'song-form' or 'ternary form'. It is undoubtedly a limiting, even limited form, and without a great interpreter – or perhaps we should say, without great interpreters, for Gerald Moore has taught accompanists to be 'unashamed' – it can readily lead to boredom. There are also many songs and Lieder which consist of two, three, or more stanzas set to exactly the same melody. Schubert's *Luisens Antwort* (Louise's answer) has nineteen!

For that reason, many composers favour the second type of *Kunstlied* – the modified strophic form. This form is, as the name suggests, part strophic, and part what I have called 'through-composed', that is, the composer follows the differing emotions of the poem rather than the dictates of the strophic pattern. The mould is broken from time to time

8

to introduce new melodies which more satisfactorily reflect the poet's thoughts.

Lying at the opposite extreme from the strophic is the 'through-composed' or 'durchkomponierte' Lied. In this type of *Kunstlied*, the type made immortal by Franz Schubert in his settings of Goethe's poems *Erlkönig* and *Gretchen am Spinnrade*, the composer follows every twist and turn of the poet's thought in his attempt to illuminate the poet's meaning. When he succeeds, when the music catches the glint of the poetry and matches it, then the result is beauty beyond compare. When he fails, we have a succession of disjointed musical phrases with no unifying thread running through the setting. It is by far the most intellectualized of vocal forms, since the composer takes it upon himself to understand the poem so well that he can interpret almost every detail – but the singer-interpreter has to bring this to musical life through his or her own intelligence. It is erroneous to believe that the 'durch-komponierte' Lied is necessarily superior to the strophic type. There are clearly cases where a composer has shown more skill in finding a melody which suits all the verses of the poem than another composer whose setting meanders through the various lines of the poetic work. We shall see in the succeeding pages how the Lied-form developed from the simple strophic through to the more complicated 'durchkom-ponierte' form – but also how there are jewels to be found in all three types.

It was mentioned above how Gerald Moore had taught us to look on the accompanist as an equal partner in this musical adventure. We call the Lied-form in German properly 'Lied für Solostimme mit Klavierbe-gleitung' – a 'Lied for a solo voice with a piano accompaniment', or sometimes just *Klavierlieder*, literally, piano songs. In the earliest pre-piano days, songs would often be sung either without accompaniment (as with much British folk-music from the Celtic-speaking areas of Scotland, Wales and Ireland), or later with lute or guitar accompani-ment. But in those early times, the voice was the important factor; the accompanist, when there was one, simply kept the rhythm going or duplicated the vocal line. All the emotions of the text were carried by the voice. We shall see that it was not until the early 18th century and the invention of the pianoforte with its wide dynamic range and wealth of possibilities of harmonics and modulations, that the accompaniment eventually took on a more equal rôle and allowed the composer to interpret the poem in the instrumental as well as in the vocal part. Indeed, the story from the 18th century is of the development of the piano part to a point where it was no longer capable of carrying the composer's grandiloquent ideas – and the 19th century orchestral accompaniment was born, which in turn killed the domestic Lied.

Clearly the development of the accompaniment runs parallel with the development of the Lied-form itself. The move away from the simple strophic form through the modified strophic to the 'durchkomponierte' form is mirrored in the move from the simple, almost strumming accompaniment following the vocal line, to the complicated harmonic and rhythmic patterns of the 'durchkomponierten' Lieder. Hand in hand with these go, of course, the immeasurably greater demands made on the interpretative skills and vocal techniques of the singers. And these improve as the opportunities for solo voices to perform in public increase. The first true 'song recital' (*Liederabend*) was not given until the middle of the 19th century after all – by Brahms' friend Julius Stock-hausen, who was also the first singer to perform Schubert's song-cycle *Die schöne Müllerin* as a cycle, in May 1856.

The path from the early simple *Volkslied*, which told a story or described a sylvan scene, to the complicated rhythmic patterns and psychological refinements of a Hugo Wolf setting, is a long and fascinating one. Our succeeding chapters will attempt to guide the reader and the listener on the journey, stopping here and there to point out those details worth observing and helping them to stand back now and then to observe the whole scene. The German Lied is a world in itself large enough to bring a new discovery every day for the true *aficionado*. It is a world of beautiful melodies and gripping narratives, a blend of poetry and music, of aria-like *bel canto* and stentorian heroics, which ranges over the whole gamut of vocal possibilities for all types of voices, as well as providing enormous joy and interest for the accom-panist. Lieder can be sung by professional and amateur alike; not all of us have the range, the technique or the interpretative genius of a Janet Baker or a Dietrich Fischer-Dieskau, yet anybody with the slightest pretensions to the name 'singer' can attempt a Schubert or a Schumann Lied to his or her own immense satisfaction. Every local library contains scores of vocal selections – usually for 'High' or 'Low' voice – many supplied with (alas!) rather ageing Victorian or Edwardian translations abounding in 'thee''s and 'thy''s, 'maidens', 'bowers' and 'flow'rets'. If one can stomach these, or, better still, replace them with some of the modern translations found or mentioned in this book, or on record sleeves and in concert programme-notes, much of the alienation and terror of the foreign language will be taken out of the exercise. German is a fairly easy language for Anglo-Saxon learners – to pronounce at any rate – and the effort to conquer it is so worthwhile. Lieder in translation have their place, of course, in the scheme of things, but they really are a poor substitute for the real thing, and all who are truly interested in

obtaining the greatest enjoyment from the world of Lieder should learn
at least to pronounce German. There can be no greater helpmate to this
than the many Lieder recordings made by the greatest of modern Lieder
singers, the German baritone Dietrich Fischer-Dieskau – but his example
has spurred many other singers, German and non-German, to strive to
emulate him and to take pains to pronounce and enunciate the German
language as accurately and as clearly as possible. I am certain that it is in
part at least due to him and his example that the great British singers
Dame Janet Baker, Heather Harper, Margaret Price, Sir Peter Pears,
Benjamin Luxon, John Shirley-Quirk and many, many others – not
forgetting that gifted group who have brought Lieder to so many young
people, *The Songmakers' Almanac* – are able to sing Lieder with only the
merest trace of a non-German accent.

[2] THE LIED UP TO 1770

IN ONE OF the first documents in existence to tell us anything about the
Germanic races – the *Germania* of the Roman author Tacitus, written in
98 AD – we read that the only form of recorded history possessed by
these *Germani* was their songs or 'lays' in which they either celebrated
their gods or gave themselves courage to face the coming battle.

It certainly seems to be true that music has always played a leading
rôle in what might loosely be called the cultural life of these Northern
peoples. When the German language began to assume something like
the shape and form we know today, that is, round about 1100–1300 AD,
we find even there a strain of lyric poetry and song which connects
directly with the Lied of our own times. Indeed, the word Lied (or 'liet'
as it was spelled in the 13th century) which is connected to the Latin
word *laus, laudis* = praise, or *laudo, laudare* = to praise, was used in that
period by those poets whom the Germans call the 'Minnesänger';* it was
a song which had three sections: the first two were called 'Stollen' (or

---

* 'diu minne' was the Middle High German word for 'love', and the Minnesänger were the
German equivalent of the English minstrels or French troubadours of the period. The
Wolfram von Eschenbach (c.1170–c.1220) who sings *O Star of Eve* (*O du mein holder
Abendstern*) to his harp in Wagner's *Tannhäuser* was a real-life Minnesänger who
composed in fact the original *Parsifal* – or *Parzival*, in the original Middle High German.

'props') of eight bars each, while the concluding section was called 'Abgesang' (literally, the 'end-song') or coda, ending with a snatch of the 'Stollen' melody. The two 'Stollen' (= the 'Aufgesang' or 'opening song') and the 'Abgesang' became a recognisable song-form as the years went by.

From these earliest times, music has played an important rôle in the psyche of the Germanic peoples. Those of us who learned German before the Second World War were introduced to a great corpus of *Volkslieder* which, when we eventually went to live and study in German-speaking countries, gave us an *entrée* into Youth Hostelry or club-and-pub functions. It is of course true that many of these *Volkslieder* were old songs put to new, more sentimental settings, such as those of the very popular Friedrich Silcher (1789–1860), remembered above all by his immortal setting of Heinrich Heine's poem *Die Lorelei* ('Ich weiss nicht, was soll es bedeuten' – 'I do not know what it means') which tells the story of the seductive maiden combing her hair on the rock above the Rhine, luring sailors to their doom in the whirlpool beneath – but many of the old songs were deeply embedded in the folk-memories of the Germanic peoples. These songs were, perhaps significantly in the light of Germany's tragic history, predominantly sad, often, as I have said, sentimental, but practically always *tuneful*. That must be the major characteristic of German *Volkslieder* – they are tuneful, the melodies are irresistible, once heard, rarely forgotten. Here is one of the loveliest: *Innsbruck, ich muss dich lassen* (Innsbruck, I have to leave you), dating from the 15th century:

From the 13th to the 16th century, the *Volkslied* was a powerful influence in German musical life. Its themes – like its forms and its melodies – were simple. The singers sang of Love, Birth, Nature, Home and Death in simply-constructed verses to a simple harmonic accompaniment – or to none at all. Carols too were just another form of folk-song, not necessarily connected with religious festivals. The carol has been defined as 'a song of joyful character, in the vernacular, and sung by the common people', which places it firmly in the folk-song tradition. Many so-called 'Christmas carols' are simply examples of new wine having been poured into old bottles. The words of *Good King Wenceslas*, for example, were set to a 17th century melody *Adest tempus floridum* (Now the time of flowers is here). Like so many folk-songs, the carol was originally meant to be danced to – indeed the Italian form 'carola' means a 'ring-dance'. Again the Germanic nations have a particularly rich treasury of carols, particularly of those cradle-song types connected with the Nativity, most of which date from mediaeval times.

From then on, however, the birth of new musical instruments such as the viol and the lute, and, in Europe, the growing desire to sing in two or more parts instead of just one, led to the development of polyphonic music, seen at its finest flowering in this country in the great English madrigal composers, John Wilbye, Thomas Weelkes and Orlando Gibbons. (Here, too, there developed however, side by side with part-singing, what I have already called the 'art-song', the 'ayres' of John Dowland, above all.) In Germany, the most popular type of vocal music was the polyphonic 'tenor song' written for a 'middle voice' which 'held on', as it were, to the melody. ('Tenor' derives from the Latin *teneo, tenere* = to hold.) The melody itself was called the 'canto fermo' or 'fixed song'. From the middle of the 16th century in Germany, however, great composers like Orlando Lassus (or di Lasso) (from Mons) (c.1532–1594) and Hans Leo Hassler (1564–1612) began to write much more flexible polyphonic music and the consequent increase in harmonic possibilities paved the way for the more adventurous music of the 18th and 19th centuries.

Yet it must be added straightaway that it was the very existence of the *Volkslied* which at first barred the progress of its more sophisticated brother, the *Kunstlied*. The development of opera and oratorio and the all-powerful influence of the Catholic, as well as the Lutheran Church in the 18th century led composers to look down rather on the homely, rustic *Volkslied*, even although, as we now know, many of the melodies which graced their works were in fact borrowed from those humble folk-songs. In addition, where, in Renaissance times, the poet and the musician were often one and the same person, (a concept reborn in the folk-singer of today), the rise of tonality in the 17th century brought about an interest in the development of new musical forms – without words. Indeed, it has been suggested that one might think of the madrigal as an extreme case of the apparent (and growing) lack of interest in the text of a work as the words are thrown back and forth to serve the dictates of the music. And was it not John Milton who praised the 17th century composer Henry Lawes for actually paying attention to the words in his settings? 'Thou honourest verse', he wrote!

Here, I think, is the beginning of what I noted as the 'Wort-Ton' problem, the problem of words *versus* music. Which should prevail? Certainly for most of the 18th century there was no doubt that the *music* took pride of place. In the 18th century opera, the librettist had to tailor his text to fit the demands of the *da capo* aria for which there were strict rules of tonal relationships and modulations. This often led to near-nonsense appearing in libretti. As the French writer Voltaire put it, 'What is too stupid to be spoken is sung'!

It also made composers adopt a technique which bores some and puzzles many – the seemingly almost pointless repetition of words; one can find many examples in Bach's writing for the voice where the singer has to sing long *melismata* on one or two words or, as late as 1791, in Mozart's *The Magic Flute*, where the composer adapts his libretto to suit his musical idea at the conclusion of Tamino's beautiful aria *Dies Bildnis ist bezaubernd schön* (This picture is wondrously beautiful). The tenor exclaims that the girl in the portrait, Pamina, 'would be his for ever', if he could but find her – and he sings the words 'Und ewig wäre sie dann mein . . .' But what Mozart actually wrote is 'und ewig wäre sie dann mein . . und ewig wäre sie dann mein. . .' *five* times in all. What does the listener gain from the repetitions? Is Tamino's love for the girl made more evident or more real? It is doubtful. The listener is hearing the most magical music sounds framing words which happen to fit the music. The music does not seek to 'interpret' 'ewig' or 'mein', although one might *just* claim that the beautiful top A on the final 'ewig' does express an exultant longing. (Later we shall hear the poet Tennyson complaining bitterly about some settings of his poems: 'Why do these damned musicians make me say a thing twice when I said it only once?')

In Bach's writing for the voice we find the words of the text set to frighteningly difficult instrumental-like runs or *melismata* (from the Greek word for 'songs', but used to describe vocal cadenzas). An interesting example would be the following from Bach's church cantata *Wo Gott der Herr nicht bei uns hält* (No. 178), where the text tells of the 'wild waves of the sea', 'die wilden Meereswellen'. Bach sets the word '-wellen' to the following fearsome run:

14

gleich-wie die wil - den Mee - res-wel - - - len

There are sixty-three separate notes there. Of course, there is an element of 'the wild sea' about the wave-like movements of the semi-quavers, but the composer is truly much more interested in displaying the quality of the *instrument* – which happens here to be the human voice – than following the sense of the libretto.

On the whole then, the 18th century composer was much less interested in the *words* than in the *music* of a vocal work. Where Schubert and the post-Schubertian composers were 'setting' the words to music, the 18th century composer was mainly concerned with writing music to a supplied text. The instrument was King in an age where composers were after all essentially servants to a patron – 'valets de chambre', as the French court musicians were actually called. These patrons might be Dukes, Counts, Kings or Emperors, an enlightened, artistic, flute-playing King like Frederick the Great of Prussia, or a narrow, crusty Archbishop, like Mozart's Archbishop of Salzburg. The composer's task was to supply music on demand for festivities, religious or secular, essentially 'background music' which was not always heard and certainly not always appreciated. It is true too that the orchestral playing was not of the standard to which we are accustomed nowadays; exceptions such as the great Mannheim Court Orchestra (directed by the various members of the Stamitz family) only prove the rule. Mozart's letters, written to his family while on his European travels, pay eloquent testimony to his distaste for many of the inadequate performances of his works:

I was very nervous at the rehearsal, for never in my life have I heard a worse performance. You have no idea how they twice scraped and scrambled through it . . . (3rd July 1778)

'It' was his new 'Paris' symphony (No. 31 in D, K.297).

The love of the voice as an *instrument*, as a medium for the display of vocal technique rather than as an interpreter of *words*, is seen most clearly, of course, in the operas of the 18th century, whose popularity overshadowed the more modest art-song. Indeed, Esteban de Arteaga, the Spanish 18th century historian of Italian opera, declared that the poet must surrender all his rights – without question – to the musician, and Antonio Salieri (1750–1825), the teacher, conductor, composer and hated rival of Mozart, who gained 20th century fame from the portrayal in Peter Shaffer's play *Amadeus*, wrote an opera with the title '*Prima la musica, pòi le parole*' ('First the music, *then* the words'). It is not without significance for our theme that Salieri was the teacher of Beethoven, Schubert and Liszt, and was on friendly terms with Gluck and Haydn. Thus, although songs continued to be written throughout the 18th century, the literary standard of poems set and the nature of the music did (and do) not allow a singer the employment of the same range of interpretative skills as is available in post-Schubertian music. It is true too that German literature in the earlier part of the 18th century was more concerned with prose works than poetry – the fine poetry that *was* written tended to the epic, the 'Miltonian', which was hardly suitable for a musical setting. (Yet, strangely enough, it was Franz Schubert himself who made best use of what pre-Goethe lyric poetry there was, setting poems by major writers like Herder, Uz, Klopstock, Kosegarten and Jacobi.)

In religious music, too, and particularly in the works of the two greatest German composers of the period, Johann Sebastian Bach (1685–1750) and George Frideric Handel (1685–1759), the voice is treated more as an instrument. Bach, a deeply religious man, we know, always thought – musically – in terms of the church organ, and although it is plain that he was sincerely moved by the words he had to set for his great Passions, the B minor Mass and his two hundred or so church cantatas, here too he makes little association between words and music, many of his greatest melodies being used indiscriminately for religious and secular works. In the same way, Handel, less devout and perhaps more dramatic than Bach, though still a religious man, would transfer his music willy-nilly from a religious oratorio to a secular dramatic work or from a secular number to an oratorio. ('For unto us a child is born', so well known from *Messiah*, was originally a duet for two sopranos, *Nò, di voi non vuò fidarmi*, known as 'No, I will not trust you, blind Love').

To avoid any misunderstanding, I am not, of course, asserting that either of these great composers did not write well for the voice! No composer indeed has surpassed either man in the beauty of their vocal compositions. The point at issue is simply that their Age did not, on the whole, interest itself in the smaller-scale Lied – it was a social age, an age of great occasions, of pomp and circumstance – and the composer had to provide the musical feast. That is not to say either, of course, that there are not peaks among the foothills. A study of 18th century German song reveals that there is a not inconsiderable and rather surprising wealth of material available for both the professional and the amateur singer, which is not heard as often as it might be. The music is undeniably difficult to sing and some of the accompaniments may not be as immediately attractive as Schubert's or Schumann's, but the effort is worthwhile.

J.S.Bach left only five Lieder, found in Anna Magdalena Bach's *Notenbüchlein* of 1725. (She was his second wife.) Indeed it has lately been discovered that the best-known song in the collection *Bist du bei mir* (If you are with me), was in fact written by a contemporary, Gottfried Heinrich Stölzel (1690–1749), but, rather as 'Purcell's Trumpet Voluntary' (by Jeremiah Clarke) resolutely refuses to change ownership on concert programmes, this song continues to appear under Bach's name. It is a song well worth the attention of a soprano with a good trill and can be taken as one of the first of those 'staging posts' on the way to the Schubert Lied. Bach's own contribution to the corpus of German Lieder might be the *Erbauliche Gedanken eines Tabakrauchers* (Edifying thoughts of a tobacco-smoker)! – a none-too-hilarious moralising comparison of the brevity of life and tobacco-smoke. 20th century audiences would be quick to note a more causal connection, no doubt!

Yet one wonders what Bach would have made of the *Kunstlied* had he turned his attention seriously to it. His cantatas and other religious works abound in such beautiful melodies that it seems inevitable that he too would have made an outstanding contribution; and it must be added, the fairly unskilled singers at his disposal in his choirs might well have preferred less tortuous music to sing than the music of his weekly cantatas. (The best professional singers were only to be found in opera-houses in 18th century Germany.) However, the *Zeitgeist*, the Spirit of the Age, willed it otherwise, and it was left to a collection of two hundred and fifty strophic songs, the so-called *Singende Muse an der Pleisse* (The Singing Muse by the Pleisse) by an insignificant Leipzig musician, one Johann Sigmund Scholze, known as, in the 18th century manner, Sperontes, to herald (in 1736) the birth of the modern *Kunstlied*, since these songs were the first attempt to provide, as Dietrich Fischer-Dieskau puts it in his preface to *The Fischer-Dieskau Book of Lieder*, 'vocal communication for the emotions bound up with the poem'.* He adds,

---

* *The Fischer-Dieskau Book of Lieder* (with English translations by George Bird and Richard Stokes (Gollancz, 1976)), a translation of Dietrich Fischer-Dieskau's *Texte deutscher Lieder: Ein Handbuch* (dtv, München 1968).

17

and rightly, I believe, that the songs are scarcely performable nowadays, although they are indeed historically among the first Lieder to attempt to supply varied accompaniments to the varied settings of the different verses of the poems. Sperontes' collection ended what is called in Germany the 'liederlose Zeit' (the 'song-less age') and supplied some competition for the imported Italian operas which had flooded Germany during the first years of the 18th century.

Much more significant Lieder are available for the modern performer in the works of Carl Philipp Emanuel Bach (1714–1788), Bach's third son, whose settings of the *Geistliche Oden und Lieder mit Melodien* (Spiritual odes and songs with melodies) (1745) of Christian Fürchtegott Gellert (1715–1769) fulfil what Sperontes' unperformable songs promised. Of the three hundred songs which C.P.E. Bach has left us, these ones most nearly anticipate the Schubertian and post-Schubertian Lied with their concern for word-setting and independent accompaniment. Bearing in mind too that C.P.E. Bach himself wrote that he had composed his songs for 'Liebhaber von verschiedenen Fähigkeiten' ('amateurs of varying abilities'), it can be seen how attractive they might be to the modern amateur performer. I believe that Lieder like *Morgengesang* (Morning song), a lovely strophic song, or the attractive *Demut* (Humility), or the tuneful *Wider den Ubermut* (Against arrogance) deserve to be resurrected – and would give great enjoyment to performers and audience alike.

These songs are contemporaneous with those Lieder of the so-called 'First Berlin School' of German composers, who moved away from the traditional modes of song-writing and prepared the way for the innovations of the later 18th century composers. As all students of history know, 'movements' do not start on a given date. One cannot (or should not) 'date' the beginning of the Industrial Revolution or the onset of the 'Romantic Movement'. These are often simply convenient labels which historians, looking back with hindsight, can pin on events for purposes of classification and alignment. With such hindsight however we could agree that the composers of the 'Second Berlin School', Johann Friedrich Reichardt (1752–1814) and Carl Friedrich Zelter (1758–1832), with Johann Zumsteeg (1760–1802), did indeed prepare the way for Schubert, but we dare not forget, firstly, that other composers, great composers like Haydn, Mozart and Beethoven, continued to write songs in the 'old' tradition side-by-side with their efforts and, secondly, that they were still writing in the 18th century social milieu described earlier. Their Lieder have to be understood against this background.

Listening to Haydn's music, one wonders if he ever wrote an ineffectual melody? Tunes poured out of him, and, like J.S. Bach, had he lived in a different tradition, it is certain that he too would have written maybe hundreds of Lieder, given his melodic fecundity. As it is, Haydn left us only about forty at the end of his long life (1732–1809 – Schubert was twelve when Haydn died). Haydn was a child of his century and saw and felt his music instrumentally. It would of course be utter nonsense to suggest that he 'took no notice of the words' – as some have done – one has only to think of the awesome setting of that majestic phrase in *The Creation*: 'Es werde – Licht' (Let there be – light!), or that haunting melody for Adam and Eve at the end of the same work: 'Von Deiner Güt', o Herr und Gott/Ist Erd' und Himmel voll' (Earth and Heaven are full of Thy goodness, O Lord and God), but we can see from the original scores of some of his songs that he was not really very interested in the whole process, since his music is written out on two staves only. (Haydn's *XII Lieder für das Clavier* were published in 1781.)

Although trying to trace in this chapter the development of the German Lied, I am also hoping to introduce the reader to undiscovered treasures which he or she might venture to hear or sing for him- or herself. On a visit to London in 1791, Haydn met Mrs Anne Hunter, a socialite and wife of the London surgeon who, Haydn hoped, would remove the nasty polyp from his nose. Haydn set six of Mrs Hunter's poems to music in 1794, six 'canzonettas', as they were called. These 'Lieder in English', with some additions, are among Haydn's best and loveliest songs. One of the additions, my own favourite Haydn Lied, is his setting of Shakespeare's *She never told her love* from Act II Scene 4 of *Twelfth Night* where Viola talks about her 'sister' – actually herself. This is a fine song, as is one other, from a later date (1804), arguably the Haydn song which is most recognisably a *Kunstlied*, viz. *The Spirit's Song* by an anonymous poet. Many a good judge would rank this remarkable song, with its beautiful lines 'all pensive and alone/I see thee sit and weep', as the equal of a Schubert Lied. As has already been said about Bach, had the *Zeitgeist* willed it otherwise . . .

Wolfgang Amadeus Mozart, who was born when Haydn was 24 (in 1756), is not known to have sung his own songs in public as Haydn is reputed to have done at royal banquets in London! (Composers' voices tend to be as notorious as poets' – or conductors'!) But, like Haydn, Mozart was certainly not unaware of the problems and possibilities of setting words to music. In Mozart's case, however, the words were mainly to be found in operatic libretti. He wrote thirty-four songs in all – between 1768 and his death in 1791 – most of which are, in that most uncharitable of descriptions, 'very interesting'. Yet here too genius would out, and a song like *Das Veilchen* (The little violet) (1785) can now be recognised as one of the most innovative written to that date. *Das*

Veilchen gives singer and audience alike the genuine article – a 'through-composed' song, in which the music makes the (successful) attempt to follow the emotions of the poem and to add something to the original words. Here is perhaps the first *true* example of a musician thinking of voice and accompaniment independently, yet as one. The pianist accompanying *Das Veilchen* need feel neither inferior nor 'ashamed' – but he must also be on his guard, as the staccato notes of 'mit leichtem Schritt' (with a gentle step) are suddenly sprung upon him. No other music would suffice here – no 'improvisation' à la Haydn is permissible.

Das Veilchen is a poem by a great poet – but it appears that Mozart was not aware that it was by Goethe – and it is fairly clear that Mozart's general lack of interest in great poetry must have something to do with his lack of interest in song-writing, for few works by the great German poets were found in his library on his death. Indeed, I believe that it takes an age of great lyric poetry to produce great Lieder composers. It is really no surprise to find so many first-rate composers of songs in Elizabethan days in England – and so few today!

Song-writing for Mozart, as for Haydn, and to a slightly lesser extent for Beethoven, was a pastime – time away from the composition of more important instrumental and orchestral works. Nevertheless, I believe that a recital-programme could benefit from the inclusion of Mozart Lieder such as *Abendempfindung* (Evening emotions) (1787) a lyrical scena, 'through-composed', and written during the composition of *Don Giovanni* and best sung by a high soprano, *Das Lied der Trennung* (The song of separation) (also 1787), and *An Chloe* (To Chloë)(1787), a surprisingly explicit poem about an eager lover and his passionate lass which *should* be sung by a male voice, of course, but is often (indeed *usually* in Britain) sung by a woman. (There will be more to be said about the matter of male and female – and 'unisex' – songs later.)

These three, along with *Das Veilchen*, and perhaps the tiny gem *Das Traumbild* (The dream vision)(1787) with its appealing accompaniment, would certainly not be out of place at the most distinguished of Lieder evenings.

It will be clear that I have been dealing so far with a type of music which, by and large, stood apart from the mainstream of 18th century musical development. The composers mentioned (and I could have included others, such as Gluck) were engaged on other musical tasks, symphonies, piano or harpsichord works, operas, masses and oratorios; the Lieder fell from these high tables like crumbs and have been picked up only over the years by avid collectors. The courts employed their musicians, who, in turn, earned their bread-and-butter (or sausage-and-beer in Germany) by turning out – even churning out at times –

20

hundreds of pieces of music, many similar to their earlier pieces, many borrowed from other composers, or indeed from themselves. To look at a tome like the *Bach-Werk-Verzeichnis* (hence *BWV*), the catalogue of J.S. Bach's works, or the *Köchel–Verzeichnis* of Mozart's works, (hence *KV*), is to marvel at the industry of those 18th century composers, and to envy the good fortune of their listeners. The King in his palace and the 'poor man at his gate' seemed to have been surrounded by music – although the former would have heard considerably more than the latter, usually thought of as 'der dumme Bauer', 'the stupid peasant'. Yet it is curious that the birth of Germany's greatest musician coincided with the earliest burgeonings of a literary movement, one of whose aims was to move the centre of social gravity away from the courts by singing the glories of Nature in lyric poetry whose beauty inspired Germany's greatest song-writers for a hundred years or more to come.

[3] STURM UND DRANG: THE POETIC REVOLUTION

LUDWIG VAN BEETHOVEN was born in Bonn, then a little village on the left bank of the Rhine, in December 1770, the year in which Johann Wolfgang Goethe, who was to become Germany's greatest poet, and who was twenty-one, had gone to study at the University of Strasbourg in Alsace. There he met Johann Friedrich Herder, who was then twenty-seven, and it was he who encouraged Goethe to study nature, Shakespeare – and *Volkslieder*. From these and other sources, Goethe set out on a path which was to lead to a new German literature – one freed from formal dogma, from classical rules and regulations, a literature full of 'storm and stress'. This was the name – *Sturm und Drang* in German (taken from the title of a contemporary play) – which was given to this literary 'movement', a group of young poets and dramatists who believed that, in the words of Goethe's *Faust* which was begun in these years, 'Gefühl ist alles' (Feeling is everything).

Herder, born in 1744, had early been interested in the study of languages and above all in the songs of the peoples of the world – *Stimmen der Völker in Liedern* (Voices of the peoples in songs) was the name that his publisher gave to Herder's collection of folk-songs published in 1778–9. Thus the *Volkslied*, of which I have spoken so

21

much, suddenly became respectable; Rousseau-like calls to 'return to nature' could be heard on all sides – the countryside was no longer simply a place for rude peasants and pig-sticking parties, but became 'God's creation', an object of wonder and veneration. (Not that these poets thought much about the 'rude peasants' – their feud was to gain for themselves equal rights with the nobility – think of Beaumarchais' and Mozart's Figaro – not to win freedom for the underpaid and overworked farmhand.)

Yet it is true that, slowly but surely, 'Nature' began to be depicted in painting, poetry – and music. Goethe's verses – he was a poet of the very first order whose equal is still sought in Germany – inspired composers from Beethoven to Hugo Wolf to write the most beautiful Lieder that we possess. Yet there is a paradox here, for Goethe, during his long life – he died in 1832 in his eighty-third year – never really believed that music could be put on the same plane as poetry. So, yet another 'revolution': where Mozart, for example, to the end of his life in 1791, believed that the poetry should be a 'dutiful daughter' of the music, Goethe, even although he called his poems *Lieder*, had no doubt that the music would – and could – only gild the verses, yet he was not at all distressed by settings of his poems, or at any rate, not by strophic settings. Schubert's 'through-composed' version of *Erlkönig*, on the other hand, was of the type to fill him with dismay. 'To paint tones by tones; to thunder, to crash, to splash, to smack is detestable', he said to his faithful 'court composer' Zelter in May 1820.

Indeed, Zelter and Reichardt were very much the arbiters of Goethe's musical taste. The great poet was not himself unmusical – he made many attempts at musical composition, some, like his drawings, very respectable efforts – but he let himself be guided by these two powerful leaders of the 'Second Berlin School'. Little is heard of either man nowadays – only at an infrequent recital or on a record such as Dietrich Fischer-Dieskau's 'Frühe Goethe-Lieder' (Polydor DG 2533 149) do we hear examples of the sort of setting that Goethe loved to hear. In a letter to Goethe on 10 January 1824, Zelter wrote:

> Above all, I respect the form of the poem and try to see my poet in it, since I can imagine that he as a poet thought of a melody hovering in front of him. If I can enter into rapport with him and recall his melody, then our melody will satisfy us both . . . That this melody should fit all the verses is something that not even the better composers understand. I know the objections to this; you, my dear friend, will know by now that I am not in favour of the 'through-composed' way of setting poems. Others will take a different view – they may do as they wish, although a melody which one does not enjoy hearing several times is probably not one of the best.

Of course, not all of Zelter's or Reichardt's songs are purely strophic; a good many of them are what I called 'modified strophic', that is,the melody recurs, but there are variations in the tempo, the dynamics, the rhythms, and, of course, in the melodic pattern. And even where their songs *were* strophic, the story of Goethe interrupting the well-known singer, Eduard Genast, when the latter was singing Reichardt's setting of Goethe's poem *Jägers Abendlied* (Hunter's evening-song) in 1824, shows how well the poet understood the theory behind the setting. According to the tale, he interrupted the singer with some vehemence, telling him that verses one and three had to be sung with vigour, whereas verses two and four were to be sung much more gently because the emotions were different. *Mutatis mutandis*, the advice holds good for today – and shows how important it is for singers to understand the *words* of a strophic song. In a 'through-composed' song, the composer has already given the singer some indication of the emotions being described.

Lest it be thought that song-writing in German-speaking countries began with Schubert in the 19th century, it is just worthwhile recalling that Reichardt himself wrote nearly fifteen hundred songs, one hundred and sixteen of them to poems of Goethe. Most of his settings are fairly unadventurous by 19th century standards, but when he was caught up in a great poem – like Goethe's *Rastlose Liebe* (Restless love) – the accompaniment and the melody are beginning to take on a subtlety previously unknown in German song-writing:

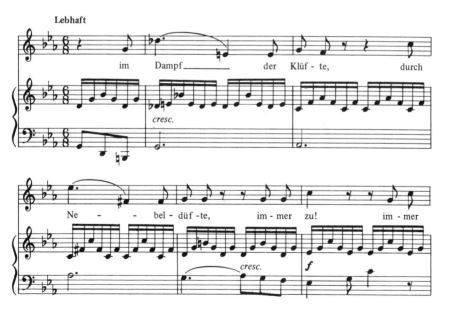

23

He also set those poems from Goethe's novel *Wilhelm Meister* of which Schubert, and later Hugo Wolf, were to make immortal music, *Kennst du das Land. . .?* (Do you know the land. . .?), *Nur wer die Sehnsucht kennt* (Only the one who knows yearning) (which Schubert set no fewer than six times), and *Wer nie sein Brot mit Tränen ass* (The one who never ate his bread with tears). There are *in toto* eighty-four settings of *Kennst du das Land. . .?*, fifty-six of *Nur wer die Sehnsucht kennt* – Tchaikovsky's 'None but the lonely heart' is still the best known – and forty of *Wer nie sein Brot mit Tränen ass* in existence!

Reichardt often becomes a mere footnote in a history of music, but the amateur singer could do worse than try out Reichardt's *Die schöne Nacht* (Lovely night) or *Rhapsodie* (Rhapsody – the poem set later by Brahms as his *Alto Rhapsody*). Both show imaginative use of the accompaniments (especially on the 'Hammerflügel', an 18th century instrument played by Jörg Demus on the Fischer-Dieskau recording mentioned above).

Zelter, likewise, a master-mason by profession and a choral director by choice, was a prolific writer of songs, setting some four hundred poems, seventy-five of Goethe's alone. The poet thought highly of Zelter, nine years his junior, and told him once that, 'Your compositions are identical with my poems: the music simply takes the poem aloft, as gas does a balloon', and reminded him on another occasion that the important point about a setting was to put the listener in the same mood as the poem had done. He felt that the listener's imagination would then be made to conjure up the same images as in the poem – and he would not be aware of how the trick had been done!

Like Reichardt's Lieder, Zelter's might well have sunk beneath the flood of Schubertian and post-Schubertian Lieder, but there must surely be a case for an occasional performance of charming songs like *Um Mitternacht* (At midnight), where Zelter obeys the Master's dictum of bringing out 'the most contrasting meaning of the different verses' by cleverly varying the setting of each verse. One is always charmed by that extraordinary plunge to the low note at the end of the strophes on the closing words *Um Mitternacht*.

TO RETURN to Goethe: it is difficult to over-estimate the effect of this great writer, not only on the future development of the German Lied, nor even on German literature, but on the whole German nation. Goethe dominates German literature today as much as he did in his own day. Indeed, one of the most remarkable 'movements' in modern German theatre has been the attempt to come to terms with the German 'classics', those works that all Germans study in school, and which have loomed large in the theatre, in film and on television, and in the worlds of music and painting. Goethe's major plays, *Götz von Berlichingen* (1773), *Egmont* (1775–1788), *Iphigenie auf Tauris* (1787), his novels *Die Leiden des jungen Werther* (1774), *Wilhelm Meister* (1795–1796) and *Die Wahlverwandtschaften* (Elective Affinities) (1809), and, above all, his epic poem *Faust*, parts I and II, 'the *Ulysses* of German literature', have all been re-assessed, revamped and reworked for all the media. One of the literary 'hits' of recent years was the East German Ulrich Plenzdorf's version of Werther, *Die neuen Leiden des jungen W.* (The new sorrows of young W.), which 'adapted' Goethe's theme to modern GDR circumstances.

With his fellow 'Classic', Johann Christoph Friedrich von Schiller (1759–1805), Goethe has presented an eternal challenge to all German writers since his death in 1832. He was arguably the last universal man, having attained eminence not only as a poet, novelist and playwright, but also as a philosopher and scientist. If in this book we are mainly concerned with his poetry as it affected the development of the German Lied, we dare not forget the effect of his persona on the artists with whom he came into contact. Even as a young man, let alone as the 'Olympian' that he became, he was worshipped by his contemporaries: Haydn, Mozart, Beethoven, Napoleon, Sir Walter Scott, Byron, Schubert, Wordsworth and Coleridge and many, many others came to pay homage to the Great Man of Weimar. He exercised an extraordinary, almost magic attraction on his immediate entourage and not least on a large number of beautiful young women! Unlike some poets, Goethe wrote love poetry based on personal experience. Passion throbs through his verses and it set composers alight throughout the world. And even when Goethe believed that he had left the 'Storm and Stress' of his youth and had arrived in the safe haven of 'Classicism' – in the 1790's – the rest of the world, particularly the musical world, heard in the works of this period, too, the dark passion and unbridled emotions of that most German of movements, Romanticism. A seemingly chaste work, like Goethe's 'classical' play *Iphigenie auf Tauris*, could be characterised by Anselm Feuerbach's lovely painting entitled *Iphigenie*, which shows the heroine casting longing looks back at her homeland, Greece – and that word 'longing' (*Sehnsucht* in German) is at the heart of the Romantic movement in Germany. It will occur countless times in the Lieder of the 19th century which I shall be examining.

It was not only by his *Faust* that Goethe attracted most of his admirers – and detractors. His passionate epistolary novel *Die Leiden des jungen Werther* (1774), the story of the unhappy love of a young man for a married woman, became the epitome of the sighing, dying lover for the 19th century, and an object of moralising suspicion for every British Victorian, giving Goethe, and Germans generally, the sort of reputation that France 'enjoyed' through its 'gay Paree' image in the early 1900's. Even Thackeray's derogatory verses aimed at de-mythologising this legendary figure in his blue coat, yellow waistcoat and top boots, achieved little; writing of Werther's death, Thackeray depicted Charlotte, the married woman, watching the dead body of her lover being carried out of the room:

> Charlotte, having seen his body
> Borne before her on a shutter,
> Like a well-conducted person
> Went on cutting bread and butter.

No one writing on German music in the 19th and 20th centuries can overlook Goethe and the Goethean influence. There was not a single one of the great 19th century composers – from Schubert to Mahler – and very few of the 20th century ones – who was not attracted by Goethe's poems or the songs in his plays. His name appears in every Lieder collection from 1780 to 1980.

So, where does the fascination of this poetry lie? And why has it moved great composers to try to 'gild the lily'? For that is of course the view of some – like Michael Tippett, for example – who believe that a great poem cannot be improved upon. 'The music destroys the verbal music of a poem utterly', he felt. Yet many composers would agree with the English composer Gerald Finzi, who died in 1956 and who

'. . . wanted to associate himself with something that moved him greatly', and believed that the view that one should not set great poetry was 'bunkum' – as his friend Howard Ferguson reported on the BBC3 Music Weekly programme in September 1981. The musical setting of a great poem – think of Schubert's incomparable setting of Goethe's poem *Über allen Gipfeln ist Ruh'* (O'er all the mountain tops is peace) – only enhances the poem and gives a double pleasure, if not a quadruple one: the words of the poem, the sound of the music along with the voice of the singer, and the playing of the accompanist.

It was clear that Goethe's contemporaries were moved by the beauty of his verses. Although Reichardt and Zelter are by any standards *petits maîtres*, and we have seen that Mozart set only one and Haydn none of these extraordinary poems, the greatest musical genius that Germany has ever produced was set on fire by the passion that he found in Goethe's poetry. Beethoven was born in the year that heralded the onset of the 'new' poetry – 1770 – and as a young man he was deeply affected by the naturalness and the freedom-loving and freedom-demanding calls of its adherents. Beethoven read widely: Homer, Ossian (the 'fake' poems of the Scottish bard), Schiller and Goethe were among his favourites, and he too had an abiding interest, as did Goethe, in the *Volkslieder* of the world, going so far indeed as to set almost two hundred English, Scottish, Welsh and Irish folk-songs for George Thompson, an Edinburgh publisher. Yet Beethoven was also a child of his times, instrumental times, and his songs betray his Age.

It should be mentioned at this point that I am discussing 'revolutionary' times in all senses of the word: Goethe's and his colleagues' poems from 1770, the breaking-up of autocratic society in the American and French Revolutions of 1776 and 1789, and, in music, the replacement of the harpsichord by the newly-developed pianoforte with its astounding possibilities in harmonics, dynamics and tone colours. Indeed, without the pianoforte (or fortepiano as it was also called) the 19th century Lied would be unthinkable. There had been wishes for some time throughout the 18th century for an instrument which somehow might combine the ability of the clavichord to give *crescendi* and *diminuendi* and that peculiar singing quality, and the brilliant sound, albeit somewhat reticent – Richard Capell called it 'wiry and glittering' – of the harpsichord. (Whether any 18th century composer actually shared Philip Hope-Wallace's view – that harpsichord continuos sounded as if someone were thrashing a bird cage with a tuning-fork – is not known!) In 1709, Bartolommeo Cristofori in Florence had invented what he termed a 'gravicembalo col pian e forte', a harpsichord which had both soft and loud qualities. The hammer-blows in place of the harpsichord's plucked strings gave the resonance and power demanded. John Broadwood's pianos produced during his lifetime (1732–1812) were widely exported to the Continent – the so-called 'square pianoforte' – and, with others, produced the revolution that we are discussing, for, from now on, composers could strive for, if not always achieve, a balance between voice and accompaniment. The 'piano' could act as a true partner, and we shall be following from now on how the different Lieder composers managed to blend the two.

Beethoven is not to be imagined without the new piano. As is well known, many of his 'violin sonatas' are really for piano with violin accompaniment, and surely no composer has so exploited the piano's 'warmth and rich quality', to speak with Richard Capell again. It is this 'singing quality' in the piano accompaniments which makes Beethoven's contributions to the development of the *Kunstlied* so intriguing. Contrary to what many still believe, Beethoven was interested in vocal music from his earliest years as a composer and composed songs all his life. Indeed, he wrote his first song, *Schilderung eines Mädchens* (Description of a girl), when he was thirteen. The 'singing quality', the *bel canto* music that we hear in Italian operas, is present in all his early sonatas and re-appears in his corpus of Lieder. Beethoven wrote some eighty Lieder, some for inclusion in plays or operas – in Goethe's play *Egmont*, for example, where the 'heroine' Klärchen has two splendid songs to sing: *Die Trommel gerühret* (Beat the drum!) and *Freudvoll und leidvoll, gedankenvoll sein* (To be joyful, sorrowful and pensive), wonderful gifts for the resonant mezzo-soprano voice like Dame Janet Baker's or Christa Ludwig's, since both poems echo Klärchen's wish to be as masculine as her lover Egmont.

Although Beethoven said once to his friend Johann Friedrich Rochlitz, 'I don't like writing songs' (*Ich schreibe ungern Lieder*), he certainly seems to have been able to overcome his prejudices without much difficulty; a Beethoven *Liederabend* is certainly an artistic possibility, although, truth to tell, few impresarios have the courage to mount one, even in Germany, and it needs artists of the calibre of Dietrich Fischer-Dieskau, who recorded two discs of Beethoven Lieder as far back as 1954 (ALP 1317/1318), to encourage other singers to include some Beethoven Lieder in their repertoire. Unlike Mozart or Haydn, Beethoven could be profoundly moved by great poetry, and Goethe's dramatic bid to give the Germans the premier position on the European literary scene which had always eluded them, had the composer's whole-hearted support. He first set a Goethe poem in about 1790, the quirky, 'macaronic', i.e. half-French, half-German, song *La Marmotte* (the marmot is a type of squirrel), and then he set eight more between 1792 and 1810, including the very beautiful *Mailied* (or *Maigesang* as Beethoven titled it) (May song), and went on in later years to set nine more of the poet's finest poems, including the *Song of the Flea* (*Floh-Lied*) from Part I of *Faust* (in 1809). Although Beethoven clearly writes in an 18th century idiom and many of his Lieder are either strophic songs, where the piano, in the 18th century manner, often simply repeats the melody given to the voice, or the 'recitative-and-aria' type, where the voice declaims some (usually pious) sentiment before launching out on a broad *cantabile* melody, the great exceptions occur, it seems to me, in the Goethe settings. *Mailied* is possibly the finest representation bar none of the freshness and vigour of the young *Sturm und Drang* movement. Not even a Schubert could match the gaiety and drive of this beginning:

which dances on to the triumphant 18th century conclusion on the repeated words 'Sei ewig glücklich, wie du mich liebst' (Always be happy just as you love me), while the later, on-driving *Neue Liebe, neues Leben* (New love, new life), a setting of Goethe's 1775 poem, is a superb example of the 'through-composed' type of song which captures all the emotions of this youthful paean to the rapture of love. Beethoven manages to marry the music to this pulsating text right from the very first breathless urgent plea to the man's heart: 'Herz, mein Herz, was soll das geben? (Heart, my heart, what does all this mean?)(See p.123 below.)

These songs, along with the more sombre *Wonne der Wehmut* (Bliss of sadness) (1811), the beautiful strophic *Andenken* (Memory)(1809), where the lover sees his girl mirrored in all the natural phenomena, birds, forest and evening, and the long scena *Adelaide* (1795), which Jussi Björling recorded so memorably as the cantata it really is, would make a splendid addition to any (probably male) repertoire. (Beethoven's writing for the female voice is often criticised – largely because of those appalling high A's given to the sopranos in the final movement of the Choral Symphony! But many of the songs lie well for this voice too, and, if the texts are suitable and do not specifically indicate a male singer – for, alas, many do – then a female singer can perform these Lieder with relish.)

Apart from Beethoven's impressive 1803 settings of six religious, very 18th century poems by Christian Fürchtegott Gellert (op.48) which are

29

wonderful material for a rich baritone voice, or in the case of the famous No.4, *Die Ehre Gottes aus der Natur* (The heavens extol the glory of the Eternal One), for four-part choral singing – the composer's most important contribution to the development of the *Kunstlied* is indeed a major one. Beethoven is often credited with having written the first song-cycle (*Liederkreis* in German, literally, 'song-circle'). The Concise Oxford Dictionary of Music defines a song-cycle as 'A string of songs of related thought and musical style, thus constituting an entity and being capable of being sung as a series', and there is indeed room for the argument that Beethoven's song-cycle *An die ferne Geliebte* (To the distant beloved)(op.98, 1816) is one of the very few *true* song-cycles, since the songs are thematically bound together and the melody from the first song, *Auf dem Hügel sitz' ich spähend* (I sit gazing out, on the hill-top), re-appears in the last song to create the link. The six songs (to poems by a young Viennese Jewish doctor, Aloys Jeitteles) 'tell a story' of a forlorn lover sitting gazing into the far beyond, thinking of his departed beloved – the original title of the cycle was 'An die entfernte Geliebte' (To the absent beloved). The songs cannot really be taken out of their context, since the piano accompaniment continually bridges the 'gap' between the songs and supplies the necessary key and tempo changes. For those who only know the Beethoven of the great symphonies or the towering last quartets, this small-scale cameo will be a wonderful discovery. The verses themselves are true Romantic out-pourings; Jeitteles was no Goethe. Yet one meets all the familiar Romantic themes: *Seufzer* (sighs) – *Geliebte* (beloved) – *Pein* (pain) – *Wald* (wood) – *Bächlein* (little brook) – *Vöglein* (little birds) – *Liebesflehen* (protestations of love) – *'es kehret der Maien'* ('May returns') – *Laute* (lute) – *Dämmrungsrot* (the red of the sunset) – *Sehnsucht* (longings) – all united by a piano accompaniment which at times makes us think that we are listening to a piano work with voice obbligato.

Hans Joachim Moser in his celebrated book on German Song, *Das deutsche Lied seit Mozart* (The German Lied since Mozart)(1937), claims that Beethoven's remarks at the introduction to his song *Resignation* (1817) can be applied to all of his Lieder: Beethoven wrote that the Lied was to be sung 'mit Empfindung (with feeling), jedoch entschlossen, wohlakzentuiert und sprechend' (yet decisively, well-accentuated and as if you were speaking). When one considers that *An die ferne Geliebte* was written as late as 1816 and that Schubert's first great Lied, *Gretchen am Spinnrade*, was written in October 1814, one sees how central Beethoven's position is in the history of the *Kunstlied*.

[4] FRANZ SCHUBERT: THE GOLDEN AGE
OF LIEDER

I HAVE TRIED to trace the development of the 'art-song' from its beginnings in folk-song through the various refinements of succeeding centuries up to its treatment by the great Austro-German-Hungarian masters at the end of the 18th century. In whatever age, however, and in whatever country, song as such has remained one of the most vital and one of the liveliest aspects of German music; indeed, I doubt if there would be much disagreement if I claimed that the one factor which binds all the German masters of music has been – melody. 'They could all write such good tunes', a student once exclaimed delightedly! And, as we have seen, many of the greatest melodies derived from folk-songs long known to their rural communities and handed down through the ages. Many of these songs are of course in ballad form. The ballad was originally a 'song to dance to', from the Latin *ballare*, from which we have the modern word *ballet*. From Shakespeare's time on, however, and in all countries, the 'ballad' became something like a news-sheet where the singer sang his listeners a story, usually about some famous event, to an old familiar tune. These were often published, decorated by simple woodcuts, as 'broadsides' or 'broadsheets', many of which can still be found in good libraries around the country.

Perhaps the most remarkable German example of the form is the ballad *Lenore*, written in 1773 by Gottfried August Bürger, a 26-year-old North German poet. It tells an Erlking-like tale of a young woman, distraught at the news of the death of her lover in battle, who is then bidden by a ghostly rider in the guise of her lover to abjure God and gallop with him through the night – only to find that her ghastly companion is Death himself. This poem swept through Europe like wildfire and inspired not only many musical settings, but other ballad-writers. Sir Walter Scott, born in 1771, was to be fired by the work and to produce his own important Scottish epic poems and novels in the early years of the 19th century, which in their turn did so much to influence the growth of the Romantic Movement on the Continent and to attract musicians as varied as Schubert and Donizetti.

Many of the ballads from German-speaking lands were to be found in Herder's collection *Stimmen der Völker in Liedern* (see p.21 above), which sought to reveal the truth of the remark of the German philosopher J.G. Hamann that 'poetry is the mother-tongue of the human race'. Many of the ballads in Herder's collection were translations from other languages, particularly of British ballads, since, on the one hand, the influence of Shakespeare on the 18th century German writers had been particularly strong, and, on the other, Romantic imaginations had been set alight by the Celtic effusions of one James Macpherson (1736–1796), a Scot who claimed to have discovered the poems of an ancient Gaelic bard named Ossian and published them as *Fragments of Ancient Poetry Collected in the Highlands of Scotland and Translated from the Gaelic and Erse Tongues*. It was this volume, published in translation in Germany in 1764, which, without any exaggeration, can be held to be the *fons et origo* of later German Romantic poetry – and music. (That Macpherson was eventually unmasked as a fraud and had to admit that the poems were, in fact, his own seems not to matter any more! The *effect* might have been the same, since the soil was clearly ready for the seed, and it was not until 1805 that the final collapse of the Ossian myth was signalled – strangely enough, only shortly after Herder's death.)

The wave of ballad-writing that subsequently spread over central Europe gave great impetus to productions for the 'solo voice with piano accompaniment', and, in a sense, the vogue has never waned. The songs of Pete Seeger or Simon and Garfunkel 'tell a story' – to a guitar – much as these 18th century ballads did. Many of these modern ballads point a moral or recount some famous contemporary incident, e.g. 'Where have all the flowers gone?'!

Beside Reichardt and Zelter in the 'Second Berlin School' stood Johann Rudolf Zumsteeg (1760–1802), who, a close intimate of Goethe's friend, Schiller, set many of the latter's ballads to music. No one would say that Zumsteeg claimed a high position in the hierarchy of German musicians, but he can be the link for us between the world of 18th century ballads, *Volkslieder* and *Kunstlieder* – and the new, magical world of the man Gerald Moore called the Prince of Lieder composers – Franz Schubert. Schubert, born in Vienna in 1797, took an early interest in Zumsteeg's ballads and among his first compositions were ballads, some of inordinate length, and as a result rarely heard in recitals nowadays. Indeed No. 5 in Otto Erich Deutsch's *Schubert: Thematic Catalogue of All His Works* (which should by now have replaced the often erroneous opus numbers which have been used for years),* is a ballad *Hagars Klage* (Hagar's lament), attributed to 30 March 1811 when Schubert was fourteen, and modelled on Zumsteeg's ballad *Hagars Klage in der Wüste Berseba* (Hagar's lament in the desert of Beersheba) (1797). Since Hagar was a woman, Dietrich Fischer-Dieskau did not include it in his monumental enterprise of recording all the Schubert Lieder for male

---

* *Schubert: Thematic Catalogue of All His Works in Chronological Order* by Otto Erich Deutsch, Cambridge 1950.

voice – twenty-nine L.P.'s in all – but Schubert's seventh composition, *Eine Leichenphantasie* (A fantasy by the grave)(D7), *is* included – all nine, ten-lined verses, which take some twenty minutes to perform! Schubert, like all other composers that we have mentioned, lived in, from and by his Age, and although he was later to strike out on absolutely new paths and literally to *create* the German *Kunstlied* as we know, understand and love it today, he, like his predecessors, was first of all bound to the traditions that had long prevailed. The prerogative of genius however is to be like the Roman god Janus and to be able to look forward and backward at the same time, and to transmute the dull metal which he inherits into the gold of the future.

Books continue to be written on the phenomenon Franz Schubert; born the son of a poor schoolmaster on 31 January 1797 in Lichtental, a suburb of Vienna, he became a schoolmaster himself, hardly left Vienna except for holiday excursions, never married, and died in that same Vienna, aged only 31, on 19 November 1828. It is fatally easy to become sentimental about Schubert – legions of stories, anecdotes and operettas bear witness to that fact: the two 'hit' operettas *Blossom Time* (1921) and *Lilac Time* (1923) gave a very inaccurate picture of Schubert as a romantic dreamer chased by – and chasing – buxom, be-dirndled maidens singing his cheerful lays the while. The truth was much more sombre: Schubert spent a good deal of his life in introspective contemplation, smarting under the close censorship of the reactionary Austrian authorities of the day, unhappy in love – his one great *innamorata*, Therese Grob, married another – and finally succumbing to typhoid fever after having gone through the pain and indignity of a bout of venereal disease, during which he lost all his hair. Schubert was possibly the first great composer to be independent – even of his family. No great Prince or King engaged him to write salon music – no Maecenas financed his various artistic projects; ironically, his family made more money out of his works after his death than he ever did during his life-time.

He *was* blessed of course with friends, without whose encouragement many of his songs would never have been written, let alone performed or published, and it is from their testimonies – many of them living, also ironically, into ripe, comfortable old age – that we know what we do about Schubert.

Most artistic movements are connected in one way or another with the social, economic or political tendencies of their age; the great Dutch portrait painters of the 17th century found patrons made wealthy by the flourishing of Dutch industries after the union of the Provinces; the rich French and German courts of the 17th and 18th centuries gave employment to those 'valets de chambre', the musicians who could play and compose for them, while the rock, soul and punk movements of the 1960's, '70's and '80's were born of the frustration of the coloured and unemployed youths of America and Britain. In Schubert's Austria, the passing of the great court occasions and the popularity of the newly-introduced pianoforte led to an intense interest in domestic music-making, 'do-it-yourself' performances of popular music, vocal and instrumental – and particularly of dance music. The Viennese were insatiable dancers; the country dance known as the *Ländler* was soon to gain world-wide fame, particularly in the later 19th century under the Strauss family as the more sophisticated waltz, and the remark of the Austrian soldier, Charles Joseph de Ligne, about the 1814–1815 Congress of Vienna is probably well known: 'Le Congrès danse, mais il ne marche pas!' (The Congress is dancing, but is making no progress (literally, 'is not walking')). The $^3/_4$ rhythm was, and still is, in every Viennese's blood – listen to Willi Boskovsky's recordings of the New Year Concerts with the Vienna Philharmonic Orchestra in the Grosser Musikvereinsaal – and Schubert was no exception; many of his Lieder are written $^3/_4$ or $^6/_8$.

We can now see how these various threads became woven into Schubert's development. From his early interest in Zumsteeg's ballads, he learned how to run a wide gamut of dramatic expression, setting poetic works which were not in truth amenable to musical settings. Zumsteeg's ballads also encouraged him to wander into, and out of, strange keys: the infamous *Hagars Klage*, already mentioned above, begins in C minor and ends in A flat – which was certainly not taught in the music conservatories of the day. Devastating modulations, 'sudden swerves into new keys', the Schubert scholar Maurice Brown used to call them, became Schubert's trademark.

Why Schubert, the undistinguished son of an undistinguished family, with no musical reputation or background, should become the most celebrated composer of Lieder, will probably never be explained – although there has certainly been no lack of attempts. Was it a sure sense of literary values? Did he perhaps 'hear' the music as he read the poetry? Did he perhaps *sing* the poetry to himself? We shall never know for certain. What is clear from a study of his other works is that there has never been another composer with such a fecund storehouse of melodies, nor, perhaps, one who could make so much of a melody, once discovered. No one could have taught him this, it seems; it was clearly God-given, as was his extraordinary ability to set words to music. Add to that his wonderful sense of rhythm, which may well have come from his Viennese background. As he grew older, he was much in demand as an accompanist, not only for evenings of Lieder, but as the equivalent of the 'pub pianist', thumping out tunes for the dancers. Schubert would play happily for hours for his friends' entertainment – having often composed the tunes himself.

It was mentioned earlier that it is dangerous, even impossible, to say that 'such-and-such a literary movement' began on 'such-and-such a day', since ideas float about in the air and different people seize them and develop them in different places, often at the same time. But by common consent of critics and musicologists, the German 'art-song', the *Kunstlied* as we know it, that genre developed through the 19th century and which now forms the staple diet of the countless *Liederabende* held throughout the world, west and east nowadays, was born on 19th October 1814 with Schubert's *Gretchen am Spinnrade* (Gretchen at the spinning wheel), when Schubert opened Goethe's *Faust, Part I* and set to music Gretchen's tremulous response to meeting the rejuvenated professor. Gretchen, a simple lass, is swept off her feet by the worldly-wise Faust's attentions – she cannot get him out of her mind and, as she sits spinning, his handsome bearing and seductive voice force themselves into her thoughts.

No musical setting had as yet enhanced any poem so much; the vocal part mirrored and explained the words to an uncanny degree, while the accompaniment, quite separate, no longer simply doubling the voice, lent a depth of texture unimagined by any composer to that date. Gretchen's throbbing heartbeats were reproduced exactly in the opening lines:

and it has been noticed how every other melody in the song derives from one or other of these phrases.

After over one hundred and fifty years, *Gretchen am Spinnrade* (D118) remains *the* model of the 'through-composed' song. Schubert had written quite a few songs already in 1814, but this was his first setting of a Goethe poem – he was to set more than seventy Goethe poems in all, many in several versions – and they changed the face of vocal music. Although later composers, particularly Schubert's fellow Viennese, Hugo Wolf, were to make a fetish of psychological word-settings, Schubert's music for Gretchen blazed the trail to the future. Composers realized the potential satisfaction to be gained from writing this type of song instead of just supplying a 'rum-te-tum' accompaniment to words, and there are few German composers of the 19th (and indeed also of the 20th) century who have not tried their hand at writing songs.

Schubert's astounding fecundity – Otto Erich Deutsch tells us for example that Schubert wrote eight songs (D312–319) on 19 October 1815, and one hundred and fifty in that year alone – enabled him to write over six hundred songs before his all too early death in 1828. It means that a Lieder singer could spend his career on the performance of Schubert's Lieder alone! Every taste in vocal music is catered for here: the short, meditative lyric poem, the ballad, the merry ³/₄ *Ländler*, the cantata-aria type, and of course, the innocent *Volkslied*. Indeed, Schubert could write the last type so well that many native German-speakers believe to this day that songs like *Heidenröslein* (Wild rose) (D257), to a poem by Goethe, and *Der Lindenbaum* (The linden tree) (No. 5 of D911) (or *Am Brunnen vor dem Tor* (At the well in front of the gate), as it is more popularly known – a song from the song-cycle *Winterreise*) are indeed folk-songs, so 'folksy' are the tunes. That well of *Volkslieder*, the three volumes known as *Des Knaben Wunderhorn* (The youth's magic horn), collated and published in the years 1805–1808 by Achim von Arnim and Clemens Brentano in that arch-Romantic German town on the River Neckar, Heidelberg, proved to be an inexhaustible source of inspiration for all composers. In these volumes, the German *Volkslied* was 're-produced' – unlike Herder's 'original' *Volkslieder* – with the aim of producing a song-book for the people, literally a 'Volksliederbuch'. Not a poet, not a musician since has failed to be inspired and influenced by them, from Goethe (to whom the first volume was dedicated) through Schubert and Brahms to Gustav Mahler.

That area of central Europe influenced by all the various cross-currents of melodic invention – German, Italian, Eastern European, Russian – even Oriental to a certain extent, when the Romantic Movement's love for 'chinoiserie' developed – could not but influence a young musician whose ears were so wide open as Schubert's. Nor can we forget that when he entered the Imperial Seminary ('Das k.k. Stadtkonvikt', in the officialese of the day, a boarding-school in which the choir-boys of the Imperial Court Chapel were also trained – the forerunners of today's *Wiener Sängerknaben*, the Vienna Choir Boys), at the age of ten in October 1808, the melodic influences of the great Viennese masters of music were still being felt. Mozart had died, aged 35, in 1791, so was of as recent memory as, say, Igor Stravinsky, who died in 1971, will be in the 1980's for our young musicians; Haydn was 76 in 1808 and was to die the next year, while the mightiest Titan of them all, Beethoven, was at the height of his musical powers – albeit totally deaf – and only aged 38.

Thus, by 1812–1814, when Schubert really began to put pen to paper, his musical mind would be brimming over with the wealth of impress-ions from all sorts of sources: folk-music, the music of these great predecessors, the religious music which he had to sing in the Seminary, and, of course, the settings of Goethe's poems by the Master's 'court composers', Zelter and Reichardt. It is difficult to underestimate the importance of Goethe in Schubert's development. The attraction was not however reciprocal; the ageing Olympian – he was sixty-five in 1814 – hardly knew of the existence of the tiny, corpulent Austrian genius. They never met, and when, in 1816, a few of Schubert's friends persuaded him to allow them to send Goethe a selection of Schubert's settings of his poems accompanied by a rather fawning letter from one of the friends, Josef von Spaun, there was no reply, although the songs *were* eventually returned. And yet the first parcel in 1816 contained among others the scores of *Gretchen am Spinnrade*, *Rastlose Liebe*, *Nähe des Geliebten*, *Wanderers Nachtlied I*, *Heidenröslein*, *Erlkönig* and *Der König in Thule*! There must be many singers in many countries in the world who regularly sing *Gretchen* or *Erlkönig* with enormous pleasure – and never give Goethe a thought! We do not know whether Goethe even looked at the songs, although some authorities give him the benefit of the doubt by claiming that the poet would have had difficulty in finding an accompanist in his immediate entourage who could have done justice to, say, *Erlkönig*!

Be that as it may, Schubert worshipped the Weimar Master to his dying day, and his Goethe settings bear witness to the extraordinary impulse that these poems gave to his musical imagination. Their sonorous language, the burning passion of this 'new' poetry, added to the harmonic possibilities of the 'new' piano, drove this most un-Romantic of men, an impecunious, plain, stout, tiny – his 'official' height was 1.567 metres = 5 feet 1 inch – Viennese schoolmaster to flights of musical fantasy hitherto undreamed of.

At a much lower level of poetic fancy were the numerous poems offered to Schubert by his poetaster friends. Their devotion to their friend is indeed touching to read about; it was genuine, deep and founded on the utmost respect for his genius. They befriended him in his worst moments, and what pleasure he had from his short and uneventful thirty-one years was found in their company. The famous Schubertiaden at which Schubert's music was played and sung in the milieu for which it was composed, that is, for a few friends in a house round a piano, were organized by friends like Josef von Spaun, Franz Bruchmann, the Sonnleithners and others whose names can be found at the head of Schubert's songs, for many of these songs are settings of poems by those few close friends. Again and again, the question has been asked: why did Schubert set so much second-class poetry? The question is asked perhaps more often by non-German critics, and perhaps *most* often by non-German critics who have no German. The latter confuse the frequent appearance of what Germans call *Knittel* verse – in German poetry, and in Schubert's settings, four-beat couplets, rhyming ABAB or AABB where the number of unaccented syllables can be freely varied – with what is often thought of as 'doggerel' outside Germany. But Goethe's great epic poem *Faust* is written in a mixture of *Knittel* verse (which goes back to Hans Sachs and the sixteenth century), and the more austere 'Madrigal' verse-form from the seventeenth and eighteenth centuries – and it would be a brave man who would call *that* doggerel! Take for example these splendid lines from Faust's opening monologue, *Nacht* (Night):

> Habe nun, ach, Philosophie,
> Juristerei und Medizin
> Und leider auch Theologie
> Durchaus studiert, mit heissem Bemühn.
> Da steh ich nun, ich armer Tor,
> Und bin so klug als wie zuvor!

In a prosaic translation: 'Oh, I've worked hard and long studying philosophy, law, medicine, and, alas, theology too. Now here I am, a poor fool, as clever now as I was before I started!'

Some of the most sublime verse to be found in German poetry was written for the form best suited to the language. Ignorance of the strength and subtlety of the *Knittel* verse has led many an unwitting foreigner to condemn a German poem for the very lack of these qualities!

SCHUBERT'S life was spent in very simple surroundings; there were no fine court diversions, no beautiful Countess to be obeyed, no tyrannical master to write for. He and his friends shared the most modest, often uncomfortable, cramped and cold rooms, and Schubert set whatever poems his friends would find for him – in anthologies, almanacs of the day and those selections of poems that they could lay their hands on.

38

There were many masterpieces among them which fired Schubert's imagination – but it was also fired by much poorer poetry which – somehow – contained that vital spark which was all that Schubert seemed to need. Such poetry was often supplied by friends or friends of friends; sometimes it would be a poem for a birthday, another time, congratulations on an engagement or a marriage or a birth, very often a threnody on a death or on a parting or on the memory of a beautiful scene in the country. But if in the dross of mediocrity there was a line, a phrase, a word even, which Schubert saw as gold, then a Lied would follow. And if *all* the poem were gold . . .

If *Gretchen am Spinnrade*, composed on 19 October 1814, was one milestone, *Erlkönig* was another. The story of how this extraordinary masterpiece came to be written has been questioned, but this is how Josef von Spaun related that he witnessed the birth of this most famous of Schubert Lieder on 16 November 1815:

> We found Schubert all aglow, reading the *Erlkönig* aloud from a book. He walked up and down several times with the book in his hand; suddenly he sat down, and in no time at all, the wonderful song was on paper. We ran to the *Konvikt* with it as Schubert had no piano, and there on the same evening, the *Erlkönig* was sung and wildly acclaimed. Old Ruzicka (The teacher, *KSW*) then played through all the parts himself carefully, without a singer, and was deeply moved by the composition. When one or two of the company questioned a recurring dissonant note, Ruzicka played it on the piano and showed them how it matched the text exactly, how beautiful it really was and how happily it was resolved.

And *Erlkönig* is written in *Knittel verses*!

Wer reitet so spät, durch Nacht und Wind?	(Who rides so late through the night and wind
Es ist der Vater mit seinem Kind,	It is the father with his child,
Er hat den Knaben wohl in dem Arm,	He holds the boy in his arms,
Er fasst ihn sicher, er hält ihn warm.	He clasps him firmly, he keeps him warm).

(Incidentally, it is worth adding that the late Maurice Brown, the eminent Schubert scholar, always cast doubt on the truth of that tale, since he felt that it would have taken three hours or so for Schubert just to have written the song out. Dietrich Fischer-Dieskau however, in his book on Schubert, felt that, since Schubert never wrote out the repeats in the accompaniments, and given that there are few key changes, it could have happened just as Spaun related it.)

Schubert was known to sing his own songs at these Schubertiades; his friend Anselm von Hüttenbrenner said of his voice: 'It was weak but very pleasing. When he was nineteen, he sang baritone and tenor; in cases of necessity, when one of the ladies failed to turn up, he used to take over the soprano and contralto parts, for he could sing a wide range of falsetto parts. . .' But his own singing could never have made his songs popular, and there is little doubt that we owe the spread of the popularity of Schubert's songs to their championing by an operatic baritone just retired from the Vienna Court Theatre at the age of forty-nine. Johann Michael Vogl, a lyric baritone, was taken almost immediately by Schubert's innovative talent, and he befriended and supported the young composer until the latter's death. Schubert undoubtedly had Michael Vogl's voice in mind for many of the post-1820 songs – and it is to Vogl in turn that we owe some of the more peculiar embellishments in the extant scores of the Lieder, and in the editions of Schubertian scholars such as Eusebius Mandyczewski's *Gesamtausgabe* (Collected Edition) of 1884–1897 which first revealed that Schubert had left us 603 songs – and a few have come to light since.

Erlkönig was one of the songs that Vogl popularized – indeed, with one other, *Der Wanderer* (D489/493), *Erlkönig* was the song that most contemporary music-lovers associated with Schubert's name. It was one of the very few Lieder to be published in his lifetime – as 'opus No. 1.' on 31 March 1821. (On Schubert's death his publications had reached opus 89; in the Deutsch catalogue, *Erlkönig* is listed as D328 and it has remained one of the most famous Schubert Lieder.)

It is perhaps the independence of the piano part that makes *Erlkönig* such an innovative song – the vocal part is in a traditional ballad or declamatory style. It is in this wholly new attitude to the accompaniment that Schubert's true genius lies. One of the most interesting experiments that I have ever made was to have the Schubert piano parts recorded separately on cassette, so that the songs could be sung when no piano accompanist was available. How complete these piano parts sound in themselves! Look, for instance, at the opening of the accompaniment to the lovely *Frühlingsglaube* (D 686):

This 'music minus one' could be the opening of a piano sonata. Yet, in the very finest Lieder, these wonderfully 'independent' piano accompaniments blend with the vocal part to form a new, exciting and – often – enriched experience of the original poem.

I believe that Schubert must have possessed an extremely subtle sense of what the Romantics called 'synaesthesia', a blending of sensations. He must have heard music as he read the words (just as some people can 'smell a taste'), so that a combination of vowels and consonants in a certain emotional framework emitted musical patterns which he notated. The very fact that he was not writing for talented professional singers, but, on the whole, and at the beginning certainly, for domestic purposes, meant that his writing rarely strays beyond the 'comfortable' vocal compass of the amateur. Yet, even in his own time, the need for 'interpretation' was soon recognized, since Schubert took great pains – through his notations – to indicate where the melodic line was to be pure and where it had to be coloured, subtly or dramatically. The most famous Lieder singers all claim that the secret of great Schubertian singing and interpretation lies in reading the music faithfully – after having studied and understood the poem. It is very difficult to do this with, or through translations, where the notes lie to different vowel sounds or harder or softer consonants, let alone to words with different meanings. It seems to me to be quite wrong to sing any Schubert song in translation nowadays – yes, even the Shakespearean *Hark, hark, the lark*, which was written, after all, to the German translation *Horch, horch, die Lerch.*

This practice is particularly to be recommended when one is tackling the two great song-cycles. *Die schöne Müllerin* (D 795, 1823), traditionally translated as 'The Fair Maid of the Mill', but clearly the girl here is 'The miller's beautiful daughter' – and *Winterreise* (Winter's Journey)(D 911, 1828). Although *Winterreise* was Schubert's own title on the manuscript, Wilhelm Müller's cycle of poems is titled *Die Winterreise* (*The* Winter's Journey).

We saw how Beethoven has been credited with having written the first true song-cycle *An die ferne Geliebte* (1816). Schubert must have known this beautiful cycle of songs – he studied everything that Beethoven wrote – when he came upon the poems of Wilhelm Müller (1794–1827) in a book entitled *Seventy-seven Poems from the Posthumous Papers of a Travelling Horn-player*, published in 1820. The twenty-three poems are now known to have been written for a charade performed in Berlin in 1816 and called 'Rose, the miller's beautiful daughter', which was intended to be a parody of the poorer type of 'Romantic' folk-poem, as can be seen from the ironical Prologue and Epilogue to the collection.

However, as Schubert omitted the Prologue and the Epilogue and also carefully refrained from setting three other poems which contained ironic references, we can fairly assume that he wanted us to take the 'story' at its face value as the tale of a young miller's lad who, wandering by the banks of a brook, is led to a mill, finds work with the miller and falls in love with his pretty daughter. On to the scene comes however a virile hunter who takes the girl away from the ineffectual lad, who then finds solace – and death – in the comforting arms of his only true friend – the brook.

The *Liederzyklus*, the song-cycle, is a 'string of songs of related thought and musical style, thus constituting an entity and being capable of being sung as a series'. We shall find various composers using various German terms to describe it: Schumann, for example, was to use *Liederkreis* (= song circle) or *Liederreihe* (= series of songs), and there is also a word *Liederkranz* (= wreath of songs), but they all have in common a 'link', either musical or narrative.

In the case of *Die schöne Müllerin*, the musical links often lie in the last and first notes of the accompaniment – which makes transposition of some of the songs *only*, a dangerous game. These 'links' will then be lost, along with the deeper meaning, and, sometimes, the magic of the entity. The same holds for singing the songs out of context – not *all* will be lost, of course; the song will remain beautiful or sad or powerful, but the essence of the song, what Schubert meant it to be when he wrote it, will be lost, irrevocably so. But perhaps only those who have lived with, and loved these cycles for years are able to assert this. The average singer is no doubt happy to have found another lovely song to add to his repertoire.

The full *Die schöne Müllerin* was finally published, in five separate books, by August 1824 – the five books attempting to make a small drama of the cycle, so that Book 1 (or Act 1) contained songs 1–4 up to the boy's arrival at the mill; Book 2, his burgeoning love for the girl (songs 5–9); Book 3, songs 10–12, their short spell of bliss; Book 4, the boy's jealousy of the hunter and his growing anguish (songs 13–17) and Book 5, his resignation and suicide (songs 18–20). Not the least attractive feature of the great song-cycles for singer, accompanist or listener, is their ability to catch all participants in their thrall and hold them spellbound from start to finish – even, strangely enough, in inadequate performances. One of the finest and most enthralling performances of *Die schöne Müllerin* that I have experienced was by a young Methodist minister in a church hall in the north of England; his sincerity, and love for the music, conquered the unlikely ambience.

This cycle sounds best in the tenor register for which it was written;

Schubert dedicated the cycle to a baritone (Karl Freiherr von Schönstein) however, and many fine baritone singers have made it their own. It would be nonsense of course for a woman to sing this cycle – and only a few have attempted it, arguing that 'lovely music is for all'. But only a singer who never listens to the words of a song could do this – a Lied is above all a human experience.

This is not the place to attempt to give a full analysis of this wonderful music; there will be opportunity for further discussion later. In addition, many books have been written on the work; I mention Gerald Moore's *The Schubert Song-Cycles*,* because it is an excellent book, and, as Dietrich Fischer-Dieskau said of Gerald Moore once, he is probably the only pianist in the world who has accompanied *every* Schubert Lied! His opinions on Schubert's Lieder can fairly be taken as authoritative.

For our purpose here, it is worth noting Moore's remark that the miller boy's songs 'run the gamut from exultation to despair' in a variety of keys and tempi; thus the three participants mentioned above have their minds and senses continuously exercised as the music and the drama lead them now here, now there. We are walking along with the young lad by the rushing brook at one moment (No. 2 *Wohin?* (Whither?)) – the next, we are witnessing the young lad after his daily work (No. 5 *Am Feierabend* (After work)), then listening to his love-song (No. 9 *Des Müllers Blumen* (The miller's flowers)), and so on to the last song, No. 20 *Des Baches Wiegenlied* (The brook's lullaby), where we gaze down on the body of the drowned boy now in the arms of his beloved stream, his one constant un-fickle friend. Of the twenty songs, sixteen are either strophic or 'modified strophic', and four could be termed 'through-composed', where Schubert marries the words most closely with the music, e.g. No. 2 *Wohin?*

Die schöne Müllerin takes about sixty minutes to perform. Great singers and accompanists, like Fischer-Dieskau and Moore or Peter Pears and Benjamin Britten, used to sing the closing words of the cycle 'und der Himmel da oben, wie ist er so weit' (And Heaven up above/How broad it is) *pianissimo* into halls where a dropped pin would have reverberated – and the audience might have numbered up to two thousand:

* Hamish Hamilton, 1975.

How was – and is – the miracle worked? I have never agreed that it is *all* due to Schubert; Wilhelm Müller's verses are much much more than the 'artless rustic lays' that some commentators have made of them. They are the lineal descendants of the great *Sturm und Drang* lyrics of Goethe and his friends of the 1770's. Müller had a true poet's eye and voice for the unusual image, and the artist's ear for the unusual juxtaposition of images and sounds – listen to:

Ihr schlummertrunk'nen Äugelein
Ihr taubetrübten Blümelein . . .

in verse three from No. 8 *Morgengruss* (Morning greeting). The 'slumber-drunk eyes' and the 'dew-troubled flowers' images married to the magic of a Schubertian C major melody:

are a near-perfect synthesis and bear out the prophetic nature of Müller's remark:

> I can neither play nor sing, yet when I write verses, I *do* sing and play after all. If I could produce the tunes, my songs would please better than they do now. But courage! A kindred soul may come along one day who will hear the tunes behind the words and give them back to me.

And it was Schubert who 'came along' – and who must have realized that this was, if not a 'marriage of minds', at any rate a 'marriage of feelings', for, having found Müller, he stayed by him, and, in 1827, four years later, returned to the poems of the 'travelling horn-player', and, right at the end of his pitifully short life, chose another twenty-four of Volume II to form his last great song-cycle, *Winterreise*, which Benjamin Britten would have placed beside the Bach B minor Mass as one of the 'twin peaks of Western culture'. The *Winterreise* Lieder were published in two groups of twelve, the first in January 1828 and the second, the proofs of which Schubert corrected on his deathbed in November 1828, in December, after his death.

Although some critics have sought to 'prove' by examination of the key sequences and the recurrence of poetic images that the two cycles are in some way linked, I feel that the true integration is within each cycle. The betrayed lover in *Winterreise* drags himself away from his unfaithful girl-friend's house and sets out on his tortuous winter's journey accompanied by the ominous black crow, passing ice-bound rivers, sleeping villages guarded by barking dogs, and comes to his journey's end outside a village, where, accompanied now by the strange old organ-grinder, undertakes his last journey into – perhaps, madness? We never know.

If an 'inadequate performance' of *Die schöne Müllerin* can still give us pleasure, the same cannot be said of *Winterreise*. And that may well be the measure of the difference between the two cycles. Where the first is a sad little story, shot through with shafts of sentimentality and humour, the second borders on the existentialist 'nothing-ness'; there is a starkness, a terror, almost a madness in the artistic unity of *Winterreise*. Again, not all is due to Schubert – the Müllerian images in the poems which Schubert chose to set for the cycle have a sparseness and tautness akin to the images of a 20th century Kakfa. It is the great (Czech-) German writer who continually comes to mind as one follows the stumbling progress of Müller's betrayed lover through ice, snow and bitter cold. Some of the poetic images in the poems have that same ambiguity, the same opaqueness of Kafka's *Angst*-ridden prose images, and, although unlike Kafka's Josef K. in *The Trial*, who, 'without having done anything wicked', was arrested one morning, and who spends the rest of the novel trying to find out *why* he was arrested, Müller's 'Geselle' (journeyman) *knows* why he has had to set out on this winter's journey, the alienation of his surroundings, both physical and human, is just as great. Somehow this becomes much more than the conventional story of a heart-broken Romantic, pining away for his lost love. 20th century writers and audiences rarely smile at the 'poetic conceits' in *Winterreise* as they might do in *Die schöne Müllerin*. Schubert's extraordinary futuristic music and Müller's moving verses in a 'modified strophic' Lied like No. 16 *Letzte Hoffnung* (Last hope), for example, create a remarkable tension between performer and audience. This is a man wagering his life as he bets on whether the last leaf hanging from the wintry tree will fall. As the wind soughs through the bare branches, he trembles lest this 'last hope' should leave him – and when it does:

> Ach, und fällt das Blatt zu Boden,
> Fällt mit ihm die Hoffnung ab,
> Fall' ich selber mit zu Boden
> Wein' auf meiner Hoffnung Grab.

45

(Ah, and if the leaf falls to the ground/then my hopes will fall with it/And I too shall fall to the ground/and weep on the grave of my hopes.)

Those who know and love the cycle wait, as I know that I do, for the almost animal-like cry of pain on the word 'wein" (weep) that the truly great singers can produce to herald the beginning of the end of this Winter's Journey. Schubert's music for this song reaches an undreamt-of intensity of emotion and sound. Gerald Moore calls the passage a 'blaze of genius' – how right he is! As the singer comes to that final phrase, 'Wein' auf meiner Hoffnung Grab', he knows that he must sing *through* a tear – because the repeat on 'wein" – where the voice is taken up to a high G – needs all the breath and voice control that he can muster to slip down on to the E flat which expresses the wounded cry:

There are many great moments in the literature of Lieder – but few greater than this.

It is strange that Schubert's setting makes *Letzte Hoffnung* such an important song, because, although it is No. 16 of the twenty-four songs of the cycle, and is 'central' in so far as it heralds the first sight of the downhill slope to the boy's derangement, it is in fact the *twelfth* poem in Müller's original series of twenty-four poems, that is, it *is* the central poem and the turning-point of the poetic cycle. Schubert must have felt instinctively that this poem, with its imagery of 'last things', the metaphor of the last leaf representing the boy's last link with the happier past, when 'the trees all had their leaves', required music of the most tragic dimensions.

To sing the *Winterreise* cycle over an unbroken period of some eighty minutes or so requires a fine vocal technique, superlative interpretative skills and sheer physical strength; it is doubtful whether there are many operatic rôles that demand as much from a singer. Within that space of time, he has to allow the audience to run the full gamut of emotions, from the mocking tones of No. 2 *Die Wetterfahne* (The weather-vane) when the lad asks why his girl's family should worry about *him*: ('Ihr Kind ist eine reiche Braut' – Your daughter will be a rich bride) to the doom-laden journey to 'the inn' (No.21) which is, in effect, the cemetery. There can be no letting-up of the emotional tension, and, if there is none, then, as Fischer-Dieskau wrote in his book on Schubert, when performers and audience come to the last song, No.24, *Der Leiermann* (The organ-grinder), they will find that 'life has little more to offer in these lines. The effect on the listener is paralysing'.

(Strangely enough there are no 'through-composed' songs in this impressionistic cycle – two-thirds are what I have termed 'modified strophic'; they have a basic melody with a variant for one of the middle or last verses of the poem.)

Over the nearly one hundred and sixty years since the cycle appeared, it has been sung more often by the lower-voiced baritones than by the tenors for whom it was written. Certainly, Schubert's baritone friend, Michael Vogl, was its first interpreter, but it is doubtful whether that significantly influenced the singers of later years. One would imagine that it was rather the darker hues that both the number of songs in minor keys (sixteen out of the twenty-four), and the generally more sombre nature of the verses cast over this cycle, that has made it more of a baritone preserve than the earlier cycle is.

What it clearly *cannot* be is a woman's preserve! Although the great dramatic mezzo-soprano Elena Gerhardt recorded some of the *Winterreise* songs with her accompanist Coenraad V. Bos for the Schubert Centenary in 1928, and her recitals of *Winterreise* in that and subsequent years persuaded the distinguished critic Desmond Shawe-Taylor to remark that 'one had no impression of the incongruity of a woman's voice in this tragic story of a man's broken heart',* I can only say that this incongruity is the foremost impression that I have as I listen to these often moving recordings. It seems to me to destroy the imagery by raising associations which Müller could never have had in mind. A female voice can sing Schubert's *music* of course; but *Winterreise* is much more than 'music'. Here more than anywhere else in the entire history of the Lied, a composer went beyond the mere success of blending 'Wort' with 'Ton', word with music, and presented us with a psychological study of a man in the last stages of despair – but in so doing, made a general statement, valid for all time, about the male soul in travail after the bitter experience of rejection by a woman.

When Schubert said to his friends in January 1828: 'Come to Schober's today. I shall sing you a cycle of frightening songs . . . They have taken more out of me than was ever the case with other songs', he knew that he had composed something extraordinary which, as Arnold Feil put it, was 'to set music on a new path'.

---

* cf. *Elena Gerhardt and the Gramophone*: in Elena Gerhardt: *Recital*, pp 168–180 (Methuen 1953).

And there was more to come: the musical innovations found in *Winterreise*, like No.23, *Die Nebensonnen*, and No.24, *Der Leiermann*, were taken further in the last group of songs that Schubert composed; grouped by his publisher Haslinger and given the rather sentimental, but undeniably apt title of Swan Song (*Schwanengesang D.957*), this 'cycle' of fourteen songs includes settings of six poems by Heinrich Heine (1797–1856), a German-Jewish poet who was to rank with Goethe throughout the 19th century. Had Schubert come across Heine's poems sooner, who knows what might have resulted? The bitter, humorous, cynical, despairing verses of the Düsseldorf poet might just have struck the chord in the Viennese genius' heart that it did in Schumann's, and later Hugo Wolf's. There are those who argue that Schubert never understood Heine's bitter irony, born of personal and social failure. But few surely would deny that a song like No.13 of the group *Der Doppelgänger* (The double), with its three declamatory verses, each rising to a frightening climax, represented a new departure in music and pointed the way to the 20th century and its melody-less atonalism? It takes a great singer to do true justice to the Doppelgänger's heart-rending cries on the *fff*'s of the top G on 'Gestalt' in the line 'Der Mond zeigt mir meine eigne Gestalt' (The moon reveals my own self) at the end of verse two:

This Lied takes us into the world of naturalistic opera of non-Romantic pain and grief as we were to experience them in the operas of Alban Berg (*Wozzeck* and *Lulu*) in the 20th century.

Yet it must not be forgotten – amidst this welter of pain and grief – how happy the vast majority of Schubert's songs are! If one would wish to stress that he was not just a happy-go-lucky Austrian peasant singing about flowers, brooks and woods, it would be equally wrong to *over*-stress the gloom and despair of some of his music. For the professional and amateur alike, there is in the six hundred and three songs that he left us a 'song for every occasion', and, if there are not all that many that can be thought of as 'female' songs, there are a few – and enough that might be thought of as 'unisex' – for women singers to feel that they have a fair share in the Schubertian inheritance. Songs like *Gretchen am Spinnrade, Berthas Lied in der Nacht, Der Hirt auf dem Felsen* (really a small cantata), *Die Forelle, Die junge Nonne*, the *Mignon*-Lieder and the *Suleika*-Lieder – all these give a soprano or contralto a fine opportunity to show the most appealing qualities of their voices.

What was Schubert's major contribution to the development of the Lied? No one before him – and not all that many after him – fused the words and the music more admirably together. Many books have been devoted solely to an examination of Schubert's song-writing methods and it would be arrogant to pretend that an explanation could be given in a few lines, yet three examples from well-known Schubert Lieder might give some idea of what I am trying to claim: The opening bars of *Der Musensohn* (D764), for example, where the composer pictures Goethe's Son of the Muses gaily dancing through the fields – what bounce there is in the music as he sings 'Durch Feld und Wald zu schweifen' (What fun to dance through the woods and fields):

One can actually see the lad piping away, exciting the young people to get up and dance with him. Or, in more pensive mood, the opening of *Im Abendrot* (At Sunset) (D 799), by Carl Lappe, where we are asked to listen to the poet's hymn of praise to God for his beautiful world. Schubert's melody and accompaniment breathe perfect peace:

and lastly, one of the most remarkable examples of sound-painting: Schubert's evocation of a 'still sea', his 1815 setting of Goethe's poem of that title *Meeres Stille* (D216). No one would have dared to write such 'motionless' music before him – and what art is needed to sing the long legato phrases without disturbing the calm:

It was such a concern for verbal values which then predominated throughout the 19th century, the 'Golden Age of Lieder'. Drawing on the enormous reserves of lyric poetry in German, which Goethe's example had inspired, the great 19th century composers almost all tried their hand at Lieder-writing, some, certainly, with more success than others. Each age revalues the art of the past; Schubert's symphonies are valued much more than in the 1880's, when Sir George Grove could write that they get 'into all kinds of irregular keys and excrescences' (in a letter to Mrs Edmond Woodhouse.)

Similarly, Brahms' songs are now seen to form a much more important part of his *oeuvre* than was formerly believed to be the case. But nearly all – Schumann, Mendelssohn, Liszt, Brahms, Wolf, Mahler, Richard Strauss – even Richard Wagner – felt compelled to follow in Schubert's footsteps and contribute to the literature of the Lied.

It is not insignificant that, on Schubert's death, Franz Grillparzer, the leading Austrian dramatist and poet, when asked to compose an epitaph for Schubert's tombstone, produced the following:

He bade poetry and music speak; not as a mistress, not as a servant, but as sisters, the two embraced above Schubert's grave.

The form, more than the sentiments, was criticised, and Grillparzer was prevailed upon to change this to the final version now to be seen on Schubert's tomb, which lies beside Beethoven's (and Hugo Wolf's) in Vienna:

Die Tonkunst begrub hier einen reichen Besitz, aber noch schönere Hoffnungen.

('Music buried here a rich treasure, but many more beautiful hopes'.)

[5] ROBERT SCHUMANN TO
HUGO WOLF

IT IS USUALLY claimed that Schumann took Schubert's 'concern for verbal values' a stage further, and that his settings of Lieder show even more sensitivity to words than Schubert's did. If this is true, then it is perhaps not too surprising, since Robert Schumann, born in 1810, was the son of a bookseller and author, and in 1834 he himself became the distinguished editor of his own *Neue Zeitschrift für Musik* (New Periodical for Music), in which he became possibly the first true 'music critic'.

The troubled love affair between Schumann and his beloved Clara Wieck before their blissful marriage in September 1840 is probably well known; was it the near prospect of marriage that made Schumann, who had confided in 1839 that all his life he had ranked songs below instrumental music and had never considered them great art, write one hundred and thirty-eight Lieder out of his total of two hundred and fifty or so in that *annus mirabilis*? Whatever it was, it undammed a flood of vocal music that, at its best, equals the finest of Schubert's. If I write 'at its best', it is because it is hard to appreciate those Schumann Lieder which are what the Germans call 'zeitbedingt' (conditioned by their times), songs which mirror that age known to Germans as 'Biedermeier' (perhaps 'early Victorian' to us), of simpering girls and moustachioed cavaliers plighting their troth in chintz-covered bourgeois salons. Schumann wrote quite a few of these – he too was a child of his Age – but, these apart, his genius at its finest, expressed in his settings of great poetry – he could never see the sense of wasting his efforts on inferior poetry – and in his expressive piano preludes and postludes, left us with some of the greatest and loveliest Lieder.

Not surprisingly perhaps, when one thinks of his happy life with Clara (who was herself an excellent concert pianist), many of Schumann's Lieder, certainly more than was the case with Schubert, were written for the female voice. It is practically certain that no professional male singer has ever sung – in public – Schumann's opus 42, *Frauenliebe und –leben* (A Woman's Love and Life) – the title is really *Frauenliebe und Frauenleben*. It is even difficult for some women to bring themselves to sing this cycle of submissive poems these days; it inhabits a world vastly different from that of today's independent woman, telling as it does of the wife's selfless adoration of her husband-to-be, 'the most wonderful of all':

Er, der Herr - lich - ste von al - len, wie so mil - de, wie___ so gut!

Frauenliebe und –leben is, in effect, really a series of eight songs which takes the listener from the meeting of the lovers, through the wedding and the birth of the baby, to the tragic death of the husband. Adelbert von Chamisso, the poet of the cycle, married a girl of eighteen when he was forty, and we in this country will think involuntarily of the contemporary love-story of Queen Victoria and her adored Albert – they also married in 1840! – and I feel fairly certain that von Chamisso's widowed heroine would have secreted herself away from the public gaze as Victoria did after Albert's death in 1861. It would seem fairly certain too that the Cosima Bülow/Wagner who wrote in her diary for 29 March 1869: 'Die Frau darf und soll alles dem Geliebten aufopfern' (The woman must and should sacrifice everything for her beloved) must have enjoyed this cycle!

The songs lie beautifully for the powerful contralto or mezzo-soprano voice; but, as with all great Lieder, the singer should ideally have histrionic abilities, too, to portray the varying moods of the character. Truth to tell, Chamisso's verses do not belong to the first division of the poets' league, but, after having lived for years with the cycle, it becomes difficult to be critical of poems which could inspire such wonderful music; all female singers will be eternally grateful for lines like 'Du Ring an meinem Finger, mein goldenes Ringelein' (Ring on my finger, my little golden ring) in No.4:

Du Ring an mein - em Fin - ger, mein ___ gol - de - nes Rin - ge - lein, ich___

or the splendidly heady 'An meinem Herzen, an meiner Brust' (At my heart, at my breast) in No.7:

which perfectly expresses the happiness of the young mother suckling her first child. There is a wonderful union here of words and music, a certain inevitability, which one feels only with the greatest art. Schumann's accompaniments are very special, particularly the preludes and postludes, which, like Beethoven's codas, do not just bring the work to a close, but add new material, new thoughts and ideas, or, as in the very last postlude to this cycle, by returning to the melody of the first song, *Seit ich ihn gesehen* (Since I saw him), make the series of songs into a true cycle by 'closing the ring'. We return with the widowed woman to the days of the first happy lovers' meetings.

In many ways, Schumann was the archetypal Romantic, although Hans Keller is always careful to dub him (curiously, with Mendelssohn) a 'classical Romantic' – nevertheless his profession, personal life and tragic death all bear the stamp of what Hollywood certainly would have thought romantic (with a small 'r'!). From 1853 on, Schumann showed signs of insanity and, after attempting to drown himself in the Rhine in 1854, he died in a mental home near Bonn in 1856.

By the time that Schumann was writing songs, from 1840 on, the literary Romantic Movement in Germany had lost a good deal of its impetus, but Schumann's Lieder are, in the main, settings of poems of unimpeachable Romantic provenance: unrequited love, dreams, 'Romantic' ruined, mediaeval castles, ladies in high towers, moonlight nights, all the literary *topoi* of the period are to be found there.

Yet if, when one has studied all of Schumann's Lieder, one feels that there is much more 'art' than 'nature' in them, compared to Schubert's, it really would be perverse to wish to criticize a song like *Mondnacht* (Moonlight night) No.5 from the *Liederkreis*, opus 39, on such grounds. An almost perfect example of a 'modified strophic' Lied, *Mondnacht* is arguably Schumann's most singable song – and it is 'unisex'! The three stanzas of Eichendorff's poem tell of Heaven kissing the earth in the starry-still night and of the poet's soul taking wings to fly exultantly to God. The tremulous opening piano phrase from the B in the bass to the high C sharp in the tenor:

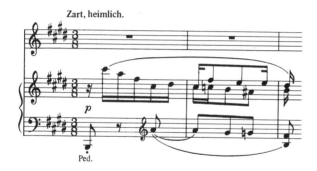

betrays the pianist-composer like no other, and the swell of the voice on 'Flog durch die stillen Lande' ((My soul) flew through the quiet countryside) betrays the consummate skill of the word-painter:

This could well be the song which best meets Schumann's own demand that his songs please best, 'when sung alone at evening'.

Schumann's greatest contribution to the development of the song-cycle was however his opus 48, *Dichterliebe*, songs written in a single week in May 1940, shortly before his marriage to Clara. Like Schubert in his last years, Schumann became fascinated by the poetry of Heinrich Heine, not only his exact contemporary, but also a native of Düsseldorf, where Schumann became Municipal Director of Music in 1850.

In 1827, Heine had published his *Buch der Lieder* (Book of Songs), which contained in the section titled *Lyrisches Intermezzo* the sixteen poems which Schumann re-constructed into his song-cycle *Dichterliebe* (A Poet's Love). Curiously enough, the artistic stimulus for the *Lyrisches Intermezzo* seems to have come from Heine's reading of Wilhelm Müller's 'travelling horn-player's' poems which were Schubert's source for *his* two great cycles. Heine, in a letter to Müller in 1826, shows quite clearly that it was the 'lesser' poet who had demonstrated that it was possible to recapture the 'pure sound and the true simplicity' of the *Volkslied* in modern poetry. The *personal* stimulus for the *Lyrisches Intermezzo* came of course from Heine's unhappy experience of being 'jilted' by his cousin, Amalie Heine in 1820 – and when Schumann came to compose his cycle in 1840, he knew that Heine had been crossed in love again – this time by Amalie's sister, Therese!

A singer aware of these autobiograhical details would, I think, be in a much better position to interpret *Dichterliebe* than otherwise. Of the sixteen songs of *Dichterliebe*, eight could be called strophic, five 'modified strophic', and three 'through-composed', and the main effect on the audience is of continuous tunefulness. There should be no breaks in the performance, since the listener is led on from one song to the next by the relationship of the keys. In Schumann's arrangement of the poems, we are taken from the passion of the lover (songs 1–6) to the poet's first anguish – No.7, the great outburst, *Ich grolle nicht* (I shan't complain) where the tenor (it really *should* be a tenor!) vents his spleen on the faithless girl. When he comes to describe the serpent that gnaws at her heart, Schumann takes him to the most dramatic point of the cycle – or rather he gives the singer a choice of being dramatic, or *very* dramatic, by writing alternatives, either a D or a top A on *Herzen* (heart) in the line

It *is* an alternative, but, as Gerald Moore writes in his recent book on Schumann, 'the top notes in the score are printed as alternatives, but they must be sung'!*

After this outburst, the jilted lover subsides into melancholy, into mention of bitter dreams, lost hopes, even in the last song, No.16 *Die alten bösen Lieder* (The old bad songs), of coffins, and only in the wonderful piano postlude is the listener's grief assuaged and hope renewed as we return to the melody of – what? Gerald Moore seems to be on the right lines when he suggests that the melody heard in the right hand in the conclusion reminds us of *Hör' ich das Liedchen klingen* (No. 10), 'the air the beloved sang'.

When introducing young people to the 'wonderful world of the Lied' I often choose *Dichterliebe* as a guide. The poems are good as poems, the music is tuneful, dramatic, touching and breathtakingly lovely by turns, the range is within the amateur's compass – and the accompanist has plenty to do. He (or she) must sing with the singer to make the most of this perfect cycle.

There is an enormous wealth of tuneful music among Schumann's Lieder; the *Liederkreis*, (opus.39), from which *Mondnacht* comes, does

---

* *Poet's Love,* Hamish Hamilton, 1981. P. 9

relate the songs in key and mood and allows them to be performed as a set, if not as a cyclical unity. We shall see from the examples dealt with in Part Three that Schumann could also control the larger vocal unit, the ballad – so well indeed that he went on to write an opera (*Genoveva*, 1848) and a remarkable work built on *Scenes from Goethe's Faust*. It is worthwhile remembering this when performing Schumann's Lieder, because it explains the extraordinary *dramatic* nature of many of the songs. 'Das Lied ist ein Drama im kleinen' (The Lied is a small drama), said a famous singer of yore, and although, as we shall see later, that must not give a concert singer licence to (*over*)'act' the song on the concert platform, it should encourage him or her to realise that the words must be understood and then clearly enunciated. Lieder composers, much more than operatic composers (who have the resources of a huge orchestra for dramatic support), have to 'make the words work' – an audience's participation is increased a hundredfold when the words are clearly understood.

It seems therefore particularly important that this should be remembered when performing Schumann, whose Lieder are thought of by some as piano pieces with a voice obbligato! This is, of course, not the case; on the contrary, Schumann's choice of poets makes a study or performance of his Lieder a very special pleasure for the listener *au fait* with German literature. His *Liederkreis*, opus 24 – the first songs of 1840 – to nine poems by Heine, although again not a song-cycle in the sense of *Frauenliebe und -leben* or *Dichterliebe*, does have some organic unity, since the songs are related by key sequences, and Heine's poems tell of the pining lover. Similarly, opus 35 to twelve poems by Justinus Kerner contain two particularly lovely Lieder, *Stirb, Lieb' und Freud'* (Die, love and joy), which echoes the Bach-like construction of the great *Im Rhein, im heiligen Strome* (In the Rhine, the holy river) No.6 of *Dichterliebe*, and the noble *Stille Tränen* (Silent tears), with the most spectacular set of crescendi in all of Schumann's Lieder.

Chronologically, therefore, Schumann did carry on the Schubertian inheritance; we know that he admired Schubert above all others – we know indeed that he cried all through the night when he heard of Schubert's death – and we know too that it was Schumann who, on his first visit to Vienna in 1839, discovered the score of the 'Great' C major symphony (now No.9, D944). The first performance was conducted on 21 March 1839, in Leipzig by Felix Mendelssohn-Bartholdy who shared Schumann's regard for Schubert and whose own works contain several interesting contributions to the development of the Lied which probably could not have been made without Schubert's pioneer labours.

Mendelssohn, born in 1809 and only thirty-eight when he died, is certainly not one of the great innovators among song-composers, not least because he had been one of the last pupils of Goethe's great friend, Carl Friedrich Zelter in Berlin. Zelter's dislike of 'through-composed' songs was transmitted to his pupil. There are some examples of these, of course, but the recitalist or listener who is looking for a 'typical' Mendelssohn Lied will choose a lilting melody like *Leise zieht durch mein Gemüt* (A sweet sound of bells rings softly through my mind) – the song is actually titled *Gruss* (Greeting, op.19a, No.5) and the poem is by Heine – than, say, his attempt to write a 'durchkomponiertes' Lied like *Reiselied* (op.34, No.6), also by Heine, with its strophic memories. When one examines concert programmes and record catalogues, however, the one Mendelssohn Lied that seems to be widely known is *Auf Flügeln des Gesanges* (On wings of song)(op.34, No.2), also to a poem by Heine; it is nevertheless a beautifully constructed, modified strophic song whose melody perfectly fits the text, both structurally and psychologically – one wonders why Heine, on hearing the setting, declared that it had *no* melody?!

Mendelssohn's rather refined salon-music contrasts strongly with another contemporary song-writer whose output is just as ignored, but a few of whose songs should really be better known and performed more often – Carl Loewe. Loewe, un-Romantic in one sense, in that, born in 1796, he lived for some seventy-three years – was an arch-Romantic in another sense since, a fine singer himself, he made his name as *the* composer of ballads, turning the ballad into an art-form of high quality. As we have seen, there was plenty of material to work from and on – Herder's, Bürger's, Goethe's, and Walter Scott's collections were all available. The deep bass or baritone voice looking for something stirring for the repertoire need look no further than Loewe's ballads: the most famous is probably *Edward* (op.1, No.1) of 1818, included by Herder in his 1779 collection, but originally, of course, a fine ballad from the Scottish Borders, 'Why dois your brand sae drap wi' bluid, Edward, Edward?'

The ballad takes the form of a cross-questioning of Edward by his mother, who wants to know why his sword is stained with blood. After he admits that he has killed his father, we discover that it was his mother who had driven him to the awful deed – in the Scots: 'Sic counsels ye gave to me, O!' At their worst, Romantic ballads can be inexpressibly dreary – and very long; at their best, as here, and in Loewe's *Herr Oluf* (op.2, No.2), a sixteenth-century Danish legend, they are very fine indeed. Essentially 'through-composed' Lieder, these ballads are the epitome of the 'Drama im kleinen', the miniature drama, and it is not surprising that many people hear in them fore-sounds of the later Wagner, since they too tell of heroic deeds, and unite the lyrical, declamatory and dramatic in what could be thought of as a sort of *Gesamtkunstwerk*, the Wagnerian term 'complete art-work', which was meant to unite all art-forms. Loewe's ballads must approach most closely too to Goethe's ideal ballad: 'The ballad', he wrote, 'requires a mystical touch, by which the mind is brought into that frame of undefined sympathy and awe which men unavoidably feel when face to face with the miraculous or with the mighty forces of nature'. Schumann, too, had tried the ballad-form – his setting of Heine's version of the Belshazzar story – *Belsatzar* (op.57) – is skilful and dramatic, but Loewe mastered all the problems inherent in the genre better than any contemporary composer. The great *Archibald Douglas* (op.128) of 1858 is almost a symphony in itself, with a myriad of contrasting themes, motifs, and tempi, while a much more gentle setting, and one of Loewe's most appealing ballads, indeed the one I should choose as an introduction to Loewe's songs altogether, is *Tom der Reimer* (op.135) of 1867. The theme is Scottish again (Tom the Rhymer), but Loewe took the poem from a book by the Berlin author Theodor Fontane, *Jenseits der Tweed* (1860). Loewe's version tells of Tom's meeting with a fairy, 'the heavenly queen', and his pledge to stay with her for seven years. This is Goethe's 'miraculous', 'through-composed' to music which never fails to illuminate the touching thoughts. When the pair plight their troth to 'Er küsste sie, sie küsste ihn/Ein Vogel sang im Eschenbaum' (He kissed her/She kissed him/A bird sang in the ash tree), Loewe's music for the bird is incomparable:

Loewe's most interesting setting – interesting for our theme particularly, as we trace the development of the German Lied – is undoubtedly that of Goethe's *Erlkönig*, no.3 of his opus no.1 of 1818. (Schubert's, it will be remembered, was written in 1815.) Where Schubert wrote a passionate, driving setting, with that famous, unbelievably difficult accompaniment of pounding triplets, Loewe took it all much more gently; he too set the ballad as a horse-ride, but his piano figures represent more than just horses' hooves – they are somehow more ghostly!

No one could deny Schubert's setting its originality – but some might deny its pre-eminence in the concert hall and suggest that not only might we hear Loewe's version more often, but that it is, in truth, a more skilful setting than Schubert's. It certainly agrees more with Goethe's intentions. It is not perhaps generally known that this seemingly dramatic – and very masculine – poem was in fact written for a female character in one of Goethe's Singspiele (a play with spoken dialogue, interspersed with songs). This play, *Die Fischerin* (The fisherwoman), written in 1772, opens with the main character, Dortchen, mending the nets and singing *Erlkönig* which is clearly meant to be a well-known folk-song. In the first performance at Weimar, the actress Corona Schröter, playing Dortchen, sang her own, very simple setting marked 'Langsam und abenteuerlich' (slowly and mysterious):

which certainly reproduces the 'mysterious' in the marking and obeys Goethe's own suggestion that this should be a song that 'the singer has learned by heart somewhere and manages to bring into some situation or other. These (songs) can and must have definite rounded melodies which are striking and easily memorized'.

Certainly the conclusion of Loewe's version with the great climax on 'tot' of 'In seinen Armen, das Kind war tot' (In his arms, the child was dead):

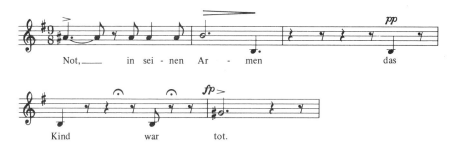

seems to me much more impressive than Schubert's rather melodramatic ending. *Erlkönig* really means 'King of the Elves' (from the Danish word *ellerkonge* or *elvekonge*). Both Herder and Goethe took it to mean 'King of the Alders', hence their translation *Erlkönig* from *Die Erle* = the alder tree, in German.

Loewe also wrote a number of very beautiful and very singable Lieder – the finest is another Goethe setting from his *Faust Part II*; it is a rather strange poem given to Lynkeus the watchman as he stands on Faust's observation tower, and that is the title of the song, *Lynkeus der Türmer auf Fausts Sternwarte singend* (op.9). This song alone would, I think, convince anyone with a musical ear of Loewe's stature as a song-writer. Now that 'Victoriana' are popular again and evenings of drawing-room songs and ballads a feature of concert-hall recitals – by Benjamin Luxon and Robert Tear *inter alia*! – complete with grand piano and table-lamp against the chintz curtains, a *Loewe-Abend* might prove extremely attractive.

In much the same way, one could construct a very attractive programme of Lieder by composers who are perhaps better known for their work in other musical fields, but whose many Lieder bear out the truth of the statement that Schubert's example tempted many to follow. Indeed, Franz Liszt, who was born in 1811, can be given the credit for popularizing many of Schubert's songs by his remarkable piano transcriptions, vulgar and 'showy' as they are to the true Schubertian. Yet the man who described Schubert as 'le musicien le plus poète que jamais' (the most poetic musician ever) could himself write the most delicate of accompaniments: listen for example to the piano in *Es muss ein Wunderbares sein* (There must be something wonderful) that, allied to the very fine melody, puts magic into Oskar von Redwitz's nondescript poem. Liszt's seventy or so Lieder are set to poems in five different languages – German, Hungarian, French, Italian and English; it is perhaps stretching my 'terms of reference' rather far to include his beautiful setting of Victor Hugo's *Oh, quand je dors* (Oh, when I sleep) as a 'Lied', but those who need to be convinced that the Liszt of the E flat piano concerto is not the only Liszt, should try to hear this song with its miraculous conclusion in the lover's cry to his Laura:

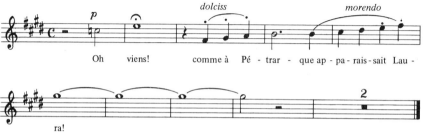

The same mastery of the medium is shown in *Ihr Glocken von Marling* (You bells of Marling) which is Schubertian in many places. Liszt's real love – the piano – is of course discernible in the prominence given to the accompaniments, and, in this respect, he is more Schumann-esque than Schubertian. Accompanists should not neglect Liszt! He can be rather tiresome at times however in his careless setting of words – witness the sad mess he made in 1843 of Goethe's exquisite poem *Wanderers Nachtlied I* (*Der du von dem Himmel bist*)(Thou which art *from* Heaven). Liszt not only changed the first line to a near-approximation to the wording of The Lord's Prayer in German, viz. Der Du *im Himmel bist* – *which art in* Heaven – but also does the final poignant line, 'Komm, ach, komm *in meine Brust'* (Come, oh come *into my heart*) to death by repeating it no less than seven times. (His third – 1860 – version is much less frothy, much more accurate – and much more appealing.)

It is perhaps not generally known that Richard Wagner too, born in 1813, two years after Liszt and three years after Schumann, tried his wings out as a Lieder composer. He never approached Liszt's total of seventy Lieder, but anyone interested in the development of the Lied would have to consider Wagner's contribution, particularly the group of five songs written in 1857–1858 for one of his extra-marital favourites, Mathilde Wesendonk, wife of one of Wagner's patrons. These 'sketches for *Tristan und Isolde'* are written for a strong soprano voice – Kirsten Flagstad has recorded them – and the poems and the music reproduce to perfection the overcharged, superheated Wagnerian atmosphere. It is not insignificant that one of Frau Wesendonk's poems was titled *Im Treibhaus* (In the greenhouse)! However, the female singer with a firm technique and a sense of Wagnerian grandeur can make *Schmerzen* (No.4) sound very thrilling.

Female singers might also like to sample the works of Robert Franz, born in 1815, whose three hundred or so songs suit the mezzo-soprano range best of all. If his best-known song (perhaps the only song of his to have made a name outside Germany) is his setting of Heine's poem *Aus meinen grossen Schmerzen* (From my great sorrows), it is recorded that, by 1890, when he was seventy-five and stone-deaf, he was astonished to find his songs as popular in Germany as those of Schubert, Schumann and Brahms. The reason for both these phenomena is probably the same; the Germans feel that his settings of words are as skilful and as sensitive as any, whereas the foreigner, while possibly accepting this, feels that Franz set the same poems, and less well, than his great contemporaries. Goethe, Heine, Eichendorff, von Chamisso, Rückert and Mörike figure largely among his poets too.

If only because one of them has become such a favourite with baritone singers in English churches at Christmas time, one should mention here Peter Cornelius' six tuneful *Weihnachtslieder* (Christmas Songs) (1856). Cornelius, born in 1824, was, like many other composers, also a poet, and there are many of his own poems among his seventy or so songs. The *Weihnachtslieder* however, with that peculiarly attractive final *Christkind* (Christ-child), exude that very German Christmas fragrance of pine-needles and burning candles which is why they are often paired on recordings with Gabriel Josef Rheinberger's *Star of Bethlehem*, set for soprano, baritone, chorus and orchestra.

MANY university courses which deal with 'modern times' might consider the year 1870 to be a very suitable *point de départ* for their opening lectures. The unification of both Germany and Italy, the growth of international industrialisation, the expansion of transport facilities, and the acceptance of more democratically-controlled and representative government, all contribute to lending the last third of the 19th century a 'modern' air.

Yet Johannes Brahms, who was only thirty-seven in 1871 and who died as late as 1897, nevertheless seems nearer in spirit to Haydn, Beethoven and Schubert, who died in 1809, 1827 and 1828 respectively. This 'conscious classicist', as Brahms has been called, is however a classicist only in the musical sense, i.e. one who composes more with *form* in mind than with *emotion*. In music, the 'Romantic' composers are those whose works are often large (or 'sprawling') – Liszt, Berlioz, Wagner – often strongly influenced by the burgeoning calls to national feeling heard in the 19th century – in Dvořák, Verdi, Glinka, Tchaikovsky – and, as often as not, based on themes taken from literary works – and that would include *all* the composers named. It would also account for the growing popularity of the Lied-form in the 19th century, since, by definition, the composer of Lieder has a close affinity with literary works.

It is therefore not easy to tease out the Classical from the Romantic; it was Goethe who said – as categorically as Olympians are allowed to! – 'I call what is healthy, the Classical; I call what is sickly, the Romantic'. We see what he meant, however; the 'Classical' virtues are those of balance, control, proportion, economy of form, harmony, the light of day; the 'Romantic' virtues (or 'vices', to many) are those of instability, emotional fervour, disproportion, extravagance of form, discord, the dark of night, dreams and the supernatural. It was the German writer Ludwig Börne who, on 30 October 1830, wrote from Paris about Victor Hugo and the French Romantics:

... Romantic poetry is wholesome for the French, not because of its creative, but because of its destructive principle. It is a joy to see how the industrious Romantics apply the match to everything, tear it down and push great wheelbarrows of rules and classical rubbish away from the scene of the conflagration.

These are, of course, two sides of the same coin – we all have aspects of both in our make-up, as do nations and art-forms. One could say, indeed, that the history of 'art' is the history of the swing of fashion from one of these poles to the other. At any given time, custom decrees that the prevailing art-form will be nearer one pole than the other.

These thoughts make Brahms a fascinating case-study, particularly when one is trying to examine him as a composer of Lieder. We have seen the *Kunstlied* develop from the artless *Volkslied* with a basic accompaniment, through the 18th century with its attention firmly fixed on the *music* while the text – libretto or poem – was by and large merely an excuse for the development of instrumental variations, into the early 19th century where literary values assume much greater importance because of the strength of literary Romanticism. (By the middle and end of the century, we shall see that the Wagnerian-Lisztian demand for a 'fusion of the arts' had brought about a change in the composer's attitude to Lieder.)

Brahms, like Schumann, worshipped Schubert and he knew the Austrian's songs well – indeed it was Brahms' friend, the baritone Julius Stockhausen, who gave the first complete performance of *Die schöne Müllerin* (in 1856), and who sang Schumann's *Dichterliebe*, with either Brahms himself or Clara Schumann as accompanist. (It will probably be known that Brahms befriended the widowed Clara Schumann to her death in 1896 and one of his greatest contributions to the corpus of Lieder was the *Vier ernste Gesänge* (Four Serious Songs), written as an expression of his sorrow at her impending death.)

Brahms is known as a classical Romantic, probably because his interest really lay with the form of the *music* rather than with the words; he set a large number of poems by what I have called 'second-division' poets; August von Platen, Ludwig Tieck, Ludwig Hölty and Detlev von Liliencron for example. He set only five poems by Goethe, but one of these, *Dämmrung senkte sich von oben* (Twilight sank from above) is a jewel; the beginning portrays the peace of the evening to perfection:

schon   ist   al - le   Nä - he   fern,

But, on the whole, the two hundred or so Brahms' Lieder do not present us with that marvellous fusion of 'words' and 'music' that the greatest Lieder composers, Schubert and Wolf, achieve. Writers on Brahms usually present the beautiful musical beginning of *Wie bist du, meine Königin/Durch sanfte Güte wonnevoll!* (How blissful you are, my queen, with your gentle goodness)(op.32, No.9) as a particularly striking example of how Brahms often stressed the wrong syllable of the poem in order to make it fit his musical phrase. Thus, Brahms' setting emphasizes the words *Wié* bist du *méine* Königin:

Wie   bist   du,   mei - ne   Kö - ni - gin,

where, they would claim, the more normal German stress would be on *bíst* and *Königin*. It is a point that would have to be made in any scholarly study of Brahms' Lieder, but not one to disturb the average singer, who would find this one of the loveliest and most melodious of all Lieder; the often-repeated word *wonnevoll* (literally 'bliss-full'), to which Brahms seemed remarkably drawn, is given a dropping ecstatic phrase which is the epitome of the Romantic lover's sigh to his beloved:

won - ne - voll,   won - ne - won - ne - voll!

It is often said that because of his earlier interest in folk-songs and as a director of choral groups, Brahms favoured strophic settings rather than 'through-composed' or 'modified strophic', believing them to be superior because of the strictness of their form, and, incidentally, also because it was more 'difficult' to find a melody that would fit and suit every verse. In actual fact, of Brahms' two hundred or so songs, only one third are purely strophic. Nevertheless, it is true that such a regard for symmetry is one of the major features of his four great symphonies. We find however that it is precisely the modified strophic songs which contain some of the finest of Brahms' inventions. The song-cycle *Die schöne Magelone* (Beautiful Magelone)(opus 33), to not-too-inspired 'mediaeval' verses by Ludwig Tieck, contains many fine examples of these, none finer than No.9, *Ruhe, Süssliebchen, im Schatten der grünen, dämmernden Nacht* (Sleep, my love, in the shadow of the green, twilit night). It *should* be sung by Count Peter, one of the male singers in the cycle, to the fair Magelone – in theory, there are two male and two female characters – but it has often been borrowed as an out-of-context single soprano Lied. The song is a beautiful lullaby which, based on the opening melody,

leads on to a wonderfully evocative refrain on a rising phrase *Schlafe, schlaf ein* (Fall asleep, do)

which needs to be sung with the gentlest half-voice. Since one rarely hears this cycle in the concert-hall, it would be a great pity to lose such a marvellous song by insisting that it should only be sung in context, for these fifteen 'Romances' do, in truth, just sound like a collection of songs on a theme. Tieck wrote the poems in the Romantic manner as interludes in a prose narrative, and one would really have to have read that to understand the true significance of the interspersed poems.

Brahms' nine songs of opus 32 (1864) would probably form the best introduction – albeit a melancholy one – to his Lieder – although the singer who knows the mighty *Von ewiger Liebe* (Of eternal love)(Op.43, No.1) of 1868, might disagree! This splendid love-song, with its strangely futuristic peroration, 'Eisen und Stahl, man schmiedet sie um' (One can re-cast iron and steel'. . . but our love must endure for ever', it goes on) is always a favourite when sung as the last song of a Brahms' group – and it is 'unisex', since there is a short narrative passage which leads to a declamation of love by first the boy and then the girl, who ends the song on the ringing phrase 'Unsere Liebe muss ewig bestehen' (Our love must endure for ever):

Brahms' Lieder are undeniably pessimistic, on the whole – Hugo Wolf said once that 'Brahms could not exult' – and he showed the light touch of the other great song-writers only infrequently, partly because of his own rather gloomy, introverted temperament, partly because of the nature of his musical mind. He thought in dark hues, it seems, although his last great vocal work, the *Four Serious Songs* (op.121) of 1896, set to the Biblical texts of Ecclesiastes, Ecclesiasticus and St Paul, does end on an optimistic note: 'And now abideth faith, hope and love. . .' These songs, written, it must be remembered, only seven years before the death of Hugo Wolf, when Brahms was sixty-three, mirror his fears of Clara Schumann's impending death; she died in fact on 20 May, two weeks after he had finished the songs. They have become a lower register preserve – they were written for Julius Stockhausen – since their effect is made by the gravity of the voice and the piano bass, for example at the beginning of No.3 where the voice apostrophizes Death: 'O Tod, wie bitter bist du' (O death, how bitter Thou art), and the piano sinks to a low F.

But for the singer who can range from there to a ringing top G on 'Liebe' (love), this is a noble series of Lieder, which forms an essential ingredient of any baritone or bass repertoire. It is not surprising that many good judges of song feel that these songs, like other Brahms' songs, would sound most effective when accompanied by an orchestra. Certainly, they were composed at a time when the age of the solo song with piano accompaniment was drawing to a close, and they, with Hugo Wolf's last Lieder, can be regarded as the last great monuments of the Golden Age of Lieder. But even in Brahms' middle years, he, with Franz Liszt, had felt that many songs demanded an orchestral accompaniment. We know that Brahms made orchestral versions of Schubert's *An Schwager Kronos* and *Memnon*, just as Liszt had orchestrated *Erlkönig*. It is perhaps further proof that Brahms was always more interested in the *music* of a song than in the poem being set; but when one listens to the melody of a song like *Feldeinsamkeit* (see p.150 below), one wonders if it is material whether such a melody 'fits' the text or not!

Clearly, one can split hairs on the matter, and, if the listener has no German, it probably does *not* matter. But – when we are considering the *Kunstlied* as an art-form and attempting to assess the quality of the various composers, then their success or failure in producing this 'fusion' is just as clearly of paramount importance. Each of the great composers can claim perfection in *some* of their songs; by common consent however, it was the first and the last representatives of the Golden Age who achieved success most often: the two Viennese composers Franz Schubert and Hugo Wolf.

When Hugo Wolf died, *The Musical Times* reported simply: 'He wrote songs wholesale', a reference to Wolf's almost single-minded devotion to the setting of poems. The list of compositions published as Appendix II to Frank Walker's authoritative book on the composer, certainly lists many instrumental compositions, but, apart from the 1903 *Italian Serenade*, and of course Wolf's opera *Der Corregidor* (1895), very few are now heard in public.* For the concert-goer, Wolf is indeed a 'writer of songs'.

Writing fifty or so years after the death of Schubert and Goethe, Wolf knew that *fin-de-siècle* sensation that 'it had all been done before', a sensation that artists living today are beginning to experience. But, like Schubert and Müller, Schumann and Heine, Wolf too was fortunate enough to stumble upon a poet, Eduard Mörike, whose words released a stream of melodic invention. Yet the fifty years which had passed since Schubert's day had brought unimagined advances in knowledge of the human soul and mind. Wolf lived contemporaneously with those great anti-Christian movements, Marxism and Darwinism, and with the insidious growth of urban development and mechanical invention. The effect on sensitive minds was horrendous – many withdrew from the world, either into suicide or, as in Wolf's case, insanity. The last five years of his troubled life were spent in a mental asylum before he died, aged only forty-three. He lies buried beside Schubert and Beethoven in the Central Cemetery in Vienna.

Hugo Wolf believed that the 19th century Lieder composers had moved the emphasis away from the poet to the composer: the 'Wort' had lost the day to the 'Ton' – and he was determined to redress the balance. On 24th December 1880, Wolf set a poem by Eduard Mörike,

---

* *Hugo Wolf* (Dent, 1968).

Suschens Vogel; we do not know how Wolf alighted on Mörike – Schumann had set five of his poems for solo voice, Brahms two, and Wolf may well have heard the Schumann songs.

Mörike, born in 1804, wrote many of his loveliest poems while a Protestant pastor in Württemberg in south-west Germany from 1834–1843. His poems, published in 1838, have grown steadily in popularity among lovers of German literature, till he now ranks with Goethe and Heine as one of Germany's major poets. There is a soft, sweet lyricism about Mörike that is hard to resist – a touch of the *Volkslied* along with nature poetry of the highest order. Yet – as we have seen so often before – without the genius of the Wolf settings, Mörike's name, like that of so many of the German poets mentioned, might not have become known outside Germany.

An old professorial friend of mine – who indeed introduced me to both Mörike and Wolf – used to say that neither was 'for mass consumption'. The shy, retiring poet seems perfectly matched to the introspective, solitary musician. Here was a true 'marriage of minds'.

Wolf's fifty-three settings of Mörike poems have few equals in the quality of their white-hot inspiration. That Wolf thought of them first and foremost as *poems* and not as texts to be set to music, is shown by the title-page of the score, which reads: 'Poems by Eduard Mörike, for voice and piano, set to music by Hugo Wolf'. Wolf set the first poem *Der Tambour* (The drummer) on 16th February 1888, and there followed that flood of melodic inspiration up to 18th May 1888; in these three short months, he composed forty-three songs. He took up the challenge again on 4th October 1888 and finished the fifty-third song on 26th November 1888. It is not difficult to be awed by the inspirational heat in these Lieder; a lover of German poems senses here, almost more than with any other composer, a one-ness of poem and setting. The lily is often gilded – and the result is art of a higher order.

The group of fifty-three poems is not linked in any way, either by theme or by key sequence. Wolf simply proceeded from poem to poem, reacting to the emotions called forth within him; the result is a glorious *mélange* of lyrical, devotional, declamatory, even comic songs – although the latter find more detractors among critics than most of Wolf's songs. There are those who find his humour heavy and what they like to call 'Teutonic', every spade being called a shovel and every nut being cracked with a heavy hammer.

A sense of humour is a very personal matter – the reader or listener or performer is asked to go away and listen to Wolf's *Zur Warnung*, where a hung-over poet calls on the gods to help his Muse after a convivial evening – then decide whether Wolf's setting is 'comical' or not. Or he should listen to the last song in the printed volume, *Abschied*, where Mörike (and, I am sure, Wolf too) took revenge on an unkind critic, who had insulted him by drawing attention to his unsightly nose, by leading him to the top of the stairs and helping him on his way 'home' with a timely push – which Wolf sets to a descending cluster of sparkling notes, and then parodies the whole Viennese situation by writing a postlude in an intoxicating Viennese waltz rhythm! Music critics tend to sniff at these Lieder – but what joy the artist gets from singing them – and from the audience's obvious pleasure in hearing them!

But these are trifles compared to the matchless gems offered else-where. If pressed to choose the most flawless, one might select one of the few settings to match Schubert's music to Goethe's *Über allen Gipfeln ist Ruh'* (see Part Three, p.131 below): Wolf's setting of Mörike's *Das verlassene Mägdlein* (The forlorn girl). The poem had been set by more than fifty other composers up to 1888 (including Schumann), but Wolf's setting has dwarfed them all. The music traces the freezing dawn as the poor servant-maid who has lost her lover goes about lighting the morning fire. The opening bars with their distant descending melody make the scene almost cinematically real:

and the heartbroken sob at the end as the love-lorn maid wishes that the fearful day would soon be over: 'O ging er wieder' (O would it were soon over) is perfectly portrayed in the music.

In the bigger songs, and in the ballads like *Der Feuerreiter* (The fire-rider) and *Die Geister am Mummelsee* (The ghosts on Lake Mummel), Wolf's skill in the 'through-composed' idiom becomes a positive dis-advantage, since he was so able to portray scenes and emotions in music that he often went too far and overloaded the setting with too much detail.

Alongside the remarkable Mörike-Lieder, Wolf can place equally towering achievements: the settings of the one and only Goethe – there are fifty-one to savour. Wolf was unhappy about setting poems that Schubert and Schumann had already set, which often led him to choose less well-known, and, in truth, less suitable poems. Yet, where he believed that Schubert or Schumann had *not* made a success of a setting, he resolved to improve upon it. The outstanding examples are the settings of the poems found in Goethe's novel *Wilhelm Meister* when the 'hero' Wilhelm meets up with the orphan girl Mignon and her companion, the half-crazed harper. Wolf tried very hard to place the settings in the original context – but then, as Frank Walker has pointed out (op.cit.), he perversely chose to set them in the order in which they appeared in Goethe's *Collected Lyrics* – which was quite different from their order in the novel!

All the settings are flawed in one way or another, but they contain some wonderful music – none more so than Mignon's memory of her Italian homeland, *Kennst du das Land, wo die Zitronen blühn. . .?* (Do you know the land where the lemon trees blossom?) The enormous sweep of music at the end of the song eventually convinced the composer that the music was too much for the piano and he made two orchestral versions. The soprano who has battled against the Wagner-like orchestra might well prefer the piano accompaniments – and a sensitive listener might feel that this operatic portrayal is a far remove from Goethe's hapless, helpless orphan mite.

This is certainly not the case where the 'grand' setting matches the 'grand' theme: the last three settings of Goethe are of poems whose concepts, themes and language are truly gigantic: *Prometheus, Ganymed* and *Grenzen der Menschheit* (Limits of humanity). All three poems come from Goethe's defiant years of pantheistic worship – they glorify the individualistic attitude to life and therefore cry out for a heroic setting and response from the composer. This they certainly receive from Wolf. To settle the eternal argument, whether Wolf or Schubert most accurately reproduces the sentiments of these poems in music, must, in the last analysis, be a personal choice. Perhaps we should just rest happy that we have them both?

Finally, mention must be made of what were nearly Wolf's last groups of songs: *Spanisches Liederbuch* (1889–1890), settings of translations of 16th and 17th century Spanish and Portuguese poems by Paul Heyse and Emanuel Geibel, and *Italienisches Liederbuch* (Parts I and II, 1890–1896), settings of Italian poems, also translated by Paul Heyse.

The religious poems in the *Spanisches Liederbuch* take the palm: *Herr, was trägt der Boden hier* (Lord, what does this earth bear?) is a most moving poem in which Wolf encapsulated the whole Passion tragedy in a mere twenty-seven bars of deeply-felt music. The low baritone or bass voice will find here an experience which equals that found in Bach's Passion music. Again, in *Nun wandre, Maria* (Now let us go, Mary), Joseph's words of encouragement to the exhausted Mary as they journey to Bethlehem, Wolf manages wonderfully to depict the almost plodding footsteps of the Holy Couple as they cling to each other on the way:

Langsam und ruhig

Nun wan - dre, Ma - ri - a, nun wan - dre nur fort.   Schon

The pseudo-Spanish effects of the secular songs do not attract me as much as the glories of the *Italian Song-Book*. The two Books can be divided between the female and the male voice; there are treasures for both within. Complete performances of the songs are not necessary – the two singers can choose a perfectly-balanced programme from the forty-six Lieder. These songs are a mixture of secular love, jealousy, irony, humour and lyricism. There is something for everyone to enjoy, indeed, and it is quite invidious to mention but two: yet *Auch kleine Dinge* (Even tiny things can enchant us), a praise of the small, seemingly insignificant objects in life, is set to a haunting melody:

Auch klei - ne Din - ge kön - nen uns ent - zü - cken,

and its twenty-four bars are in themselves 'tiny things which enchant us'. *Auch kleine Dinge* often begins performances of excerpts from the *Italian Song-Boook*, just as *Ich hab' in Penna einen Liebsten wohnen* (I have a lover living in Penna) often brings them to an exhilarating conclusion. This high-speed catalogue of the girl's amorous conquests throughout Italy ends on a rapturous top A (on *'zehn in Castiglione'* (*ten* in Castiglione)), and then, as the singer stands back with a satisfied, contented smile on her face, the poor accompanist embarks on what he has probably been dreading all evening – Wolf's postlude, which is a helter-skelter of nine bars of rushing semi-quavers which last for thirty-two seconds –·while some of the audience (as Gerald Moore once pointed out sorrowfully) will have already started to applaud the singer!

At the very end of his creative life (in 1897), Wolf produced three of the greatest Lieder for the bass voice that we possess. Although I shall try to answer the question of 'which-voice-for-which-Lied' in Part Two, it is true that, if the text is largely disregarded, *any* voice can sing *any* Lied. (Wolf himself was fairly inconsistent in his demands, we know.) But these three settings of dark brooding poems by Michelangelo, translated by Walter Robert-Tornow – and one in particular, *Alles endet, was entstehet* (All things created come to dust) – seem somehow to be a fitting epitaph to the life of this haunted genius who more than any other composer, more even than Schubert, devoted his entire life to the German Lied.

71

[6] GUSTAV MAHLER AND THE LIED IN THE 20TH CENTURY

WITH HUGO WOLF'S tragic death in a Vienna asylum on 22 February 1903, one could fairly claim that the Golden Age of the German Lied was over. Not that Lieder did not continue to be written; we shall see shortly that they did, and that they continue to be written up to the present day. Concert-hall recitals continue to be based, however, on the Lieder of that hundred-year period – why, is a difficult question to answer. Some good judges believe that, with some notable exceptions, such as that of Hermann Hesse, the lyrical poetry that could inspire this type of musical setting is no longer being written. Others believe that Hugo Wolf took the Lied-form as far as it could go and that his orchestral versions of Lieder like *Kennst du das Land. . .?*, *Ganymed* and *Prometheus* and others written under the influence of his declared enthusiasm for the full-blown tonalities of Richard Wagner, removed the Lied from the realm of *Kammermusik* (chamber music) and made it part of the orchestral repertoire.

Whatever the reason, the fact is that performers and listeners alike will continue to be charmed by the enormous amount of music available to the Lieder-singer. Nearly four thousand songs are there to be sung and listened to; more than enough for one person's life-time. Yet, despite the belief that this Golden Age came to an end with Hugo Wolf, the influence of vocal music continued to be strong among those composers who considered themselves to be heir to the inheritance – particularly in the southern parts of the German-speaking area.

Gustav Mahler was born in the same year as Hugo Wolf, and, although he is best known to most concert-goers as a composer of tuneful and, at times, very long symphonies, he was truly Viennese in his love and affection for the human voice – in his case professionally so, since he served for ten years as the Director of the celebrated Vienna State Opera. Mahler's Lieder, unlike Wolf's, place the *music* firmly in the ascendant – he is much more concerned with the 'singability' of the melody than with the 'fusion' of word and sound. The importance that he attached to themes from *Volkslieder* underline the point. His first published songs were even divided into *Lieder* and *Gesänge* (the plural of *der Gesang*, another word for '*song*'), where the *Lieder* belonged to the Schubert-Schumann tradition of the *Kunstlied*, and the *Gesänge* more to the less sophisticated tradition of the *Volkslied*. Many of these delightful melodies found their way into his symphonies, where they were then embroidered upon out of all recognition. Debussy once wrote of this tendency that 'from east to west, the tiniest villages have been ransacked, and simple tunes, plucked from the mouths of hoary peasants, find themselves to their consternation trimmed with harmonic frills'. He might have been writing about the Mahlerian symphonies!

Nevertheless, the concert-goer or record collector should not be alienated from Mahler's Lieder by these remarks. In many ways, Mahler looked back in this genre rather than forward; his greatest achievement, in my opinion, is the *Lieder eines fahrenden Gesellen* (1883–1885), wrongly translated as *Songs of a Wayfarer: A Geselle* in German is a journeyman who, having finished his apprenticeship, sets out to perfect his craft by travelling from town to town for some years before returning home to produce his 'masterwork'. Thus, the translation should be 'Songs of a Journeyman'. Mahler wrote the four poems himself and set them to music not far removed from the world of Schubert's *Winterreise*, although *his* poems speak of Spring. The songs were set for voice and piano originally, but were clearly always intended for the orchestral arrangement probably made in 1893; in No.3, *Ich hab' ein glühend' Messer in meiner Brust* (I have a red-hot knife in my breast), the male soloist, (and it really should be a male soloist) has to override the orchestra in the great *crescendi*, making the song into a quasi-Wagnerian aria. In No. 4 however – *Die zwei blauen Augen von meinem Schatz* (The two blue eyes of my beloved), we return to the true element of the Lied, and, as the harp, pizzicato cello and woodwind lead into the final funeral march section, *Auf der Strasse steht ein Lindenbaum* (A linden tree stands by the roadside):

Mahler's late-Romantic Viennese heritage is plain to hear.

The intensely melodic strain, derived ultimately from folk-song, is heard again in Mahler's setting of five poems by Friedrich Rückert, the Romantic poet who was much favoured by Schubert, Schumann and Brahms too. These songs, written in 1901–1902 and published later with the others as *Seven Last Songs*, are also set for solo voice and orchestra and seem to me to be quintessential Mahler. Each song has a haunting melody which colours the words of the poem in masterly style. *Ich atmet' einen linden Duft* (I breathed in a gentle fragrance) – a play on the German word for lime-tree, *Die Linde* – has a wonderful weaving melody which seems to mirror the delicate spray of the lime-tree picked by the beloved. The grandeur of the last song, *Um Mitternacht*, fades rather in the piano version, since Mahler sets the words 'Herr über Tod und Leben/Du hältst die Wacht/Um Mitternacht' (Lord of Life and Death, you keep watch at midnight) to a chorus of piercing brass, again proof, if proof were still needed, of how far the Lied had 'advanced', since the days of the simple naive *Volkslied*, and the subtleties of the Schubertian Lied, expressed in voice and piano alone.

Mahler's great cycles *Das Lied von der Erde* (The Song of the Earth) (1907–1908), settings for contralto (or baritone), tenor and orchestra, of poems translated from the Chinese by Hans Bethge, and *Kindertotenlieder* (Songs on the deaths of children)(1901–1904), settings of poems by Friedrich Rückert, which can be sung either by male voice alone or in partnership with a contralto, are technically Lieder in my earlier definition, but belong exclusively to the concert-hall and its orchestral repertoire. The addition of the orchestra takes us back to the 18th century, where the 'words' were the libretti of the opera composers, and removes the Lied from the intimacy of the 19th century circle of friends round the piano; it no doubt also contributed to the holding of *Liederabende* in huge concert-halls, so that it is perfectly possible nowadays to hear Schubert's intimate confessional, *Winterreise*, sung before an audience of up to three thousand. It is of course in some measure the penalty of popularity; large audiences have wanted to hear great names – Schwarzkopf, Seefried, Baker, Ameling, Hotter, Fischer-Dieskau, Pears, Schreier *et al* – sing their favourite Lieder, and have become accustomed – perhaps because of the growth of the 'star' system, maybe even of 'pop' concerts – to sharing their intimate pleasures with hundreds, or even thousands, of others! But it is a far remove from Schumann's belief that his songs sound best 'when sung alone at evening'.

Richard Strauss' songs show much the same mixture of simplicity and grandeur; many of them were written with the voice of his wife-to-be Pauline de Ahna, in mind and sound best when sung with the crystalline soprano tones of, say, an Elisabeth Schumann. Strauss, born only four years after Mahler and Hugo Wolf, in 1864, actually lived right into our own times, dying a broken, embittered man, shattered by Germany's cultural and human losses in the Second World War, in 1949. Indeed, his last great work for the voice was his *Vier letzte Lieder* (Four

74

Last Songs), settings of poems by Eichendorff and the 20th century poet Hermann Hesse, written in 1948. Strauss was in first place an operatic composer who, in all truth, did not treat the voice with much respect! As in Wagnerian opera, many singers of Strauss fight an often impossible battle against the might of the full Straussian orchestra. By his own account, Strauss was not a natural song-composer; it was a product of lazy hours when 'good luck' threw a poem in his way; *if* the right poem came along, and *if* he were in a musical frame of mind, then a satisfactory song *might* result – but no lover of the Lied would wish to be without the twenty or so really great Strauss Lieder. His earliest group of Lieder, set actually for tenor (1882–1883), contains one of his best and deservedly most popular songs, *Zueignung* (Dedication)(op.10, No.1), to a poem by Hermann von Gilm; it is a modified strophic song of great beauty and power which, set to a rather archaic German text, gives thanks to the beloved for the purity of her love. Its charm and popularity rest in the repetition of the phrase 'Habe Dank' (Receive my thanks) at the end of each of the three verses, with the final exultant top E on the last 'Dank', accompanied by thunderous chords – and applause!

Like all the great Germanic composers, Strauss was blessed with the gift of melody, and, at their best, his songs rank in tunefulness with any of those already mentioned. His opus 27 songs, *Ruhe, meine Seele* (Rest, my soul), *Cäcilie, Heimliche Aufforderung* (Secret invitation) and *Morgen* (Tomorrow), written when he was approaching thirty, seem to come into this category. Indeed *Morgen* (No.4) must be one of the finest songs of the period. Few listeners are able to avoid succumbing to the sheer melodic charm of the long piano introduction – almost half the song – before the voice steals in with 'Und morgen wird die Sonne wieder scheinen')(And tomorrow the sun will shine again) (See p.158 below).

Strauss' operatic collaboration with the aristocratic Austrian poet Hugo von Hofmannsthal showed up his true nature in that he was often unhappy with the fastidiousness with which the poet treated his libretti. Strauss' Lieder show a corresponding *lack* of fastidiousness; many of his settings are of very poor contemporary poets. His best songs indeed are of poems whose *emotions* spoke to him as soon as he had read the poem. Otto Julius Bierbaum's *Freundliche Vision* (Friendly vision)(Op.48, No.1) is such a poem. Strauss must have been moved by the images of the man and his girl-friend walking through a meadow to the white house of their dreams. Like *Morgen*, this song moves incredibly slowly, demanding from the singer, who, to judge from the text, *should* be male, a sustained *legato* up to the concluding lines 'Und ich geh' mit einer, die mich lieb hat/, in den Frieden voll Schönheit' (And I walk with a girl, who loves me, into the beauty-filled peace). One could not deny that

Strauss had captured the *emotion* of the poem, even although he might not have achieved that magic fusion of word and sound. (That Strauss knew very well what was being aimed at in the setting of words and music was shown in the rather tiresome vocal squabble between Olivier the Poet and Flamand the Musician in his opera *Capriccio* (1942), which ends with the compromise that 'Ton *und* Wort sind Bruder und Schwester' (Music *and* text are brother and sister), and although his collaboration with von Hofmannsthal was often acrimonious, the mere fact that they worked together for six operas proved Strauss' appreciation of the importance of a good libretto.) We see this too in his final work for the soprano voice, the settings of three poems by the 20th century poet Hermann Hesse, and a fourth by the 19th century Romantic poet Joseph von Eichendorff – the *Vier letzte Lieder*. They too, especially no.4, have something of the typically Straussian 'motionless ecstasy', although they also proved the point made above that the *Klavierlied*, as the German call the song for voice and piano, was now felt to be inadequate by some composers for the expression of deeply-felt emotions.

Nevertheless, the 20th century continued to produce what wine-growers might have called a 'Spätlese', a late harvest, of such songs. Many 20th century composers, mainly, although not exclusively, German-speaking, have written Lieder which deserve more attention than they receive from performers, critics and audiences.

It was Fischer-Dieskau's recording of Lieder by the 'Second Viennese School', Arnold Schoenberg, Alban Berg and Anton von Webern, which surprised many listeners. It showed that, despite 'atonality', 'melody' lay deep in the hearts of these Austrian composers. Of course, Schoenberg's songs (opp. 1, 2 and 3) were written some years before his first experiments with atonality, but they prove the point made nevertheless. Schoenberg, born in 1874, writing here in his twenties, is clearly writing in a Wolf-ian tradition; there is a spikiness to the melodies and a fullness in the piano accompaniments which, allied to the melodic quality – listen to his setting of Richard Dehmel's poem *Schenk' mir deinen goldenen Kamm* (Give me your golden comb) – has us looking both backwards and forwards.

Schoenberg's enormous *Gurrelieder* (1900–1911) for solo voices, chorus and orchestra, might seem far removed from the Schubert-Wolf intimate chamber-music atmosphere of *Heidenröslein* or *Nun wandre, Maria*, yet the old attraction for 'solo voice with piano' is stll evident, witness that most compelling, albeit atonal song-cycle *Das Buch der hängenden Gärten* (The Book of the Hanging Gardens) (opus 15, 1908–1909) to fifteen poems by Schoenberg's German contemporary, the eccentric Stefan

George. The composer wrote about these songs in an essay in the German Expressionist periodical named after Franz Marc's art group *Der Blaue Reiter* (The Blue Horseman) in 1912, when he admitted that it was just the *opening words* of a poem which gave him the impetus for a setting – all else must follow from these initial sounds because he felt that a true work of art was homogeneous in its construction! It is an interesting thesis, and one feels when reading a George poem that a composer might well be attracted by the *sound* rather than by the esoteric *sense* of the poem. Look at the first of the fifteen poems. Among other eccentricities, George insisted that all his German nouns should begin with a small letter:

unterm schutz von dichten blättergründen
wo von sternen feine flocken schneien·

of which a rough translation might be: 'Protected by thick leafy depths/where fine flakes snow from the stars'. (The · indicates that George also demanded from his publisher, Bondi, that the full stop be printed centrally. It was a fascinating experiment!)

Alban Berg, a disciple of Schoenberg, born in 1885, is best known here for his operas *Wozzeck* and the unfinished *Lulu*. Although he wrote over ninety songs, Berg seemed to have little genuine interest in the genre. I would mention one song that *is* well worth hearing: the tiny *Warm die Lüfte* (Warm the winds) (his opus 2, No.4) of 1908–9 to a poem by Alfred Mombert, with its beautiful, almost romantic conclusion on 'Der Eine stirbt, daneben der Andere lebt:/Das macht die Welt so tiefschön (One dies, the other lives:/That makes the world so profoundly beautiful). There is something Wolf-ian here too.

The third of the 'School', Anton von Webern, born in 1883, has gained greatly in popularity in recent years, but it is doubtful whether his Lieder will ever figure largely in concert-hall programmes. Listening to Fischer-Dieskau singing his *Vorfrühling* (Early Spring), one can discern the undeniable Viennese heritage, but his later works, his settings of Stefan George, for example, are perhaps for *aficionados* only.

The performer or listener seeking worthwhile 20th century solo vocal works in German might turn lastly to four sources, two of which might yet yield future treasures. Hans Werner Henze, born in 1926, seems to have inherited the Germanic gift for melodious settings, albeit of rather exotic texts. He composed his *Fünf Neapolitanische Lieder* (Five Neapolitan Songs) in Neapolitan dialect for Dietrich Fischer-Dieskau, who has faithfully performed them on numerous occasions. Most composers have set poems in languages other than German – the fact that the composer was German-speaking seems to have been sufficient to earn the setting the title of 'Lied'. These poems are in turn witty, savage, and seductive, and the music has melodic charm which will, I believe, ensure it a place in the repertoire – of professional singers, at any rate.

Singers who are looking for a modern *Winterreise*, a cycle which paints man's grief and despair, might look at the Swiss composer Othmar Schoeck and his cycle for male voice on poems of his compatriot, the 19th century poet, Gottfried Keller, *Lebendig begraben* (Buried alive). Schoeck (1886–1957) set fourteen poems telling the story of a man who, buried alive some seven feet down, describes his life as it passes by before his eyes. The orchestral accompaniment obscures the true provenance of these songs, which is clearly the tradition of Schubert, Schumann and Wolf. This is not to say that Schoeck does not speak with a distinctive voice, but that, unlike the Viennese composers mentioned above, his four hundred or so songs almost always look backwards, which almost certainly accounts for Schoeck's neglect. (The same can be said of the Lieder of the long-lived Hans Pfitzner (1869–1949), whose works are heard from time to time in Germany as part of a 'contemporary' group).

Lebendig begraben, dating from 1927, deserves a hearing; Keller, a Swiss from Zürich, was one of the best of the 19th century poets writing in German. He had a fine ear for rhyme and metre, and his acerbic, anti-Christian temperament gave rise to poetry which is a far remove from the 'moon, love and dreams' of the earlier Romantics. Schoeck showed considerable skill in matching Keller's mixture of melancholy and anger.

The poems of the 19th century German Swiss poet Hermann Hesse have attracted over two thousand settings by great and small. The Austrian operatic composer Gottfried von Einem, born in 1918, set a group of these as a song-cycle, *Leb wohl, Frau Welt* (Good-bye, my world) in 1974. The seven Lieder *are* this time written with piano accompaniment and thus serve as a comparison with the Lieder of yore. Von Einem, who made his name mainly as an operatic composer (*Dantons Tod* and *Der Prozess*), sets Hesse's neo-Romantic verses in a modern idiom, but they seem to me to cry out for the melodious setting which is lacking here. It looks as if the modern composer is (once again) more interested in the music *per se* than in attempting to find a musical equivalent for the lyrics.

Aribert Reimann's settings of poems by Paul Celan are similarly essays in musical style. Reimann, born in 1936, sets the singer almost impossible tasks by treating the voice as one of the instruments for which he writes – much as Bach did. The orchestral accompaniment to these six Lieder (Cycle for baritone and orchestra) (1971) which swamps the voice at times, showed the way Reimann was heading. It led him to the composition of his great opera *Lear*, written for Dietrich Fischer-Dieskau in the title-rôle, which had its first performance in Munich in 1978.

I shall close this section with a perhaps surprising choice; just as German composers have set poems in languages other than German (Haydn!), so too have non-German composers set German poems, and have thus written 'Lieder'. A very worthwhile group to perform and hear is Benjamin Britten's *Six Hölderlin Fragments*, written for the tenor Peter Pears in 1958. Britten, one of the great melodists of the 20th century, achieved here a fusion of word and music such as few 20th century composers have approached. Hölderlin, a contemporary of Goethe and Schiller, spent half his seventy-three years in mental darkness in a carpenter's house near Stuttgart before his death in 1843, and it is almost as if Britten had composed these settings with this tragic fate in mind. We know of course how magnificently Britten has set English texts – *Winter Words* (to poems by Thomas Hardy), the Donne and Michelangelo settings and the eerie music to Blake's *Songs of Experience*. Here however, on foreign territory, he manages to sound as if he had been a lifelong part of the Austro-Germanic inheritance. Perhaps because of his devotion to British folk-songs, Britten was able to tap the well of melody for these strange, almost crazed poems. He had been introduced to them by Prinz Ludwig of Hesse (the 'Ludwig Landgraf' who, with Fischer-Dieskau, translated his *War Requiem* into German), and the settings are dedicated to the Prince. Indeed, the first performance was given in the Prince's castle, Schloss Wolfsgarten, in November 1958.

The songs do not form a 'cycle', but there are thematic connections: the loss of youth and hope is allied to the passing of the Greek gods, on the one hand, and the oncoming of winter on the other. The six poems are set with Britten's usual consummate skill – voice and piano move independently, each painting a picture of the winter desolation.

If *Hälfte des Lebens* (No.5)(The half of life) is the finest of the group, it seemed at first to need Peter Pears' characteristic 'swoop' to reproduce the coldness and emptiness of Hölderlin's poem. The eerie conclusion:

Die Mauern stehn
Sprachlos und kalt, im Winde
Klirren die Fahnen.

(The walls stand speechless and cold, in the wind the weather-vanes clatter), gives a true *Winterreise*-image and perhaps proves how moved Britten always was by his performances of the Schubert cycle.

The group/cycle takes only twelve minutes to perform, but it is a wonderful artistic experience and should be heard more often.

IT COULD well be that in this 'Age of the Common Man' with the democratization of all forms of society, government, education and religion, art too has been 'democratized', and that the Lied, as it developed particularly in the 19th century was considered an esoteric form of art relating only to what the German writer Martin Walser once called 'die oberen Zehntausend', the 'upper ten thousand', that stratum of German society who could afford to pay the prices demanded for seats at the great opera-houses and festivals of the world – £20 is a commonplace price for a seat in Berlin or Munich. Certainly the 'Lieder', used in the normal meaning of 'songs', which have proved most popular in the 20th century have been the bitter ballads of Bertolt Brecht which are to be found interspersed through the scenes in works like *Die Dreigroschenoper* (The Threepenny Opera) and *Mahagonny*, and which have become so famous in the interpretations of the late Lotte Lenya, the wife of the composer of much of that music, Kurt Weill. These songs – Brecht, who emigrated to America after Hitler's take-over in 1933, always called his songs by the English word 'songs' – are the forerunners of the protest-songs of the 1960's which mirror the politicization of German literature, so striking a feature of the years leading up to the students' revolts of 1968 and encapsulated in the Lieder of latter-day German 'minstrels' – complete with guitar – like Franz Josef Degenhardt and Wolf Biermann, who eventually defected from the GDR. These have largely taken the place of the highly-cultivated Lieder of Schubert and Wolf in the folk-consciousness of the German peoples and there are legitimate reasons for fearing that the Lied-form that we are discussing has become ossified and *is* the preserve of that 'upper ten thousand'. There are nevertheless some rather more favourable signs that this is not the case everywhere. The efforts in Britain of that popular group *The Songmakers' Almanac*, Felicity Lott, Ann Murray, Anthony Rolfe-Johnson, Richard Jackson and Graham Johnson, much encouraged by the doyen of Lieder accompanists, Gerald Moore, and reports of the popularity of the Lied in Japan, where enthusiasm for Western music is evident in the meteoric rise in record sales and in the appearance in Britain of so many gifted Japanese musicians, these and other signs – the number of students choosing vocal music as their special subject at colleges and universities, for example – make the more optimistic among us believe that there will always be a public for the endless beauties of this miniature art-form.

PART TWO

Performer and Audience

[1] VOICES: SOUND AND SENSE

As ALL concert-goers know, vocal music is sung usually by six types of voices; in 'descending' order – the female: soprano, mezzo-soprano and contralto, and the male: tenor, baritone and bass. Within these six basic categories, we can have sub-categories such as high soprano, 'heroic tenor' (the German *Heldentenor*), bass-baritone and other fine shadings or nuances.

In theory, any of these voices can sing Lieder; clearly, some Lieder 'sound better' in one register than in another. Where a song has a fine ringing high note – the alternative top A in *Ich grolle nicht* from Schumann's *Dichterliebe* or the glorious F sharps in *Mein* from Schubert's *Die schöne Müllerin* for example, or a cavernous bottom note such as the bottom E in Schubert's *Der Wanderer* or the alternative low D in his *Der Tod und das Mädchen* (Death and the maiden), it is a pity to 'waste' the effect by transposition. We have already seen – in Part One – that composers often took great care to match the particular song to a particular voice, even, in some cases, writing the song with a particular *singer* in mind, as Benjamin Britten did so often for Peter Pears, or, indeed, Schubert for Michael Vogl. These personal connections fade with the passing years, of course, but they do give future performers and scholars a pointer to the composer's original intentions.

Which voices cannot – or should not – sing Lieder is much more difficult to decide. As with so many aspects of music – and life – it is often a matter of personal taste. I cannot honestly admit to enjoying the great Italian tenor, Beniamino Gigli in German Lieder – his version of Schumann's *Die Lotosblume* (The lotus flower), for example, which he recorded in an Italian translation as *Il fior di loto* in 1936 (on a 10 inch record, DA 1504). The lush crooning voice with the beautiful Italianate *bel canto*, full of swooning and swooping *portamenti*, seems to destroy the fragile simplicity of Heine's poem and Schumann's music. But I would agree without hesitation that Webster Booth's fine *Heavenly Aida* (from the Verdi opera), recorded in English on C3379 in 1943, similarly lacks the fullness and ardour that an Italianate voice can give it – and I am sure that there are readers who would profoundly disagree with both statements!

It is of course not *only* a matter of taste; it is also a matter of *knowledge*. It seems to me self-evident that a performer or listener who is a native German speaker, or a foreigner who understands German fluently, will be able to get nearer to the heart of the song than one who is not. For the performer, the language of the poem must be an integral part of the whole; the ability to 'feel' the German vowels and consonants, to be able to shape the difficult German 'ü' sound, to caress the liquid 'l''s, or to spit out the 'z''s, 'r''s and 'ch''s which are such a feature of this language, is of paramount importance. For the listener, the aesthetic experience of fully appreciating the beauty of a word like 'wonnevoll' breathed out at the end of Brahms' setting of Daumer's poem *Wie bist du, meine Königin*, or of being able fully to appreciate Elisabeth Schumann's intoxicating pronunciation of 'Der Frühling will kommen' (Spring is coming) on the reprise of the melody in Schubert's *Der Hirt auf dem Felsen* (The shepherd on the rock), is comparable to the English speaker's enjoyment on hearing John Gielgud's very English 'Oh, what a rogue and peasant slave am I!' from *Hamlet*, or a Welshman's joy at Dylan Thomas' glorious Celtic rendering of 'Do not go gentle into that good night'.

I must repeat – it is a matter of taste and knowledge. It is very difficult for anyone who knows and loves the German language to approve whole-heartedly of a beautifully-sung, but execrably-pronounced version of a favourite Lied. The outstanding example that comes to mind is that of the late Count John McCormack, witnessed most memorably on his recordings of German Lieder, now available on the Pearl Company's collection GEMM 158 issued in 1979. In his lyrical sleeve-note to an earlier collection on the World Record Club label, Desmond Shawe-Taylor wrote that 'some Germans have felt unable to respond to performances which *in almost every other respect* (my italics) are of the highest calibre' because of the poor German. But that is just the point: it is a classic case of the kind. McCormack never learned to pronounce the German subjunctive forms *könnte* or *möchte* at all, and was equally weak on the other vowels. Yet - what singing! No one has sung the *music* of Schubert's *Die Liebe hat gelogen* (Love has lied) more passionately, no one floated the final pianissimo note on the word *Nachtigall* (nightingale) in Brahms' *In Waldeseinsamkeit* more evocatively – and few have sung Wolf's *Ganymed* with such religious devotion. But – for a German speaker, part of whose pleasure in Lieder is in the beauty of the *language* of the poem, the singing is undeniably flawed by the poor pronunciation of the all-important words – just as a Shakespeare sonnet would be flawed.

To sing Lieder in translation is a weak substitute for the real thing – a poor supermarket wine beside one of the great Rhine or Rhine-Hessian vintages! Attitudes towards singing in translation have changed considerably over the years. There was a time in Britain when the speaking of a foreign language was regarded as being somehow *infra dig* – it was putting one on a par with 'the foreigner'. The upper-class Englishman in particular had a well-known way of 'dealing with foreigners' who did not speak English: 'Shout louder'! Nor did modern language teaching methods in schools encourage the acquisition of a fluent knowledge of the spoken language, based as they were on the firm belief that modern languages were but a pale imitation of the classical languages, Latin and Greek, and that they should therefore be taught in the same way, viz. by translating from English, or by treating them as safe 'dead languages' and studying the literature of the great Golden Ages of literature, the 17th century in France, the 18th century in Germany. But, as Molière himself wrote in a different context, 'nous avons changé tout cela', and the proof that the British *can* learn to speak German, French, Spanish, Italian, and even Russian, at least, can be measured by the popularity of the 'modern' modern language courses at Britain's newer universities and polytechnics, and the excellent German, Italian and French to be heard from our British singers in concert-halls and opera-houses all over the world. (In a recent BBC 3 interview, Hugues Cuénod, the distinguished veteran Swiss tenor, praised the general level of the French of British singers, although he admitted that most had difficulty with that very difficult French vowel 'u' – which is not very far from the German 'ü'.)

The case for singing in English translation was well put by Richard Capell in the book which has become the Bible for English Schubertians, *Schubert's Songs*. Capell argued that 'in the most favourable circumstances of performance', the argument for singing in German is irresistible. But he could not agree that this would always obtain, and he felt that, where the German was understood neither by the singer nor by the audience, it would be sheer pedantry to insist on it.

This book appeared for the Schubert Centenary in 1928, only ten years after the fiercest of modern wars, when things German were still not fully appreciated by British intellectuals, who were mostly French-orientated. The great era of foreign travel was not yet upon us, and Capell could therefore write: 'The German language strikes the stranger as uncouth and repellent' in the fair assurance that many would agree with him. Capell appreciated that, if we did not know German, we might well be gazing into a glass darkly when we encountered German Lieder, but, on balance, and given the sparse knowledge of German among English people of the day, he favoured translation, going as far as to say that the 'BBC's broadcasting of *Erlkönig* in German is surely the crowning of pedantry'!

Fortunately, things *have* changed, and there are not many knowledge-able performers or listeners who would be prepared to accept Capell's belief that A.H. Fox-Strangway's and Steuart Wilson's translations of the opening stanzas of Friedrich Reil's *Das Lied im Grünen* (Song in the open air) is anything like the original, either in sense or in sound:

> Ins Grüne, ins Grüne, da lockt uns der Frühling,
> Der liebliche Knabe,
> Und führt uns am blumenumwundenen Stabe
> Hinaus, wo die Lerchen und Amseln so wach,
> In Wälder, auf Felder, auf Hügel zum Bach,
> Ins Grüne, ins Grüne.

> [. . . Fair sights beckon all men and sundry to follow;
> The song of the lark and the flight of the swallow,
> The carpet of bluebells that fills every nook
> Lead on by the meadow and down to the brook
> In spring-time.]

Gone is the wonderfully evocative 'am blumenumwundenen Stabe' (with the flower-twined staff) – and a 'carpet of bluebells' has appeared from nowhere! There is, of course, nothing at all wrong with the English – except that it is not a translation of Reil's verses. Like so much of Capell's writing on Schubert, there is an air of condescension behind his belief that there is in fact a *need* for translation; almost a suspicion, indeed, that the song would sound better in 'beautiful' English than in 'uncouth and repellent' German.

None of the above is meant to detract from the joy to be obtained from reading Capell's book – none better on Schubert has ever appeared; it is meant solely as an illustration that times have changed and that performers' and audiences' attitudes have changed with them. It would be the exception nowadays to find a young professional singer without reasonable-to-good German, French and Italian – and one would hope soon to find audiences unwilling to accept poor translations – of Lieder anyway. Opera in English is another matter altogether and with a quite different *raison d'être* not to be argued here. (To act the *advocatus diaboli*: if one wanted to make a case out for singing Lieder in translation, then I should put on the witness stand – or turntable – that superb perform-ance of 'The Erlking' by Peter Dawson and Gerald Moore. From Gerald Moore's inspired opening tempo and Dawson's anxious 'Who rides through the night so dark and wild/A loving father with his young child'

86

– via the singer's fine differentiation of the four voice-parts, a soft voice for the child, a deep bass-baritone for the father, a perhaps rather stentorian Erl King, and a suitably dramatic narrator for the melodramatic conclusion: '. . .but in his arms/Lo, his child – lay – dead'! It is a thrilling recording for the listener to listen to – and understand.)

The best of all roads is the *via media*, the golden mean, the middle way: to sing, or hear the song sung, in German supported by a good and accurate prose translation which will give, not a 'poetic version' (as above) but a faithful, nearly literal (but not stupidly so) rendering of what the poet actually said. Such renderings are still not to be found in the popular editions of Lieder, viz. the Peters or Schirmer editions available in our bookshops and public libraries. Henry S. Drinker has tried a more modern version of the three great Schubert cycles in the Dover series* – but again the need to match rhyme for rhyme leads to emendations, additions and even mis-translations. One example might suffice: the opening of the first stanza of No. 1 of *Die schöne Müllerin, Das Wandern:*

Das Wandern ist des Müllers Lust,
Das Wandern (bis)
Das muss ein schlechter Müller sein,
Dem niemals fiel das Wandern ein,
Das Wandern.

An accurate but not too literate translation of that might read: 'Wandering is the miller's joy, wandering (repeat); he's a poor miller who never thought of wandering, of wandering'. (To be absolutely accurate, 'Das Wandern' is 'journeying', since the young man in question is clearly off on his travels as a 'journeyman', q.v.)

Drinker's 'poetic' version – which of course matches the music is:

To wander is the miller's joy
To wander (repeat).
The best of millers loves to roam
And never wants to stay at home. . .'

This poetic version can be seen to be a good way removed from the *sense*, although I agree that the *sound* is probably better. A 'literal' prose translation is supplied by George Bird and Richard Stokes in their versions in *The Fischer-Dieskau Book of Lieder:*

To journey is the miller's joy,
To journey (repeat).
A wretched miller must he be
Who never thought of journeying. . .

---

* *Franz Schubert: Complete Song Cycles* (General Publishing Co. Ltd., Toronto, 1970) (translated by Henry S. Drinker).

It must be said that their 'journeying' is much more accurate than the usual 'wandering', 'hiking' or 'roving', since this miller's lad is clearly a 'Geselle', a travelling journeyman, as Mahler's 'fahrender Geselle' was, as we saw.*

On balance I prefer the versions in Professor Prawer's *The Penguin Book of Lieder*, which combine most successfully the 'literal' and the 'poetic':

> Wandering is what the miller enjoys,
> Wandering! (repeat)
> He must be a poor miller
> Who never thought of wandering . . .

(and the versions are printed to pair with the poetic line).**

This is what I termed 'the golden mean', if not necessarily 'the best of all possible worlds', and I should strongly recommend performers, promoters and secretaries of Music Societies to provide such non-literal translations for German-language recitals.

There has however been a new development on the scene with the publication of Lois Phillips' book *Lieder Line-by-Line* (Duckworth, 1979), strongly recommended in the Foreword by Dame Janet Baker; this is what it says it is – a line-by-line translation of each word *as it appears in the song*. The *rationale* for the book is that, by this method, the singer will know what weight of meaning each note should carry and will be able to interpret the music accordingly. It is always difficult for a performer who knows German to appreciate the value of such a book, but singers with no German to whom I have spoken about this book assure me that it is indeed invaluable. It is not meant, of course, for audiences.

Transposition is not too far removed from translation; where the latter is the rendering of one language into another – and the result might justify the poet Robert Frost's definition of poetry as 'something that is lost in translation' – the former, that is, the singing by, say, a bass of a song clearly written for the tenor voice, is thought by some to destroy the original conception of the composer by introducing a different 'sound'.

We know that it made little difference to some composers *what* voice sang their songs; some, like Brahms, often stipulated 'Low Voice' or 'High Voice', or for 'Soprano or Tenor', while Hugo Wolf was quite happy to transpose some of his loveliest songs for his friend, the amateur bass-baritone Hugo Faisst. Again, it is a matter of taste. Richard

---

* *The Fischer-Dieskau Book of Lieder* (Gollancz, 1976)(with English translations by George Bird and Richard Stokes).

** *The Penguin Book of Lieder* (Penguin, 1964) edited and translated by S.S. Prawer.

Strauss was particularly fond of the soprano voice – and not so fond of the tenor register – and when he met the German soprano Elisabeth Schumann during the First World War, he believed that he had come across the perfect interpreter of his songs. To have heard Elisabeth Schumann sing a Lied like Strauss' *Ständchen* (opus 17, No 2), finishing the last few bars on that perfectly-pitched exultant high A sharp on the word 'hoch' in '*Hoch* glühn von den Wonneschauern der Nacht', was an unforgettable experience. Yet, for some, Dietrich Fischer-Dieskau's splendid baritonal verson had its own charms, not least because Adolf von Schack's poem is clearly a seductive invitation from a man to a girl to come out and share the rose-scented night with him! (It should be added, too, that one can hear the *words* on the baritone's record more clearly than on Madame Schumann's.)

At the other end of the scale – literally – a song like Schubert's *Der Atlas* (D957, No.8) cannot really be adequately performed by a light-weight tenor or baritone, and certainly not by a female singer. This massive song, set against the pounding demisemiquavers and triplets of the piano accompaniment, needs a 'big' heroic, operatic baritone or bass voice with the strength to ride out the piano climaxes. Indeed, as with so many of the great Lieder, it is a song which should be thought of in operatic terms, and, just as one would not have a deep baritone or bass voice singing an aria like Des Grieux' *En fermant les yeux* in Massenet's *Manon* or a contralto voice singing *Vissi d'arte* in Puccini's *Tosca*, it would be folly for anyone other than a sturdy bass or a heroic baritone to essay this portrayal of this Atlas – not, of course, the mythical Atlas, but *an* Atlas who bears the grief of the world on his shoulders.

There are however many songs, the majority of Lieder by far, which *can* be sung by any of the voices. One can probably perform Lieder out of character more easily than operatic rôles. Many first visits to opera have resulted in almost permanent alienation because the Madame Butterfly, say, a bride of tender years, was an eighteen-stone mature soprano who remained 'out of character' throughout the evening. A Lied, on the other hand, is over in three or four minutes – and little permanent damage will be done!

It is a different matter with the great song-cycles, however, some of which last up to and over an hour. The very greatest, Schubert's *Winterreise* and *Die schöne Müllerin*, Schumann's *Dichterliebe* and *Frauen-liebe und -leben*, Beethoven's *An die ferne Geliebte*, Brahms' *Vier ernste Gesänge* and Mahler's *Lieder eines fahrenden Gesellen*, each presents its own problems and possibilities.

I shall be dealing with the question of male and female interpretations; at the moment I am only concerned with the timbre of the voice.

Schubert, as we know, set both his song-cycles for the tenor voice. In his book on these song-cycles, Gerald Moore gives no definite indication of his preferred voice for singing them – although he did say to me once that *Die schöne Müllerin* should always be sung by a tenor voice – except when it is sung by Dietrich Fischer-Dieskau!* Fischer-Dieskau himself, however, agrees that this cycle sounds better in the higher register, because, as he wrote in his book on Schubert, 'the brook murmurs all too frequently in the bass clef'.** The 'hero' of the cycle is clearly that young 'journeyman' leaving one place of work to travel on to another in search of experience, so he is a young-ish man. One has the feeling, too, that the miller's beautiful daughter is his first true love and that his disappointment is the disappointment of the first heart-break. In *Winterreise* on the other hand, the main character is portrayed as somehow more mature altogether, more experienced. He had been prepared to marry his girlfriend, but she (and her parents) have rejected him – *his* journeyings are not to seek work and perhaps to meet another girl, but are the wanderings of a man half-crazed with grief, through the pitiless ice and snow of winter. The deeper voice suits the character and the music. (Nevertheless, had Schubert elected to set the poems as a dramatic *scena*, he would probably have thought of the quartet in conventional operatic terms, viz. 'heroine': soprano; 'hero' (the man): tenor; 'villain' (the hunter): baritone; 'strange character' (the organ-grinder): bass. (Janáček did this with his remarkable 20th century cycle *The Diary of One Who Vanished*, which he set for tenor (the lad), soprano (the seducing woman), and a chorus of three women who act as narrator).

These are nevertheless 'counsels of perfection', and I have heard superb performances of both Schubertian cycles by tenor *and* baritone. Bass performances have pleased less, because the bass voice is less convincing in the many lyrical strophic songs, although it can be effective in the 'bigger' Lieder. But the bass voice seems unsuited to either cycle as far as 'interpretation' goes. Bass voices *do* represent maturity and/or villainy in most concert- or opera-goers' experience, and just do not convince in these two cycles about essentially young-ish men.

Dichterliebe, again, sounds best in the brighter, ringing tenor register. Here the key relationships between the songs are very important – many

---

* *The Schubert Song Cycles*: (Hamish Hamilton), 1975.
** *Auf den Spuren der Schubert-Lieder* (Brockhaus, 1971) translated as *Schubert: A biographical study of his songs* by Kenneth S. Whitton (Cassell, 1976). The translation appears in the USA as *Schubert's Songs: A biographical study* (Knopf 1977).

baritones have to transpose some of the more heaven-stretching songs and lose these musical *liaisons* – and one has to stress here too that the cycle is about a young poet and his love(s). Heine was thirty when he wrote the poems, Schumann thirty when he composed the songs; the poet was sore with grief at having been rejected by a woman; the musician was delirious with happiness at the thought of his marriage to his beloved. A high lyric baritone like Hermann Prey or Benjamin Luxon or Dietrich Fischer-Dieskau is certainly not out of character in this cycle. If they can take those splendid (alternative) high notes on 'am Herzen frisst' (eats my heart) in song No.7, *Ich grolle nicht*, or the last of the three great *crescendi* in No.16, *Die alten, bösen Lieder*, then there is nothing in the texts which would forbid a baritone voice.

. . . and with the mention of 'texts' we are back again with our major theme – the importance of the words. Mahler's cycle *Das Lied von der Erde* is set to translations by Hans Bethge of Chinese poems for tenor, contralto (or baritone) and orchestra – that last-mentioned voice has given critics much to argue about since the first performance of the work, after Mahler's death, in Munich in 1911.

In Great Britain the sentimental connection with the late and much-loved contralto Kathleen Ferrier and the story of that unforgettable performance under Bruno Walter at the first Edinburgh Festival in 1947 where the final words, the repeated 'ewig' (for ever) would move her and her audience to tears, has pre-disposed British audiences (and critics, it seems) in favour of the contralto or mezzo-soprano voice in this cycle. Nevertheless, the text does indicate a male character: the second song is titled *DER Einsame im Herbst*, that is, 'The lonely *man* in Autumn', although this poem itself is not concerned with purely masculine sentiments; the fourth song, and the second for the lower voice, *Von der Schönheit* (Of Beauty), does not specifically demand a male voice, although a close reading of the poem reveals a more masculine than feminine theme. The sixth and last song *Der Abschied* (The farewell) is however clearly the leave-taking of two *men*: the text runs: '*Er* stieg vom Pferd und reichte *ihm* den Trunk des Abschieds dar' (*He* dismounted and handed *him* the cup of farewell). These considerations would certainly *allow* the baritone voice to sing the cycle – but many good critics feel that the music simply sounds better when sung by females, perhaps because it makes a greater contrast with the almost operatic writing for the tenor.

Such an either/or leads us to one of the most hotly-disputed areas of Lieder singing: Does it *matter* whether male or female voices sing particular Lieder?

Since most Lieder were written in ages when there were simply more

91

male vocalists available – the 'Don't-put-your-daughter-on-the-stage-Mrs-Worthington' attitude held good for many centuries! – it is understandable that modern female Lieder singers feel that they have every right to claim this or that song for themselves. In her book *Eighteen Song Cycles*, the great soprano Lotte Lehmann, wrote:

> Why should a singer be denied a vast number of wonderful songs if she has the power to create an illusion which will make her audience believe in it? (op.cit.)

and she went on to suggest that, on the concert-platform, the singer must change his or her personality in every song, that is, reality must be put aside and singer and audience must 'soar away into the limitless realms of fantasy'.

Elena Gerhardt, the famous mezzo-soprano, felt too that, 'if a woman has the strength and voice to interpret a man's words rightly, it will never sound ridiculous', but she added, 'it usually does when a man imitates a woman's voice'. Madame Gerhardt granted however that it would be wrong for a woman to try to sing *Die schöne Müllerin* or *Dichterliebe* – although she insisted that, because the psychology of *Winterreise* is that of 'unhappy love in general', it could well be represented by a woman.*

Aksel Schiøtz, that fine Danish tenor-turned-baritone, would take issue with Madame Gerhardt in particular and claim that 'there are certain hurdles the imagination just can't cross', and that few poets would condone any change of sexes!** Without wishing to be too pedantic on the matter, I agree on the whole with Aksel Schiøtz; the greatest Lieder are a perfect fusion of word and music – poet and composer form the first pair of a classic quartet: singer and accompanist, the second, to interpret what the first pair have fashioned. Now, there are many great songs which are what I have termed 'unisex'; at random one could mention: Schubert: *Der Musensohn, Nacht und Träume* and *Du bist die Ruh'*; Schumann: *Mondnacht, Der Nussbaum, Die Lotosblume*; Brahms: *Von ewiger Liebe, Die Mainacht* and *Dämmrung senkte sich von oben*; Wolf: *Nimmersatte Liebe, Zitronenfalter im April* and *Anakreons Grab* – and there are, of course, many, many more. It is true to say however that the greater the Lied, and the more successful the fusion of word and music, the less possible it is for the song to be sung by the other sex. 'The singing of a Lied is about interpretation not impersonation', one can hear growled; maybe, but, as Aksel Schiøtz wrote, if a soprano were to sing, 'Wenn ich mich lehn' an deine Brust' (When I lean against your

---

* Elena Gerhardt: *Recital* (Methuen, 1953), pp. 163–4.
** Aksel Schiøtz: *The singer and his art* (Hamish Hamilton, 1970) p.44.

breast), or 'Doch wenn ich küsse deinen Mund' (Yet when I kiss your mouth)(in No.4 of *Dichterliebe*) – or a tenor 'Er, der herrlichste von allen' from *Frauenliebe und –leben* (which, admittedly, I have never heard!) – a discerning audience would realize that the poet's intentions were not being fulfilled. Thus, although it is agreed that there is a more restricted choice of Lieder for the female voice, there is surely a sufficient number written expressly for them, in addition to the 'unisex' songs, for them not to have to poach on the male preserve. (Indeed, in 1978, *Deutsche Grammophon* issued five L.P.'s of one hundred and eight Schubert Lieder recorded by the Czech-German soprano Gundula Janowitz which she felt 'were appropriate for the female voice' – *and* the box is labelled Vol. 1!)

One must add, of course, that the situation is different when the audience does not understand German well enough to *feel* these 'embarrassments'; one wonders indeed if that is why so many pre-war sopranos were able to sing songs which were clearly intended for the male. Were they fairly sure that few people in the audience would have enough German to sense the impropriety?

The ambience of the Lieder recital has changed considerably in the last one hundred and fifty years; rarely do we hold the intimate domestic Schubertiads such as are depicted on that charming sepia drawing of *Schubert-Abend bei Josef von Spaun* (A Schubert Evening at the house of Josef von Spaun) by Moritz von Schwind and which can now be seen in the Vienna Schubert Museum, formerly Schubert's birth-place. A group sit round the piano, gazing raptly at Johann Michael Vogl as he sits singing a Schubert Lied, while at the piano is the tiny composer-accompanist. As Maurice Brown has suggested, it would be pleasant to think that they were listening to that most heartfelt and intimate Schubert Lied, Schubert's setting of Franz von Schober's *An die Musik* (To music), particularly as we believe that Schober is depicted in the drawing.

Nowadays, Lieder recitals are often held in enormous concert-halls holding up to ten thousand people – surely wrong? Some agree – some singers however feel that there is more excitement, more 'electricity' – and fewer distractions – in a large hall than in a small one where the audience is almost on top of the singer. It can be exciting, too, some singers feel, to be the orchestrator of an entire evening with only your accompanist beside you.

To hold an audience like that, with the modest dynamic range of even the finest grand piano, requires an intensity of singing and interpretation far beyond that needed by the operatic singer – which is why so many operatic singers shy away from the solo recital. Yet the greatest

Lieder singers have almost all been distinguished opera singers as well. I mentioned earlier that the Lied had been called a 'miniature drama'; the Lieder singer has to be able to express and communicate emotions at the same level of intensity and with the same truthfulness as his operatic colleague on the stage. (Indeed, in a Lied like Schubert's *Erlkönig*, he has to portray four characters in the one song.)

There has always been intense disagreement among singing teachers about the amount of involvement desirable in the singing of a Lied. One distinguished contralto was once metaphorically rapped over the knuckles by her teacher for looking at her ring finger when singing *Du Ring an meinem Finger* (Ring on my finger) in Schumann's cycle *Frauenliebe und -leben*. It was felt that that was taking 'interpretation' too far. At the same time, a singer must respond to the words of the text – the greatest singers do this by the slightest movement of the body which draws the audience's attention to the meaning of the word or line: In Brahms' *Immer leiser wird mein Schlummer* (My sleep grows lighter), Kathleen Ferrier used to lean forward on the last words 'Komm, o komme bald' (Come, o come soon), as if willing the lover of the poem to come through the door. In Schubert's *Der Wegweiser* (The sign-post) (No. 20 of *Winterreise*), where the grief-stricken lover reaches the last stages of his frozen journey, Fischer-Dieskau stares blankly into space and lets his face harden on the monotone 'Einen Weiser seh' ich stehen/unverrückt vor meinem Blick' (I see a sign-post/immovable in front of me), and who could forget Elisabeth Schwarzkopf's comically quizzical glance to her left as she lets us 'see' the three very juvenile 'wise men' as they trot off-stage at the end of Hugo Wolf's song *Epiphanias*, written for the birthday of Wolf's friend Melanie Köchert on 6 January 1889.

Roy Henderson, the well-known British singing teacher, once wrote that there were four chief ingredients needed by every successful singer: voice, musicianship, ability to interpret, and personality. What he omitted is what we turn to next: an accompanist, because without an accompanist of the same or preferably a higher standard of accomplishment as the singer, no Lieder recital can be a total success.

[2] ACCOMPANIMENTS AND
ACCOMPANISTS

IN THE PREFACE to his book *Singer and Accompanist*, Gerald Moore, who was born in 1899, and has had the distinction and the pleasure of accompanying more great musicians than any other pianist in the world, quotes with approval the late Ernest Newman, the former music critic of *The Times* newspaper: 'There is no law', Newman wrote, 'human or divine, to compel the composer to limit his expressiveness to the voice alone'.* In a series of books – the latest, *Poet's Love* (on the Lieder of Robert Schumann), appearing only in 1981 – Gerald Moore has consistently represented the view that the successful performance of German Lieder, indeed, of all songs, depends on the partnership of singer and accompanist. Be the singer never so great, a poor accompanist will ruin the performance as surely as a poor sauce will ruin a finely-cooked dish. Nor is it purely a matter of *quality* of performance: *quantity* (of sound) is also of prime importance – and it was Gerald Moore who coined the phrase 'the unashamed accompanist' to right the balance between singer and pianist. An accompanist who blushes unseen and unheard is as wilful with the composer's intentions as a singer who disregards the dynamic markings of a song and persists in singing *forte* what is clearly marked *piano*.

The way from the simple strumming chords which accompanied the *Volkslied* to the psychologically highly-charged and musically complicated accompaniments to Hugo Wolf's Lieder, is a long one indeed; in the first case, the accompanist was there mainly to keep the singer on the right note – in the second, we have what is effectively a second voice with as much to say about the interpretation of the poem as the top vocal line. It is really not so surprising, therefore, that many composers have felt that the piano alone could not express fully what they wanted to say, and that they must employ the full range of orchestral tones available in order to do the poem justice. Clearly, the development of opera in the 19th century, and the consequent importance given to the aria and its place in the plot, influenced even those composers who restricted themselves to the more modest Lied-form. Hugo Wolf was one of those composers who ranged himself behind Wagner in opposition to Brahms and *his* supporters. Musicians like Wolf must have found Wagner's

---

* Gerald Moore: *Singer and Accompanist*, Methuen, 1953 (re-issued Hamish Hamilton 1982).

development of the *Leitmotif*, the motive in the accompaniment which heralds the appearance of a character or a symbol – most noticeably perhaps, Siegfried's famous horn motive in *Götterdämmerung* – extraordinarily fruitful for the writing of their own accompaniments. The *Leitmotif* aids the interpretation of the plot just as Schubert's galloping hooves aid the interpretation of Goethe's *Erlkönig*, or Schumann's *Marseillaise* motive aids the interpretation of his *Die beiden Grenadiere* (The two grenadiers)(see p.142 below).

More than one critic has been moved to remark that many Lieder are in effect piano solos with 'voice obbligatos', just as many of Beethoven's sonatas for 'violin and piano' were written, in fact, for piano with violin obbligato. This is particularly true, of course, of that 'bridging period' between the late 18th century song-composers who still believed the words to be of less importance than the music, but who were beginning to feel their way to a more 'modern' approach, and the post-Schubertian composers. Beethoven's *An die ferne Geliebte*, that first song-cycle, is the perfect example of this move towards a balance between voice and piano, where the accompaniment however still sounds in places like the development of a piano sonata movement.

Although few of the great 19th century Lieder-composers distinguished themselves as opera composers, most, with the celebrated exception of Hugo Wolf, wrote first-rate memorable symphonies and works for other instruments: Schubert's 5th and 8th symphonies and his many fine string quartets, (not forgetting the marvellous String Quintet (D956) in C major), Schumann's *Rhenish* symphony (No.3 in E flat), and his many works for solo piano, Mendelssohn's *Italian* symphony (No.4 in A), Brahms' four towering masterpieces, the four symphonies, and a huge corpus of chamber music, all these and others are standard works for the concert-hall repertoire, and the influence of these masterpieces is clearly to be seen in the level of difficulty of the accompaniments to their Lieder. It is a common belief among amateur pianists that Lieder accompaniments are 'easy' and do not need to be practised like other piano pieces. Amateur Lieder singers are often plagued by their amateur accompanists who are unwilling to take the task of accompanying them seriously, and who believe that they will be able to sit down on the night of the performance and somehow 'muddle through'. Let such people try to do this with, for example, these figures in the opening to Schubert's *Der Lindenbaum* (The linden tree)(No.5 of *Winterreise*)!

or the slow but exquisitely-timed progressions of Schumann's *Ich hab' im Traum geweinet* (I wept in my dreams)(No.13 of *Dichterliebe*) or the exultant conclusion to Wolf's *Ich hab' in Penna einen Liebsten wohnen* (I have a lover living in Penna) from the *Italienisches Liederbuch*:

These are feats of pianistic skill to be compared with some of the most difficult writing for the solo pianist, and the music must be treated with the same respect. Of course, the singer in turn must treat the accompaniment and the accompanist with similar respect and not demand – as the famous soprano Frieda Hempel once did of the young Gerald Moore – that he should finish that last Wolf song with a chord as soon as her part had come to an end! Thus, audiences have to appreciate that the accompaniment is an integral part of the song and can even be, as I have hinted, the most important part.

Of all the great Lieder composers, Schubert did most for the art of the accompaniment. He was the first to go to the heart of a poem and to find melodies in both the vocal and the piano line which perfectly expressed the sentiments of the poet. Indeed one might say that, after Schubert's *Erlkönig* was written (in 1815), the so-called 'accompaniment' had had its day! For, after *Erlkönig*, the piano part was no longer a mere incidental adornment of the vocal part, but was now established as an independent composition, often determining the interpretation.

In addition, when one examines Schubert's six hundred or so Lieder, one finds that certain rhythms recur to match particular themes. In conversation with me, Dietrich Fischer-Dieskau thought that he could detect four major rhythms:

a) the dancing $^6/_8$ rhythm which characterises most of Schubert's 'happy' songs, those which tell of the happiness of youth in love or the joys of Spring e.g. *Das Fischermädchen* (No. 10. of *Schwanengesang*, or *Halt!* (No 3 of *Die schöne Müllerin*);

b) the 'wandering' rhythm, written $^2/_4$, which typifies so many of Schubert's most 'romantic' settings, telling of journeys away from the 'Heimat' (home) to still some 'longing' (*Sehnsucht* in German), as in *Die Sterne* (D939) or *Wohin* (No.2 of *Die schöne Müllerin*);

c) the riding rhythm which reminds us of the importance of the horse and carriage in Schubert's day and age, as in *Die Post* (No.13 of *Winterreise*) or *Abschied* (No.7 of *Schwanengesang*), and finally,

d) the great 'death' rhythm for those quiet 'reflective' songs which form such a large proportion of the Lieder repertoire generally, Schubert's *Der Tod und das Mädchen* (D531) or *Über allen Gipfeln ist Ruh'* (D768), in which the accompanist plays such an important rôle in aiding the singer to maintain the long vocal line and the perfect *legato* singing needed. The truly great accompanists are great precisely because they play as a member of a chamber music duo, watching the singer's movements and breathing, as carefully as the members of an instrumental trio or quartet watch each other's bowing throughout a work, to mould the three or four instruments into one melodious and synchronised whole. It is interesting to read that Schubert is reported to have said about his partnership with his singer-colleague Johann Michael Vogl: 'The way in which Vogl sings and I accompany, *in which at that moment we seem to be one*, is something quite new to these people', i.e. his audiences.

One of the joys of attending Lieder recitals is to witness the rapport between two great artists, as they each in his or her own turn prepare to project his or her personality to the audience. One no doubt strives in vain to explain what makes a great platform performer; it was defined once by the great English singer and teacher Harry Plunket Greene, as 'magnetism' (*with* a capital M!), and we like to think of it as 'charismatic' nowadays, a word which is derived from the Greek *charis* = grace, and it *is* probably God-given. Clearly a fine physique and good looks help, as do a problem-free technique and a perfectly pitched voice, but no one has ever managed to explain why some voices can send shivers down the spine or raise the hair on the back of the head. Some believe that it is closely bound up with a sense of rhythm, the 'backbone of music', as Aksel Schiøtz wisely called it. Certainly, there are singers who seem to have a rhythmical sense built into them, so that when they sing they make the chosen rhythm seem inevitable. The two greatest modern examples of this have been for me the soprano Elisabeth Schumann and the baritone Dietrich Fischer-Dieskau. Yet it is not a cold metronomical rhythm, but one saved by another life-enhancing force, *tempo rubato*, which means literally 'robbed time', and indicates that the singer (in this case) will linger over certain notes or phrases. Many singers would compensate for this by hurrying slightly more over other phrases to rescue the song from a parade-ground uniformity of rhythm, but it is really not necessary; the *rubato* has done this already. Like perfect pitch, perfect rhythm is probably God-given too, but I am certain that it is what distinguishes a (singing) genius from a talented performer.

Strangely enough, a singer's rhythmical sense is probably best judged by his singing of those slow songs where the rhythm has to be *inside* the singer. No metronome can help here – although a sensitive accompanist can. Accompanists, on the whole, do not believe that slow songs are more difficult than the quick ones, yet many an amateur performance of, say, Richard Strauss' *Morgen* (Tomorrow) has been ruined by the insensitive accompaniment. Here, in a work whose slow thirteen-bar piano introduction takes up almost half the total song, the accompanist sets both the rhythm and the mood. Any tendency to hurry will ruin both. It is a superb proof of the accompanist's importance in the successful performance of any Lied.

Thus, one cannot over-emphasize the importance of the accompanist and the accompaniment. He has moved away from the self-effacing, mouse-like figure who crouched, score modestly in hand, behind the imposing *diva* or renowned tenor taking the rapturous applause, to the central figure like Gerald Moore, accompanist of almost every great singer of the 20th century, to whom was awarded the signal honour of a special concert at the Royal Festival Hall in London on 20 February 1967 when three singers, Victoria de los Angeles, Elisabeth Schwarzkopf and Dietrich Fischer-Dieskau, sang a programme of his favourite Lieder. On his retirement from active concert accompanying, EMI brought out a splendid record with the title *Supreme Accompanist*, on which we hear

Gerald Moore accompanying no fewer than sixteen internationally renowned singers, from Marta Fuchs to Christa Ludwig, while on his 80th birthday his protégés *The Songmakers' Almanac* arranged a fine concert in his honour at which some of these great artists were able to send him recorded messages of their regard for him and his achievement.

And from such professional accompanists as Gerald Moore, Geoffrey Parsons, Dalton Baldwin, Graham Johnson, and others, we have moved in another direction: distinguished conductors and concert-pianists like Wolfgang Sawallisch, Daniel Barenboim, André Previn, Jörg Demus and Leonard Bernstein are now happy to join with equally distinguished singers in Lieder recitals. To play in an intimate duo must be a welcome relief after the tumult of an orchestral concert, and audiences should be grateful to hear accompaniments of such distinction. The Lied is the ultimate winner.

[3] PROGRAMMES

IN HIS BOOK *The Singer and His Art*, Aksel Schiøtz makes two all-important points about song-recitals viz. that a singer has to keep his or her audience voluntarily captive for a couple of hours or so, whatever the conditions, and that a well-constructed programme is the best fare that can be offered.

The average recital of Lieder will begin at 7.30 or 8 pm – morning recitals are however a feature of the great International Festivals such as Edinburgh or Salzburg – and will consist of two sections, the first lasting about an hour, the second, about forty-five minutes, divided by an interval of some fifteen minutes. The programme chosen will depend on whether the singer is giving a 'recital', or a 'song-recital', or a *'Lieder-abend'*; if it is the first, then the purpose of the evening may well be to display a much-loved singer's vocal technique, rather than to pay tribute to certain composers, and the works chosen will be those which display the voice to its best advantage. Thus there may be a group of Italian *arie antiche* from the 17th century, then a group of Bach sacred songs (say from G.C. Schemelli's *Musikalisches Gesangbuch* (1736), next, perhaps, a

101

few Schubert or Schumann Lieder, even a few 19th century Italian operatic arias (preferably with a scattering of high C's or B flats!), and, finally, a group of more or less sentimental ballads or folk-songs, depending on the nationality of the singer and/or the audience.

If a 'song-recital' is announced, one could expect to find offered a programme which concentrated on a range of vocal music restricted to the concert-platform, as distinct from the opera house; perhaps a group of Italian *arie antiche* again, some 18th century English songs, a group of Lieder by one or more composers, a group of French *mélodies* or *chansons* (by composers such as Duparc, Debussy and Fauré), and, finally, perhaps a group of songs by modern British composers, such as Delius, Peter Warlock and Benjamin Britten. This programme would put the composer rather than the performer to the fore and would be attempting (while still entertaining) to present the audience with an interesting and varied cross-secton of the European song repertoire.

A *Liederabend*, or 'evening of Lieder', or 'Lieder recital', on the other hand, would consist solely of German Lieder, possibly by several composers and covering several periods of music. The performer would try to show the wide range of possibilities available in the German Lied, and might even try, as we shall see shortly that some singers have done, to 'instruct' their audiences while entertaining them, by introducing them to unusual juxtapositions of composer and/or poet.

Above all however, the performers must remember that they are entertainers, and that the audience has come to enjoy its evening. As Harry Plunket Greene put it in his book, the performer and his audience have the same object in view: 'To give or receive the *maximum* amount of interest with the *minimum* amount of fatigue, mental and physical'.

Plunket Greene's book *Interpretation in Song*, published in 1913, is one of the most fascinating guides to early recital programmes and early 20th century attitudes towards the art of singing.* It was written at the very height of the so-called 'Golden Age of Singing', at a time when Enrico Caruso was making the gramophone and the gramophone record popular – the 'pre-electric 78 or 80 r.p.m.', that is – and when the great singers were as familiar and as famous as Kings and Queens, Presidents and Kaiser – and treated accordingly. Not many modern singers have had a dish named after them as Dame Nellie Melba did at The Ritz – which created the 'pêche Melba' in her honour!

Harry Plunket Greene suggests ten essentials of programme building:

---

* Harry Plunket Greene: *Interpretation in Song*, Macmillan, 1913.

102

1. Variety of language.
2. Change of Composer (except in the case of a group).
3. Chronological order.
4. Change of Key.
5. Change of Time.
6. Classification of the Song.
7. Style of Technique.
8. Change of *Tempo* or Pace.
9. *Crescendo* and *Diminuendo* of Emotion.
10. Atmosphere and Mood.

(The capital letters are his!)

He then goes on to discuss each 'essential' in some detail. Throughout his discussion, he continually stresses how *fatigue* is the great enemy, and how a programme should always err on the side of *lightness*. He sums up: 'After a long first part made up of classical and art songs, ancient and modern, grave and gay, German, French, Italian or English, declamatory or *bel canto*, with, maybe, a song-cycle or two thrown in (*sic*), something is required in the second part that will allow the singer to relax his strain and the audience its intellectual vigilance'. The programme that he had in mind would be quite impossible to perform nowadays, starting, as it did, with a traditional French folk-song, then one of the 17th century Italian *arie antiche* (*Già il sole dal Gange* by Alessandro Scarlatti); four songs by Schubert, Brahms, Schumann and Hugo Wolf, and then, before the interval, four English songs. For the 'second part', he suggests seven 'traditional airs' (German, Hungarian, Irish and English) which were in effect arrangements of folk-tunes!

Although that was what a great singer has called a 'programme ranging over fields, woods and meadows', a pot-pourri in other words, one must add that Plunket Greene showed by means of an accompanying table of key, *tempi* classification, and so on, that the programme was in fact nicely varied and well-constructed,and that it would avoid both 'mental and physical fatigue'.

Such programmes were fairly common up to and even after the Second World War. When I heard the great Italian tenor Beniamino Gigli sing a recital on 19 November 1947 (at the age of 57), he began with the *Lamento di Federico* from Cilea's opera *L'Arlesiana*, went on to a very strange group consisting of Donaudy's *O bel nidi d'amore*, Caccini's beautiful *Amarilli* and *Dalla sua pace* from Mozart's *Don Giovanni*! Then came two songs by Martini and Lully – and he finished the first half with the *Flower Song* from Bizet's *Carmen*! There were three operatic arias in the second half of his programme which clearly fell into our first category, (a 'recital' by . . .), just as the Plunket Greene programme belonged to the second category – a 'song recital'.

It was not impossible however to find similar programmes announced for Lieder evenings, where the *performer* rather than the *music* was the main attraction. Programmes were often built up to display the voice or the personality of the singer as much as to concentrate the audience's attention on the music – and, of course, this was perfectly legitimate; indeed, it was what attracted the audience in the first place.

But it seems to be the case that audiences are now musically much better educated, and certainly much more sophisticated. The enormous growth in interest in music of all ages and types is undoubtedly due to the number of recordings available. First the 'gramophone', then the 'record-player', the development of gramophone recordings from those heavy 78 revolutions-per-minute shellac records, played with a steel or fibre 'needle', through to the wafer-thin, virtually unbreakable post-1951 Long Playing disc, containing forty minutes or so of music compared to the famous 'four-and-a-half' minutes of the 78 – *and* sold with informative, more or less scholarly sleeve-notes which can be studied at leisure in the home, and not as previously with concert programme notes, glanced at while the performer was singing – all this has produced a wider, much more knowledgeable, and a much more demanding public.

This has meant that a scholarly singer like Dietrich Fischer-Dieskau, for example, could attempt to revolutionize the recital programme by presenting, not a pot-pourri of Lieder loosely connected by having a 'group' of Schubert followed by a 'group' of Schumann, but rather a Schubert programme, say, with a connecting thread running through it. It might be a programme of Schubert Lieder based on the theme of 'Das Wandern' – Fischer-Dieskau once gave a concert which began with *Der Wanderer, Über Wildemann, Wanderers Nachtlied I* and *II* and *Der Wanderer an den Mond* – all songs about that very German – and Romantic – love of 'walking' and 'nature'.

Or it might be a Schubert programme based on Goethe settings, or Heine settings, or, as he did a few years ago, on poems by Schubert's own friends. Wolf's settings of Mörike poems make a satisfying and unifying evening, as do Schumann's Eichendorff Lieder.

Of course, if one does not want to have the music of a single composer, it is still possible to have some sort of satisfying unity by presenting, say, Goethe settings by *various* composers – such as those by the Duchess Anna Amalie of Sachsen-Weimar, Reichardt, Zelter, Schoeck, Reger, Brahms, Busoni and Hugo Wolf, or a Heine programme of settings by Schubert and Schumann where the singer can – as Harry Plunket Greene so charmingly put it – 'throw in' a song-cycle or two by performing *Dichterliebe*, which takes about thirty minutes, with a group of Schubert Heine settings (e.g. the *Schwanengesang* songs).

The great song-cycles *Die schöne Müllerin* and *Winterreise* should however be performed on their own – and without encores. (Gerald Moore likes to tell the Peter Pears story about *Winterreise*: when Pears and Britten were about to perform the cycle, someone came up to Pears and said to him, 'Now you *will* remember to sing *The foggy, foggy dew* as an encore?')

The twenty songs of *Die schöne Müllerin* take about sixty to sixty-five minutes to perform, the twenty-four of *Winterreise* about eighty minutes. Apart from the sheer musical difficulties of these Lieder, the emotional strain of the interpretation is extreme – *if* the cycles are 'lived through', as they must be if the performance is to convince. Elena Gerhardt said once that you had to be haunted by *Winterreise* to be able to sing it properly – and anyone who has spoken to a great artist after a performance of this work will testify to the effect that it can have.

Both these cycles are perfect examples of the 'unified programme'; they are bound by thematic key and emotional relationships; they are (by definition) settings by one composer of one poet, and they involve the audience from start to finish. There is perhaps not much 'relaxation of strain' for the singer – nor of the audience's 'intellectual vigilance' – but there is rather that feeling of *catharsis*, of purification of the emotions which all great tragedy is meant to create, according to Aristotle. These cycles are, in truth, in a different category from the songs contained in a normal recital programme and have to be listened to in a different way by the audience.

Few concert promoters have solved the problem of how to keep audiences still during these intimate Lieder recitals. When the Lieder are sung in groups, the artist normally prefers to be applauded at the end of the group, and not after each single song. Although no artist ever dislikes or disdains applause, the audience must remember that almost all singers perform nowadays without scores. At the most, they have copies of the words somewhere, either cupped in the palm of the hand, or on the piano edge, or somewhere else on their person, but, like most conductors nowadays, singers feel it incumbent upon them to have memorized the words and music for the performance, and that can mean for anything up to twenty songs. Any break in his concentration could have catastrophic consequences – such as the omission of whole lines or maybe even whole verses of the song. This can be particularly drastic in the case of a strophic song of, say, five verses, where the non-German-speaking accompanist can only know where he is by counting the verses! (One of the least honest reasons for singing in the original languages would be to have a feeling of certainty that not many of the audience would notice a mistake in the words. It must surely happen with Russian songs.)

Some concert promoters print the artist's wish for no applause 'until the end of each group' on the programme, and if they are really aware of the problem, they will ensure that the group can be sung without the audience having to turn the page of the programme. It might be remembered that the inimitable Sir Thomas Beecham once had his programmes printed on rice paper so that there would be no rustling at the turning of pages – *and* he encouraged the audience to *eat* the programme at the end of the concert!

It is slightly more difficult with the two great Schubert song-cycles, which are normally sung nowadays without a break. The singer and the audience should co-operate here, the singer, by reading the programme beforehand to know where the audience has to be given time to turn the page – and the audience, by preparing to turn the page quickly and quietly. Where *Die schöne Müllerin* or *Winterreise are* to be sung with an interval, it would seem wise to make the pause in *Die schöne Müllerin* after song No.12, (which is actually titled *Pause* anyway), and, in *Winterreise*, after No.12 *Einsamkeit* (Loneliness); but it is very doubtful whether either cycle will have the same powerful effect if performed with an interval.

If an interval is perhaps allowable in these cycles, encores after them are *not*. When Dame Myra Hess was once asked for an encore after a particularly intense performance of the last three Beethoven sonatas (opp. 109-111), she shrugged her shoulders and said simply, 'What could follow that?' The song-cycles are a quasi-dramatic performance like plays or operas, and no one would think of repeating, say, 'To be or not to be' after *Hamlet* or 'Che gelida manina' after *La Bohème*.

It is a different matter with recitals; few artists would fail to prepare a little group of encores (given separately, until the applause indicates that the audience is prepared to go home with its pound of flesh); these encores will usually, but not necessarily, be by the composer of the evening, or in the general spirit of the recital. Four or five might suffice – although one famous Italian tenor has been known to give up to twenty. Nevertheless, one always hopes that audiences will appreciate that a singer can be desperately tired after two hours of solo singing, and is longing to sit down. Audiences should not ask for more than is necessary; there are very few artists, however, who, having climbed to the top of their particular tree, look down on their audience from that advantageous position. Rather, they are only too well aware who put them up there, and know that a fickle public can likewise displace them. The relationship between artist and public is like a love-affair, in some cases, stormy and tempestuous, with scandals and disgraces, in others, long-lived and gracious, with true affection and gratitude on both sides – but whichever it is, every great artist goes to face his or her public with one question uppermost in the mind: Will I live up to their expectations?

In a fascinating interview given on the BBC and then reprinted as extracts in the brochure accompanying her records of music by Beethoven, Gluck, Handel, Haydn, Mozart and Schubert (Philips 6767 001), Dame Janet Baker described how she would take a piece of music to pieces, put it together again and then present the discovery to other people, the public. She went on:

> This process must be gone through before something can be given out; it has to be felt at the deepest levels of oneself. And when you've gone through this process and stand on a platform, no matter what happens, you have a sense of knowing that you've done all you can. Whether it goes wrong, whether nobody understands it, or whether you give a bad performance, is really out of your hands; but it's not so worrying if you have the feeling that the process has been gone through as deeply as possible beforehand. Then the difficulty is to allow the magic that you felt privately to come through. It isn't an unaided process; of course, the personality aids the process, but it mustn't get in the way.

Perhaps audiences might go to a concert similarly prepared by having 'done their homework'. It would be an excellent idea to have read the poems of the settings one is about to hear. There are so many good translations available nowadays – some have already been mentioned – one's pleasure can be doubled by a fuller knowledge of what is being sung. Audience, singer and accompanist make a partnership; each depends on the other.

PART THREE

Twenty-five Popular Lieder:
Background and Performance

IN THE preceding pages I have discussed the growth and development of German song through the ages and how various composers have dealt in general with the various problems arising from the decision to give a poem a musical setting. It will be appreciated that certain poems attract many different types of composers – I have already mentioned that Goethe's poem *Kennst du das Land. . .?* has been set eighty-four times – but it is undeniably true that certain settings by certain composers feature more widely in concert recitals than others. In this chapter, I have chosen twenty-five of these most popular settings to show where their charm and popularity seem to lie, and how the composer achieved his fusion of 'word' and 'music'.

The text of the poem has been printed in full, with an English prose translation which attempts to offer the 'middle way' discussed in Part Two (above p.87). It should be mentioned, however, particularly for students of German literature, that the poem printed here is the version chosen by the *composer* for his setting. This can vary from the version found in anthologies of poetry, since, in some cases, the contemporary musician would set the *first* version of the poem – as he came across it, say, in an almanac – whereas the poet would often prefer to have his *last* thoughts on the poem included in an anthology.

[1] J. S. BACH/G. H. STÖLZEL

Bist du bei mir, If you are with me (1725)

Bist du bei mir,
Geh' ich mit Freuden zum Sterben
und zu meiner Ruh'.
Ach, wie vergnügt wär' so mein Ende.
Es drückten deine schönen (lieben)* Hände
mir die getreuen Augen zu.

If you are with me,
I shall go to my death joyfully
And to my rest.
Ah, how happy would my end be,
Your lovely (dear)* hands would close
My trusting eyes.

---

* An alternative version.

111

This lovely song for a light soprano voice was for years thought to have been written for Bach's second wife, Anna Magdalena Bach, a gifted lyric soprano herself, whom he married in 1721 and by whom he had fourteen of his twenty children. It is usually numbered as the second of the five songs found in Anna Magdalena's *Notenbüchlein* dated 1725. We know from Therese von Brunswick's account that Beethoven thought highly of the *Notenbuch* and indeed that he used to sing some of the songs himself.

If it is not by Bach, then 'it should have been', since the slow, simple melody has all the power and sweetness of a great Bach aria, and like all the great Lieder, this simple song needs a singer who can sing long undisturbed phrases; the *legato* line must be unbroken if the singer is to convey to the audience the prayer-like sentiments of the text.

To begin with: Who is the 'you' referred to in the poem? Since the song can really only be sung by a high soprano voice, one could assume that the marital partner is indicated, although the quasi-religious mood might suggest a prayer to a beneficent God. On balance, I think that the former is the more likely and that it is an expresssion of the marital peace and contentment that the writer had experienced. The composer (whether Bach or Stölzel) has certainly succeeded in breathing just this mood of serenity into the setting.

The short song is contained within forty-five bars. The scoring is simplicity itself, bearing out what was said in Part One about song-writing in the 18th century. The song, in E flat, was scored in single line on the two staves; the lower harmonies are so plain that no figures are added at all.

The poem is treated in a very typical 18th century manner with manifold repetitions of the words. The opening melody is proclaimed without piano prelude:

Bist du bei mir, geh' ich mit Freu - de,

and this verse is repeated. The tempo should be slow, I think, although some sopranos believe that the song can bear a more 'joyful' interpretation and speed it up considerably. Certainly, from the evidence of the church cantatas, Bach's, or the 18th century's, attitude to death was not always solemn and such an interpretation could not be ruled out of court.

It is typical also of 18th century Lieder composers that the verse should be repeated a third time to drive home the point, this time with a subtle change in the melody:

Bist   du___   bei___   mir!

and the opportunity for a lovely trill on the word 'Freuden' (joy) – a touch of *Wortmalerei* (word-painting) which is undeniably more effective if and when the tempo has been slightly increased.

The middle portion 'Ach, wie vergnügt wär' so mein Ende' is set to a third and different melody, representing the more solemn aspect of the poem, and this too is repeated, although, one feels, unnecessarily. The song finishes with a return to the opening lines 'Bist du bei mir' . . ., but set to the second varied melody and the soprano once again has the 'trill of joy' on 'Freuden'. The song is a trifle compared with some of the 19th century masterpieces, but it breathes a spirit of serene devotion which makes it a great favourite with performer and audience alike. It is also a fascinating example of one of the earliest attempts to break away from the more formalized conception of song-writing.

[2] JOSEF HAYDN

She never told her love (Collected Edition No.34, 1794)

> She never told her love,
> But let concealment like a worm in the bud
> Feed on her damask cheek . . .
> She sat like patience on a monument,
> Smiling at grief . . .

IT MAY seem strange to choose a setting of English words to represent a Haydn Lied, but this song is certainly as fine an example of the genre as one is likely to hear in the concert hall.

Haydn visited England regularly and composed twelve songs, of which this is one, to be published as 'canzonettas' – with the encourage- ment of the wife of his surgeon, Mrs Anne Hunter. The words come, of course, from Shakespeare's *Twelfth Night*, Act 2 Scene 4, where Viola tells the Duke of Illyria a story of concealed love, which is really her own. Haydn omitted a line and a half of the speech, viz. '. . . she pined in thought/And with a green and yellow melancholy . . .' after '. . . damask cheek . . .' and before '. . . she sat like patience . . .', but produced a taut setting which marvellously colours the Shakespearean words.

This song too is for a soprano, although, since Viola is pretending to be a boy, those male singers with a sense of 'rightness' could claim it for the male voice, as many have done. It lies well for both types of voices, within a reasonable compass, and with an opportunity to display the singer's 'sense of long phrases'.

The most distinctive feature of the song is however the piano prelude, which removes it straightaway from the ranks of the 18th century song and places it firmly among the Schubertian and post-Schubertian corpus of Lieder, for here is one of the first attempts to present a scene, to prepare the listener for the *words* that are about to be sung. The piano part is no mere 'accompaniment', it works with the vocal line to illustrate the touching little excerpt from a beautiful speech.

The pianist has to play the fourteen bars of the introduction to Haydn's marking, viz. *Largo assai, e con espressione* (Very slow, and expressively), thus setting the tempo for the singer to enter, rather surprisingly (and on a *piano* note), on 'She never told her love':

She ne-ver told her love, she ne-ver told her__ love,

Because of the slow tempo of the song, these phrases only *look* short; they are in act a severe test of a singer's breathing technique, since, although each must be sung evenly, clearly Haydn meant both 'never''s to be stressed, especially in the repetition on the F flat, to convey Viola's indication of modesty. (That 'never' is marked *fz*.)

In effect, the song is 'durchkomponiert'; Haydn unwinds a beautiful melody which leads up to the high-point of his setting, the 'smiling' of 'smiling at grief'. This is preceded by a stroke of interpretative genius which shows us what a master of the Lied-form Haydn might have become, had he been born thirty years later. Viola tells us that 'she sat like patience (*not* Patience!) on a monument . . .' Haydn pictures the scene by bringing his song to a temporary halt: and then, by firstly stressing the word 'smiling', and immediately repeating it in a beautiful melisma, he underlines Viola's stoic reaction:

pa - tience on a mon - u - ment, smil - ing,

114

smil - ing at___ grief,

If the piano prelude recalls Schumann, the three bars of postlude remind me irresistibly of Schubert's four-bar introduction to his *Nacht und Träume* (D827). They also perpetuate the mood of the final word of the text – 'grief' – and make singer and audience hold their breath until the final note of this little masterpiece has died away.

[3] WOLFGANG AMADEUS MOZART

Das Veilchen, The little violet (K476, 8 June 1785)

Ein Veilchen auf der Wiese stand,	A little violet grew on the meadow,
Gebückt in sich und unbekannt;	bowed down and unknown.
Es war ein herzig's Veilchen!	It was a charming little violet.
Da kam ein' junge Schäferin	Along came a young shepherdess,
mit leichtem Schritt und munterm Sinn	tripping lightly and blithe in spirit,
Daher, daher,	across the meadow,
Die Wiese her, und sang.	singing.
Ach! denkt das Veilchen, wär' ich nur	Oh! thought the violet, were I only
die schönste Blume der Natur,	Nature's loveliest flower
Ach! nur ein kleines Weilchen,	Oh, just for a little while,
Bis mich das Liebchen abgepflückt	Until my darling had plucked me
Und an dem Busen matt gedrückt,	And pressed me tightly to her bosom;
Ach nur, ach nur	Oh, just for
Ein Viertelstündchen lang!	a tiny quarter of an hour!
Ach, aber ach! Das Mädchen kam	Ah, but ah, the girl came along
und nicht in acht das Veilchen nahm,	and, not noticing the little violet,
Ertrat's das arme Veilchen.	stamped on it, the poor little violet.
Es sank und starb und freut sich noch:	It drooped and died, but was still happy:
Und sterb' ich denn, so sterb' ich doch	If I die, then I am dying
Durch sie, durch sie,	Because of her, and at
Zu ihren Füssen doch!	her feet!
(Das arme Veilchen!	(The poor little violet!
Es war ein herzig's Veilchen).	It was a charming little violet.)

GOETHE had written this pastoral poem in 1775 for his *Singspiel Erwin und Elmire*; in keeping with the spirit expressed in one of his famous apothegms: 'All my works are fragments of a great confession' ('All meine Werke sind Bruchstücke einer grossen Konfession'), this tells the story in verse of his jilting of Friederike Brion, the pastor's daughter from Sesenheim, as does *Heidenröslein* (q.v.)

The original three six-lined stanzas, like those of his *Heidenröslein*, sound almost like a *Volkslied*, and Mozart's setting – written just before the composition of *Le nozze di Figaro* – is a wonderful mixture of the folk-song and the more sophisticated 18th century type of rococo song known as the 'bergerette'. This Lied has its place in musical history as the first truly 'through-composed' song; Mozart's setting guides the listener skilfully through the seemingly quasi-tragic story, firstly setting the scene through the narrator, and then allowing her (or him?) to let us hear what the little violet was thinking.

It is a song usually sung by sopranos, but there is clearly a case for a male rendition, since the narrator could be either sex – and the violet's words are 'reported speech'. I have heard beautiful renderings in all the registers – the important factor is the interpretative genius of the performer. He or she must be able to bring the scene to life by a perfect understanding of the text and a sympathetic obedience to Mozart's instructions. There is no proof that Mozart knew the deeper implications of the poem, since this was, after all, the only poem of his young contemporary Goethe that he was to set – but a singer who does appreciate that the original poem was not about a tiny flower, but was rather the symbol of a young love destroyed, might feel that she can make much of what might otherwise be taken – and often *has* been taken – as mere parodistic effects.

The Lied must be started joyfully, the voice immediately repeating the piano's happy melody:

the grace notes on 'gebückt' (bent) and 'sich' (herself) underlining the naive gaiety of the scene. The light, tripping music to 'mit leichtem Schritt und munterm Sinn' (tripping lightly, and blithe in spirit) has made many commentators certain that this could only be sung by a soprano, but one has to recall again that the *narrator* is describing the scene; a light baritone or a tenor voice can make sense here too. The scene is temporarily clouded when the text moves into the subjunctive, ('O *were* I only . . .) and the music into the minor, as the modest violet is made to ponder on what might have been, if it had only been 'Nature's loveliest flower' – only to brighten again at the thought that it might be gently plucked and worn on that charming bosom. (It is probably impossible to reproduce in the voice – as it is in translation – the linguistic pun on 'Veilchen' (violet) and 'Weilchen' (a little while) in lines one and three of the second verse, although some singers like to put a little stress on 'Weilchen' to show their linguistic awareness!)

When the narrator returns *per se* in the third verse, we hear Mozart, the operatic composer, in the quasi-recitative of 'Ach, aber ach; Das Mädchen kam . . .' (Ah, but ah, the girl came along), as he tells of the 'death' of the flower – then he moves into the almost Bach-like rapture of the flower's awareness of death at the feet of its beloved – '. . . und sterb' ich denn, so sterb' ich doch, durch sie, durch sie . . .' (And if I die, then I am dying because of her . . .):

The soaring notes on 'durch sie' are matched by the increasing intensity of the accompaniment, which has matched the song's bold and varied rhythms and harmonies throughout.

It is interesting that Mozart felt that he needed to 'improve' on Goethe by adding two lines to the original poem. Goethe ended on 'zu ihren Füssen doch' (at her feet); Mozart decided on a little 'coda' which muses on the fate of the charming modest flower and adds 'Das arme Veilchen! Es war ein herzig's Veilchen' (The poor little violet! It was a charming little violet), to the melody that we heard at the beginning of the song. This is the only repetition in what could otherwise be considered to be a perfect example of a 'through-composed' Lied – twelve years before Schubert was born.

[4] WOLFGANG AMADEUS MOZART

An Chloe, To Chloë (K524, 24 June 1787)

IT IS A cliché of musical criticism that Mozart's best songs are to be found in his operas, but, as with all clichés, there is some truth in the remark. Just as some of the less serious arias, Cherubino's or Papageno's, for example, belong more to the realm of song, so too can some of Mozart's songs be thought of as arias or, at least, scenas, through-composed as they are. Many of Mozart's best songs were written too during the periods when he was working on his best operas, *Das Veilchen* just before *Le nozze di Figaro*, *An Chloe* during the composition of *Don Giovanni*.

One does not need to read far into a collection of Mozart's letters to know that sex played a major rôle in Mozart's life. Those letters to his wife Constanze, whom he had married in 1782, written while he was away on his often frustrating concert tours, refer continually to the pleasures of the flesh and to his unashamed longing for his marital rights.

Such knowledge deepens the interpreter's appreciation of both the text and the setting of Johann Georg Jacobi's poem *An Chloe*:

Wenn die Lieb' aus deinen blauen,	When Love gazes out of
Hellen, offnen Augen sieht,	your bright blue open eyes,
Und vor Lust hineinzuschauen	and at the joy of looking into them,
Mir's im Herzen klopft und glüht;	my heart pounds and flames,
Und ich halte dich und küsse	and I hold you and kiss
Deine Rosenwangen warm,	your rosy cheeks till they glow,
Liebes Mädchen, und ich schliesse	lovely girl, and I take
Zitternd dich in meinen Arm!	you trembling in my arms.
Mädchen, Mädchen und ich drücke	Girl, o my girl, I press
Dich an meinen Busen fest,	you close to my heart,
Der im letzten Augenblicke	which will only let you go
Sterbend nur dich von sich lässt;	at the final dying moment
Den berauschten Blick umschattet	My intoxicated mind is o'ershadowed by
Eine düstre Wolke mir,	a dark cloud,
Und ich sitze dann ermattet,	and then I sit, exhausted,
Aber selig neben dir.	but blissful beside you.

'Good taste' has always led to this song being regarded as a little rococo trifle on a par with those 'bergerettes' about Dresden shepherdesses and hearty rustics. In truth, *An Chloe* is a highly-charged, sophisticated allusion to the sex-act without very much concealment. It is perfectly plain too that Mozart set the poem both in this knowledge and with the intention to reproduce the poet's allusions in music.

118

Like *Das Veilchen*, this Lied is thought of as being a vehicle for the high soprano – yet what has been written above makes us realise that this, above all, *must* be sung by a tenor or baritone! It lies perfectly well for both voices, and, if sung by an artist of the calibre of a John McCormack – well accustomed to portraying Mozart's erotic rôles in opera on the stage – it will achieve its maximum effect.

The six-bar introduction is of vital importance since it sets the urgent breathless tempo for the love-scene; indeed, the song has to be sung throughout with urgency and passion – although it is just worth mentioning at this stage that the word 'Lust' (in line three of the first verse) does not mean 'lust' in German, but just 'joy'! This song is also 'through-composed', in that the repetitions of the melody in the second verse are subjected to tiny but important modifications, almost operatic touches, cf.

sieht,____ und vor Lust, hin - ein - zu - schau - en

fest,____ der im letz - ten Au - gen - bli - cke

The second stanza paints wonderfully the lovers' moment of fulfill-ment as the music comes to a temporary halt on 'eine düstre Wolke mir' (a dark cloud o'ershadows. . .):

mir, ei - ne dü - stre____ Wol - ke____ mir,

with the telling emphasis at the *fermata* on 'mir' (me). When the passionate lovers finally separate, the man sits exhausted beside his beloved – and Mozart repeats the word 'ermattet' (exhausted) not three, but *six* times for emphasis, and the final phrase 'neben dir' (beside you) no fewer than five times. Clearly, Mozart's emphases have more than musical significance, although some might think that the hammer was

119

striking the nut here again – and Jacobi might have echoed Tennyson's complaint mentioned earlier. Still, few performers or listeners would fail to agree that this is one of the most attractive songs in the whole literature of the Lied and one which shows Mozart's increasing awareness of the significance of the *words* of a poem – or the libretto of an opera. He had met Lorenzo da Ponte in 1783; their collaboration produced *Le nozze di Figaro* (1786), *Don Giovanni* (1787) and *Così fan tutte* (1790), just the years in which our two chosen songs were written. It is doubtful whether Mozart would have agreed in those years with what he had written to his father some years previously, viz. that the poem was to be (just) a dutiful daughter of the music. In these two Lieder, we have a near-perfect fusion of *Wort* and *Ton*.

[5] LUDWIG van BEETHOVEN

Andenken, Remembrances (Grove 240, WoO 136, 1809)*

Ich denke dein,	I think of you,
wenn durch den Hain	when through the grove
der Nachtigallen	the nightingales'
Akkorde schallen!	songs echo forth.
Wann denkst du mein?	When do you think of me?
Ich denke dein	I think of you
im Dämmerschein	in the twilight of
der Abendhelle	the clear evening
am Schattenquelle!	down by the shadowy pool.
Wo denkst du mein?	Where do you think of me?
Ich denke dein	I think of you
mit süsser Pein	in sweet agony
mit bangem Sehnen	with anxious longing
und heissen Tränen!	and hot tears.
Wie denkst du mein?	How do you think of me?
O denke mein,	O think of me
bis zum Verein	till we are united
auf besserm Sterne!	on a better planet!
In jeder Ferne	However distant,
denk' ich nur dein!	I think only of you!

---

* *WoO = Werk ohne Opuszahl*, work without an opus number.

BEETHOVEN was much more interested in the voice than he is given credit for; much of the disapproval of his writing for singers stems from those frightening passages for the sopranos in the last movement of his great Ninth (Choral) Symphony. But Beethoven wrote a good deal of fine vocal music apart from that movement; the great opera *Fidelio*, the *Missa Solemnis* and the Mass in C, various other choral works, over two hundred settings of British folk-songs, and more than eighty Lieder, including, of course, what is often recognised as the first song-cycle *An die ferne Geliebte* of 1816, seven years before Schubert's *Die schöne Müllerin*.

This song, *Andenken*, is an 1809 setting of a poem by Friedrich (von) Matthisson (1761–1831) whose 'lyrical fantasia' *Adelaide*, Beethoven had set so memorably in 1795/6 as an extended *bel canto* aria. The ten pages of the score of *Adelaide* give a marvellous opportunity for a gifted tenor or baritone to display his vocal technique, since the music ranges from the lyrical to the heroic. *Andenken* is a miniature in comparison; three of the four verses of, in effect, five lines each, are set strophically. Beethoven, as always, had read his text carefully and had seen that the first three stanzas were questions, each asking the loved one for a specific answer: when, where and how do you think of me when we are apart? The final stanza is a request, or, rather, in Beethoven's urgent setting, a demand to think of the loved one. This is a 'unisex' song, in that no particular sex is indicated, and either of the separated lovers could express these sentiments.

Strophic songs are as difficult to sing as any since only the singer's and accompanist's colorations can differentiate between the stanzas. They are also the most difficult to set satisfactorily, as Brahms often noted, because it is extremely difficult to find a melody which suits all the stanzas equally well. Here, Beethoven succeeded wonderfully because the first three stanzas are bound together thematically and demand the same melody. The accompanist sets the mood with a delightful introduction in 6/8 time:

and each verse begins with the singer's opening declaration of love:

Ich den - ke   dein,__ wenn

In each of the following three stanzas, the lover then paints a picture of the agony of separation: in the song-filled grove, by the woodland pool, in the tearful longing. The great interpreters attempt to sing each verse slightly differently; verse two, with its mood of twilit peace, is sung rather more softly than the passionate, tear-filled verse three. With a stroke of near genius, Beethoven then veers away from the main melody and sets verse four, with its urgent demand, to a related tune and a quite different musical structure, with slight decorations for the voice. He gives the singer two fine climaxes, one on 'Sterne' (planet) – *fp* – and one on 'jeder' (each, every) – but *ff*; both are textually correct, since the 'planet' is high, the 'every' (distance) is far-off:

o den - ke mein, bis zum Ver - ein auf bess - erm Ster - ne! In__

je - der Fer - ne denk' ich nur dein,

The typical 18th century conclusion with repetitions of the final phrase 'denk' ich nur dein' (I think only of you) – particularly the long-drawn-out *pianissimo* final phrase 'nur dein', sung to one chord in the accompaniment – can be very touching. Matthisson's poem is no worse, no better, than many of the Romantic poems which set the beloved against a background of natural phenomena – but the difference between talent and genius is made clear when one looks at Goethe's *Nähe des Geliebten* (Nearness of the beloved), which begins with the same line 'Ich denke dein'; one might say that a comparison of this Beethoven setting of Matthisson's poem with Schubert's of Goethe's poem (D162) might show the same difference – here, between the talented and the born song-writer.

[6] LUDWIG van BEETHOVEN

Neue Liebe, neues Leben, New love, new life (op.75 no.2, 1798/9)

Herz, mein Herz, was soll das geben?
Was bedränget dich so sehr?
Welch' ein fremdes, neues Leben;
Ich erkenne dich nicht mehr.
Weg ist alles, was du liebtest,
Weg, warum du dich betrübtest,
Weg dein Fleiss und deine Ruh' –
Ach, wie kamst du nur dazu!

Heart, my heart, what can this mean?
Why are you so worried?
What a strange, new life;
I do not recognize you any more.
Gone is everything you loved,
Gone, everything that worried you,
Gone your hard work and your peace of mind,
Oh, how have you come to this?

Fesselt dich die Jugendblüte,
Diese liebliche Gestalt,
Dieser Blick voll Treu' und Güte
Mit unendlicher Gewalt?
Will ich rasch mich ihr entziehen,
Mich ermannen, ihr entfliehen,
Führet mich im Augenblick,
Ach, mein Weg zu ihr zurück.

Does this fresh young thing ensnare you,
This charming figure,
These looks full of faithfulness and kindness,
with infinite strength?
If I try to pull myself away from her,
to take courage and leave her,
Then in a moment I am led
back to her, alas.

Und an diesem Zauberfädchen,
Das sich nicht zerreissen lässt,
Hält das liebe, lose Mädchen
Mich so wider Willen fest;
Muss in ihrem Zauberkreise
Leben nun auf ihre Weise.
Die Verändrung, ach, wie gross!
Liebe! Liebe! lass mich los!

And by this magic thread
that will not be broken,
this dear, flighty girl
holds me against my will;
And now here in her magic spell
I have to live as she wants me to.
O, how great is the change!
Love! Love! Set me free!

BEETHOVEN set nine of Goethe's poems to music (some more than once) and was fascinated by his great contemporary all his life. (The relationship is examined in Romain Rolland's book *Goethe et Beethoven* (1930)). Beethoven was born in 1770, the year in which Goethe, then twenty-one, went to study Law at the University of Strasbourg in Alsace, which was then, as it has since again become, French. The University was however essentially German in character. In August, armed with the title of 'Herr Doktor', Goethe left Strasbourg – and his first great love, Friederike Brion – to live for a time in Wetzlar, where he again fell in love. Home again in Frankfurt, he met, in 1775, Lili Schönemann, the daughter of a rich banker, and, despite his dislike of her 'society' household and friends, became engaged to her. The fear of being 'caged' became too great, however, and, breaking away, he fled to Weimar in November 1775, where he was to spend the remainder of his long life.

This poem reminds us of the 'new love' and the 'new life' which the twenty-six-year-old had experienced in Frankfurt, and is yet another 'fragment' of that great confession which Goethe's works were threatening to become. (One should add in all fairness that there are many recorded conversations in which Goethe insisted however that his works were *not* 'merely autobiographical'.)

From the text, this is clearly a song for the male voice; Goethe expresses his frustration at being 'ensnared' (Fesselt dich . . .) by this beautiful girl, at having to live 'as she wants me to' (auf ihre Weise). The poem is in fact addressed to himself, partly in the third, partly in the first person – and Beethoven has admirably succeeded in reproducing the frustration and the passion. The song is 'through-composed' in a fascinating and complicated manner, in that the pulsating beginning, 'Herz, mein Herz, was soll das geben?'

sets the tempo for the whole song. The first two stanzas are in different keys (C major and G major), the latter key having been introduced by the central question of the song, the last line of the first stanza: 'Ach, wie kamst du nur dazu! (How did you come to this!), which slows down the urgent questioning of the rest of the song. There is a touch of genius in the way in which Beethoven re-introduces this question after both stanzas have been repeated, this time both in C major:

The accompanist plays a vital rôle in keeping the pulsating rhythm going, although, in truth, the piano part does not contribute much else to the setting, since the genius of this song resides solely in the vocal line. In the third and final stanza Beethoven concludes with his now familiar repetitions: 'Liebe, Liebe, lass mich los, lass, lass, lass mich los, lass, lass, mich los' (Love, set me free) which can here be interpreted either as the lover's pitiful pleas for his freedom – or simply as 18th century musical convention!

The setting admirably reproduces the breathless quality of the poem and demonstrates how well Beethoven understood the problem of setting words to music. Who knows what might have happened to the German Lied if Beethoven, rather than Schubert, had been eighteen in 1815? Although the year 1816 saw Beethoven produce the song-cycle, *An die ferne Geliebte* – the first edition actually bears the sub-title 'Ein Liederkreis von A. Jeitteles' (A Song-Circle (cycle) by A. Jeitteles) – at forty-six he was probably too set in his (instrumental) ways to react to the new poetry as the younger man did. But, in every one of his songs, Beethoven (in Richard Capell's words) 'pointed to dozens of strange ways which those with the strength could explore further for themselves' – and who could deny that Franz Schubert did just that?

[7] FRANZ SCHUBERT

Gretchen am Spinnrade, Margaret at the spinning-wheel
(D118, 19 October 1814)

GOETHE worked on his epic poem *Faust* almost all his long life; the earliest parts go back to his experiences during those days spent as a student at the University of Strasbourg in 1770–1771, and were probably drafted in 1772, while he made amendments to the final version of Part II in Weimar in 1832, only two months before his death at the age of 82.

There are many candidates for the original of young Gretchen, the simple lass who falls in love with the rejuvenated professor Faust, is seduced by him and having drowned their child, is left witless in her condemned cell, as Mephistopheles, the servant of the Devil, drags Faust away. Some commentators believe that she must be modelled on the hapless Friederike Brion, whom Goethe loved and left in Sesenheim near Strasbourg; others opt for Charlotte (Lotte) Buff, to whom Goethe behaved similarly in Wetzlar. That is not our concern here. Schubert, like most of his contemporaries, was set on fire by the 'romantic' story – Part I of *Faust* was published in 1808 – and it inspired him to produce at the age of seventeen and a half the Lied which was to revolutionize song-writing, principally because it was the first song to be given a fully integrated accompaniment:

125

Meine Ruh' ist hin,	My peace has gone,
Mein Herz ist schwer,	My heart is heavy,
Ich finde sie nimmer	I shall never find
und nimmermehr.	it again, never.
Wo ich ihn nicht hab',	Wherever I do not possess him
Ist mir das Grab,	is the grave for me,
Die ganze Welt	The whole world
Ist mir vergällt.	has turned to gall.
Mein armer Kopf	My poor head
Ist mir verrückt,	is in a whirl,
Mein armer Sinn	My poor brains
Ist mir zerstückt.	are all confused.
Nach ihm nur schau ich	I look for him only
Zum Fenster hinaus,	out of the window,
Nach ihm nur geh' ich	Only to look for him
Aus dem Haus.	Do I go out of the house.
Sein hoher Gang,	His fine gait,
Sein' edle Gestalt,	His noble bearing,
Seines Mundes Lächeln,	The smile on his lips,
Seiner Augen Gewalt.	The power in his eyes!
Und seiner Rede	The magic flow
Zauberfluss,	of his words,
Sein Händedruck,	The squeeze of his hand,
Und ach, sein Kuss!	and oh, his kiss!
Mein Busen drängt	My soul longs
Sich nach ihm hin.	for him,
Ach, dürft' ich fassen	Oh, if I might grasp
Und halten ihn,	and hold him,
Und küssen ihn,	And kiss him
So wie ich wollt',	Just as I want to.
An seinen Küssen	And in his kisses
Vergehen sollt'!	I should perish!

There must be very few female singers who would refuse the chance to sing this marvellous song in public – it lies well for all the voices, soprano, mezzo-soprano and contralto – although, textually, it would not suit the very deep, 'dark-brown' mature contralto voice, beloved of oratorio audiences, since we must think of Gretchen as a young inexperienced girl. In Goethe's *Faust*, the episode takes up an entire scene, as Gretchen muses at her spinning-wheel on her memories of meeting the handsome Faust. The words are not sung on stage, but spoken as a monologue, and are not referred to again.

The song has the wider range common to Schubert's songs for the female voice – he often had opera singers in mind when writing for the women, since few female singers would sing in public otherwise – here the song goes up to a top G on the words 'Und ach, sein *Kuss*' (and, oh, his kiss!), and a top A on 'an seinen Küssen ver*gehen* sollt'' (I should perish in his kisses):

generally accepted by those particularly interested in the writing and performance of Lieder, that there is no finer moment in the literature of the Lied than the miraculous halting of the spinning-wheel in this song on 'sein Kuss', to be followed by the, at first, stammering and then *a tempo* accompaniment:

The interpretative skill of the singer is tested by the almost whispered beginning 'Meine Ruh' ist hin' (My peace has gone); Gretchen has been sexually awakened by the dashing stranger, and Goethe's words express her wakening emotions, leading to an emotional outburst. The singer has to lead us from this peaceful beginning, through the growing excitement as Gretchen describes her hero's 'gait', his 'noble bearing', and these compelling eyes (which Goethe himself possessed incidentally!). Then the thought of his flow of words – Faust was a professor! – the touch of his hand – 'und ach, sein Kuss!' (and oh, his kiss!). It is

generally accepted by those particularly interested in the writing and performance of Lieder, that there is no finer moment in the literature of the Lied than the miraculous halting of the spinning-wheel in this song on 'sein Kuss', to be followed by the, at first, stammering and then *a tempo* accompaniment:

It is no small task for the accompanist to re-establish tempo and dynamics within three bars. But then his task overall is no mean one. The song is marked 6/8 *allegro non troppo* (nicht zu geschwind) and the accompanist has to remember throughout the song that he is in effect Gretchen's right foot, and that he keeps the spinning-wheel turning as Gretchen dreams of her lover-to-be. It can be shown that the accompaniment rises in pitch as her excitement grows – from D minor to E minor to F to B flat! – and like the hoof-beat triplets in the accompaniment to *Erlkönig*, those right-hand semi-quavers hardly cease!

Very little, certainly not words, can 'explain' a work of art; students of the Lied 'know' that *Gretchen am Spinnrade* is a flawless masterpiece, almost indestructible, and audiences seem to sense this as well. It has a stunning impact in the concert hall – which is why it should always be given an important place in the programme, either as the first – or last – song of the Schubert group. It can be accompanied by other Lieder to poems by Goethe, or connected with him, e.g. *Suleika*-Lieder I and II, to poems written in 1815 by his friend Marianne von Willemer and included in his *Divan* (collection) called *West-östlicher Divan*: I (D 720 – *Was bedeutet die Bewegung* – What does this agitation mean?) and II (D717 – *Ach, um deine feuchten Schwingen* – Ah, how I envy your moist wings) are superb examples of Schubert's writing for the female voice. They might then be followed by a group too often ignored by singers and concert promoters, but which have an immediate appeal – and not only for British audiences! – *Ellens Gesänge* (Ellen's songs) I, II and III are 1825 settings of lines from Sir Walter Scott's *Lady of the Lake*. These three songs, *Raste, Krieger* (Soldier, rest, thy warfare is o'er) (D837), *Jäger, ruhe von der Jagd* (Huntsman, rest, thy chase is done) (D838) and the celebrated *Ave Maria* (D839) would make an excellent pendant to the songs already mentioned and would display all aspects of the female singer's vocal technique.

[8] FRANZ SCHUBERT

Heidenröslein, Wild rose (19 August 1815, D257)

Sah ein Knab' ein Röslein stehn,
Röslein auf der Heiden,
War so jung und morgenschön,
Lief er schnell, es nah zu sehn,
Sahs mit vielen Freuden.
Röslein, Röslein, Röslein rot,
Röslein auf der Heiden.

A boy saw a little rose growing,
Rose in the meadow,
(It) was so young and fair as morning,
He ran quickly to look at it more closely,
Saw it with great joy!
Rose, rose, little red rose,
Rose in the meadow.

Knabe sprach: 'Ich breche dich,
Röslein auf der Heiden!'
Röslein sprach: 'Ich steche dich,
Dass du ewig denkst an mich,
Und ich wills nicht leiden'.
Röslein, Röslein, Röslein rot,
Röslein auf der Heiden.

Boy said: 'I'll pick you,
Rose in the meadow',
Rose said: 'I'll prick you,
so that you'll always think of me,
And I shall not put up with it'.
Rose, rose, little red rose,
Rose in the meadow.

Und der wilde Knabe brach
's Röslein auf der Heiden;
Röslein wehrte sich und stach,
Half ihm doch kein Weh und Ach,
Musst es eben leiden.
Röslein, Röslein, Röslein rot,
Röslein auf der Heiden.

And the naughty boy picked
the rose in the meadow.
Rose defended herself and pricked him,
No oh-ing and ah-ing helped him,
Just had to put up with it.
Rose, rose, little red rose,
Rose in the meadow.

AUTHORITIES are still at odds about the origin of this poem; some believe that Goethe heard it in his Strasbourg days and re-wrote it; others say that only the refrain is original and that the rest is Goethe's own. All that concerns us here perhaps is that the poem *sounds* like a *Volkslied* – and that Schubert certainly must have read it as such to have been able to give it such an enchantingly naive *Volkslied*-like melody and setting. This is, of course, the perfect example of the strophic Lied – three stanzas set to the same melody and the same accompaniment. (Incidentally, despite what some think, Schubert never lost his love for this type of song, and it is in fact the most 'typical' Schubert Lied-form. He set thirty Goethe poems in this year 1815 and over a dozen are strophic.)

The three stanzas contain three quite different sentiments, and the performers are well advised to study the words carefully before performing the song. As so often with Goethe's poems, the seemingly artless text contains symbolical depths; we have here once again the story of a desperate lover, first of all attracted, then ensnared, and finally rejected – with many 'oh''s and 'ah''s – by the girl. The singer

129

must be able so to point the words that the boy's joy in the first stanza is followed by the rose's defiance in the second – and the boy's rebuff in the last. This can be done by choosing the springiest of 2/4 rhythms and the brightest tone for verse one and giving the lovely refrain a good deal of body. Verse two can then be sung rather more thoughtfully, particularly where the rose promises that the boy will not be allowed to get away with any untoward behaviour! The third stanza, still sung in the same bright tempo, will find the great singers adopting a contemplative tone on 'musst es eben leiden' (just had to put up with it), and singing the penultimate line of the refrain *pianissimo* as marked. The top G sharp on the *fermata* 'rot' (red) is a fine note for a good voice:

As so often with performances of Schubert's Lieder, the best are those which obey the composer's instructions. The song is marked *lieblich* (with love, tenderness) (or, in Italian, *con tenerezza*), and there is not a *forte* to be seen anywhere. The accompanist's task is technically an easy one, as the part is simplicity itself, but a good deal of rehearsal is needed to hit just the right springy tempo. It is a song too for all voices and both sexes, since we have a narrator, a boy, and a girl, although some might think the higher voices would make more of that penultimate line.

Those who are puzzled by the archaic spelling of the words in some of the versions – *Hai*denröslein, ro*th* and so on – will realize that these are 18th or 19th century German spellings which, I believe, should no longer be used. Unfortunately, there have been so few new editions of Schubert's Lieder that we have to put up with archaic spellings and translations in Anglo-Saxon countries. One particularly unfortunate effect on those who learn German from Lieder (rather than *for* Lieder!) is that they often take over into their own learner's German some of the more common 18th and 19th centuries' archaisms: *der Knabe* (now *der Junge* = the boy), *das Mägdelein* (now *das Mädchen* = the girl), *das Bächlein* (now usually *der Bach* = the brook, stream), *das Thal* (now *das Tal* = the valley), *die Thür* (now usually *die Tür* = the door) and many, many others, while musicians writing out German from a vocal score regularly spell *die Brücke* (the bridge) *die Brükke*, because, when the word is written on two notes, the rule for word-division in the German language demands that the '-ck' becomes 'k-k'!

Similarly, translators have never been quite certain whether a '*Heiden-röslein*' is a 'little hedge-rose', a 'heath-rose', a 'wild rose' or whatever! Although the rose is said to be growing 'auf der Heiden' (on a 'heath' or 'meadow'), gardeners would assume that it is on a *bush in* the meadow, and not *on* the meadow itself – 'wild rose' seems therefore to be the correct and best translation.

Just as Schumann was to have his *annus mirabilis* later (see p.137 below), during which he wrote some one hundred and thirty eight songs, 1815 was a high-point in Schubert's career as a song-writer. In that year alone – and at the age of eighteen – he wrote one hundred and fifty songs, some of them among the finest he ever wrote; his fecundity never fails to amaze: on 19 October 1815, he wrote as many as eight songs during the day, and on 19 August 1815, he wrote five songs to texts of Goethe, of which this one, *Heidenröslein*, was the third.

[9] FRANZ SCHUBERT

Wanderers Nachtlied II, 'Über allen Gipfeln ist Ruh' (Wanderer's Night Song, 'Over all the mountain peaks is peace') (D768 c.1823)

THIS LIED appears in some Schubert editions as 'Ein Gleiches' (literally, 'a similar one'), which was the title Goethe gave to distinguish it from his first *Wanderers Nachtlied*, 'Der du von dem Himmel bist' (Thou which art from Heaven), which Schubert had set, as D224, in July 1815.

This is the Lied which most separates lovers of the Lied from lovers of poetry when the argument about 'gilding the lily' is raised. By general consent among lovers of German poetry, the eight lines of the poem are among the most beautiful that Goethe – or *any* poet who has ever written in German for that matter – wrote:

Über allen Gipfeln	Over all the mountain peaks
Ist Ruh',	Is peace,
In allen Wipfeln	In all the tree-tops
Spürest du	You sense
Kaum einen Hauch;	Scarcely a breath;
Die Vöglein schweigen im Walde.	The birds are silent in the woods.
Warte nur, balde	Just wait, soon
Ruhest du auch.	You too will be at rest.

131

Goethe wrote the poem on 6 September 1780 on the wall of a mountain-hut on the Gickelhahn, near Ilmenau in Thuringia – a priceless *graffito*! He was thirty-one at the time, and we might assume that the peace of which he wrote was the peace of night and of sleeping nature. He returned to the hut in 1813, when he was sixty-four, and renewed the inscription, which was then preserved under glass, and it is fairly certain that even at that time – and particularly on his last visit, a few months before his death when he was eighty-two – the last lines, 'Soon you too will be at rest', would have been thought of as the peace of death. (The hut burned down on 11 August 1870.)

Certainly, Schubert's setting in a solemn B flat is in what Dietrich Fischer-Dieskau called his 'death-rhythm' (*Todesrhythmus*), although the music has no sadness in it, but an ineffable peace. Schubert set the eight lines of poetry to fourteen bars of music which, marked *Langsam* (slow), progresses from the wonderfully effective piano introduction:

to the opening bars for the voice describing the peace over the mountains:

When the song describes the little birds – Goethe wrote *Vögelein*, but Schubert set the word as two syllables, *Vöglein* – there is a gentle rustling in the accompaniment as if the birds were settling down to rest:

The final two lines are repeated, each leading to a *fermata* on the word 'balde' (soon), the second time sung *piano*, and, if the singer has the breath-control, with an *enjambement* to 'ruhest du auch' in the one breath:

There is nothing in Schubert's Lieder to equal the beauty and simplicity of these closing bars, enhanced for some if the performer sings the alternative turn within the word 'balde'. Some, like the scholar Max Friedländer took this turn to be a later embellishment by performers, but Eusebius Mandyczewski printed it as an option in his *Collected Edition* of the songs (1884–1897), reprinted in 1964, and one can still hear it from time to time.

This song, of all Schubert's Lieder, is the one in which 'art conceals art'. Nothing could look simpler on paper, but to achieve this effect of breathless peace, nothing must disturb the long line of the music, nor must there be any swelling of the voice or accompaniment – the only *crescendo* allowed would be on 'warte nur, warte nur . . .' (Just wait . . .). It is a song for all voices, since it, like the poem, is time-less and place-less; all that is needed to perform it and appreciate it is a deep love of natural as well as of man-made beauty. And when one has performed or listened to it, one might well agree with Professor Jack Stein that 'in this song, if anywhere in song literature, appears the ultimate refutation of the notion that great poems should not be used as texts for art songs'.

[10] FRANZ SCHUBERT

Du bist die Ruh', You are my repose (D776, 1823)

IF ONE wanted to play the 'numbers' game' to prove that Schubert set, on the whole, poems by second- or even third-rate poets, it would not be difficult to show that, of his six hundred and three known Lieder, over half are settings of poets with whom History has dealt hard. This in itself is however no reflection on Schubert's literary taste; there must be many like me who have been led to look more carefully at a poem after encountering it first in a Schubert setting. The forty-four poems of Wilhelm Müller which make up *Die schöne Müllerin* and *Winterreise* would be cases in point. Schubert was attracted by the innate musicality of these verses and, after one has heard his matchless music, the poems themselves are somehow illuminated by its glory, while, as we have already seen with one example, *Über allen Gipfeln*, great music and great poetry can be joined to create something greater than either.

Rückert (1788–1866) was much influenced by that love of things oriental which flourished in Germany during the Romantic Age, an age which dreamt constantly of places 'long ago and far away'. Many of Rückert's poems like this one (originally without a title, then called *Kehr ein bei mir* – Come in to me) are bestrewn with oriental imagery which makes them almost unreadable nowadays. *Du bist die Ruh'* suffers only at the end:

Du bist die Ruh',	You are my repose
Der Friede mild,	and gentle peace,
Die Sehnsucht du,	Longing you are
Und was sie stillt.	And all that stills it.
Ich weihe dir	I dedicate to you,
Voll Lust und Schmerz	Full of joy and pain,
Zur Wohnung hier	As a dwelling here
Mein Aug' und Herz.	My eye and heart.
Kehr ein bei mir	Come in to me,
Und schliesse du	And shut
Still hinter dir	quietly behind you
Die Pforten zu.	the gates.
Treib andern Schmerz	Drive all other pain
Aus dieser Brust!	Out of this breast!
Voll sei dies Herz	Let this heart be full
Von deiner Lust.	of your joy.
Dies Augenzelt,	The tent of these eyes
Von deinem Glanz	by your radiance
Allein erhellt,	alone is illuminated.
O füll es ganz!	Oh, fill it to the brim!

Schubert set the poem in a modified strophic form; by joining verses one and two, then verses three and four, he made two stanzas to which he gave the same melody and accompaniment, and then he used the fifth verse as his conclusion, repeating it with a variation.

Here again is a Schubert song in the 'death-rhythm', a song which requires a sure vocal technique and enormous reserves of breath-control. The very first line indicates the 'problem'; the song is marked *Langsam* (slow) and the accompaniment starts with gentle rocking semi-quavers:

Into this lullaby-like movement steals the voice *pianissimo*, its first phrase stretched over four long bars:

Du bist   die   Ruh',   der   Frie - de   mild,

and this is only the first hurdle for the singer, since this melody is then repeated for the next two lines of the poem. The effect is to intensify the prayerful atmosphere created by words like 'weihe' (dedicate). If a singer is brave enough, there is a wonderful opportunity for displaying interpretative and vocal skill in the first line of the second verse 'Kehr ein bei mir und schliesse du' (Come in to me and close . . .) The reader will see that the phrase needs to be extended to '. . . still hinter dir die Pforten zu' (. . . the gates quietly behind you) to make sense. It would be rather much to expect *any* singer – even the great ones – to have enough breath to manage all eight bars, but one should try to make the *enjambement* to 'hinter dir' at least. The accompanist will have to be relied upon too to prevent the singer from hurrying as the breath gives out!

Kehr ein bei mir und schlie - ße du still hin - ter

dir die Pfor - ten zu.

The 'third', and final, stanza differs entirely from the first two, and it is likely that Schubert was led by the notion of 'the tent of your eyes' and the 'illumination' to set the words to a rising phrase which is repeated and which ends on a very difficult A flat on the word 'erhellt' (illuminated), written to be sung *forte*. Just as opera singers differ in their treatment of the B flat finale on the word 'sol' in the phrase 'vicino al sol' in Verdi's aria *Celeste Aida* – most sing it *forte*, a very few *pianissimo morendo* as Verdi wanted it – so too do singers vary the repetition of Schubert's final climbing phrase. Those with the vocal technique needed – like Fischer-Dieskau – let the phrase end *pianissimo*, since as he points out in his book on Schubert, the top note (his high G) is a *diminuendo*, 'something often gladly overlooked because of the general difficulties of execution'.

There are few songs which can so move singer, accompanist and audience alike. As Richard Capell wrote in his book on Schubert, 'it remains one of the most difficult songs in existence, taxing the technical control as severely as the singer's taste', since two-thirds of the song have to be sung *mezza-voce* and the last part with a *crescendo*. It is a song to be performed by the greatest singers with love and respect – and by the amateur in the stillness of his or her own room!

[11] ROBERT SCHUMANN

Der Nussbaum, The walnut tree (op.25 no.3, 1840)

IT HAS already been mentioned that one of Schumann's closest friends, Emil Flechsig, heard Schumann weep through the night after hearing of the death of Franz Schubert in 1828. Schumann was then eighteen years old, and was not to know that the mantle of the 'Prince of Lieder' (*der Liederfürst*), as Schubert was later called, was to fall upon his shoulders. Schumann had shown little interest in song-writing until fairly late in his career as a composer, and, indeed, it was not until his love for the pianist Clara Wieck seemed at last to hold out prospects of fulfillment in marriage, that the doors of the treasury were unlocked and the riches within displayed – which Schumann himself was surprised to find in his possession. Although the pair did not finally marry until September 12th (on the eve of Clara's 21st birthday), the year 1840, the *annus mirabilis*, brought forth one hundred and thirty-eight Lieder, the best of them surely among the finest in the song repertoire.

Der Nussbaum belongs to a cycle of songs called *Myrten* (the old spelling *Myrthen* is still to be found) (opus 25), settings of twenty-six poems by various composers which Schumann had intended as a wedding-gift for his bride – and which she duly received. (German brides used to wear a head-band of myrtle blossom). It must be admitted that there are some people who still feel that Schumann's passionate love for Clara led him into sentimental paths, and that some of his songs have just a little too much of the early-Victorian (called *Biedermeier* in German) 'sighing swain' atmosphere about them. I find myself sharing this view from time to time – but not when singing, or listening to *Der Nussbaum*:

Es grünet ein Nussbaum vor dem Haus,
Duftig, luftig breitet er blättrig die Blätter aus.

A walnut tree stands green in front of the house,
spreading its airy, perfumed leafy branches.

Viel liebliche Blüten stehen dran;
Linde Winde kommen, sie herzlich zu umfahn.

Many lovely blossoms are on it;
Gentle breezes come to embrace it lovingly.

Es flüstern je zwei zu zwei gepaart,
Neigend, beugend zierlich zum Kusse
die Häuptchen zart.

Paired together, they whisper,
bending their heads delicately
to kiss.

Sie flüstern von einem Mägdlein, das
Dächte die Nächte und Tage lang,
Wusste, ach, selber nicht was.

They whisper of a girl who
would meditate day and night,
but did not know herself, alas, about what.

Sie flüstern, wer mag verstehn so gar
Leise Weis'? flüstern von Bräut'gam
und nächstem Jahr.

They whisper, but who can understand
such a gentle song? They whisper about the
bridegroom – and next year.

Das Mägdlein horcht, es rauscht im Baum;
Sehnend, wähnend sinkt es lächelnd in
Schlaf und Traum.

The girl listens, there's a rustling in the
tree; longing, hoping, she sinks smiling
into sleep and dreams.

137

Although one will find the title of the song variously translated as 'The hazel tree' or 'The almond tree', it is in fact a walnut tree. The poem by Julius Mosen, a friend of Schumann, originally had the word *Äste* (branches) in the second line, which Schumann (quite knowledgeable on botanical matters) changed to the more accurate, though less euphonious, *Blätter* (leaves), a small example of a Schumann trait which makes his song-texts dangerous ground for students of German litera-ture, since he treated most of his texts in a rather cavalier fashion. It must be added, however, that his literary sensitivity was, on the whole, so fine that the substitutions were often an improvement on the original!

This song is a perfect vehicle for the high soprano voice which can 'represent' the girl smiling in her dreams as the leaves whisper their comforting message to her. The song is marked *allegretto*, and its swaying gentle 6/8 tempo paints to perfection the scene of the gently swaying tree outside the girl's window:

This swaying tempo must be maintained throughout the song – up to the point where the 'secret' of the leaves' message is revealed on the words 'flüstern von Bräut'gam' (whisper of a bridegroom) – here the melody changes for the last ten bars of the song. The message has been received and the girl can settle down to dream of her coming marriage:

seh - nend, wäh - nend sinkt   es   lä - chelnd in Schlaf und Traum.

As in so many of the great Lieder, the accompanist's task looks – on paper – deceptively simple, but he must play a major rôle in maintaining the tempo, or re-establishing it after the few *ritardandi*, and, above all in this song, maintaining the *piano* marking at the beginning.

Despite the fact that Schumann arranged the songs in key-sequence, *Myrten* is not really a true song-cycle, and each of its twenty-six songs can be extracted and performed independently. *Der Nussbaum* would fit very neatly into a group of songs which deal with the flora and fauna of nature, for example; indeed, it is often performed with another Schumann Lied, *Die Lotosblume* (The lotus flower), the seventh song in the *Myrten* group.

[12] ROBERT SCHUMANN

Mondnacht, Moonlit night (op. 39 no.5, 1840)

WHEN Schumann returned to Leipzig after a visit to his beloved Clara in Berlin in May 1840, it would seem that the combination of Spring and love in bloom led in that month of May to two of his most inspired compositions: settings of twelve poems by Joseph von Eichendorff, the arch-Romantic poet, grouped under the title *Liederkreis* (Song-circle)(opus 39), and, of course, the cycle of poems by Heinrich Heine, *Dichterliebe* (Poet's Love) (opus 48).

The *Liederkreis* does not 'tell a story', as does *Die schöne Müllerin* or *Winterreise* or *Dichterliebe*, but the poems are linked by the common theme of 'romance in nature'. Eichendorff (1788–1857) was *the* German poet of nature, and there are few poems which paint so sensitively and evocatively the peaceful charm of a moonlit night as this one does:

Es war, als hätt' der Himmel
Die Erde still geküsst,
Dass sie im Blütenschimmer
Von ihm nun* träumen müsst'.

Die Luft ging durch die Felder,
Die Ähren wogten sacht,
Es rauschten leis' die Wälder,
So sternklar war die Nacht.

Und meine Seele spannte
Weit ihre Flügel aus,
Flog durch die stillen Lande,
Als flöge sie nach Haus'.

It seemed as if the sky
Had gently kissed the earth,
So that in a shimmer of blossom
She now had to dream of him.

The winds soughed through the fields,
The ears of corn swayed gently
And the woods rustled softly,
The night was so starry-clear.

And my soul spread out
its wings wide,
Flew through the peaceful countryside,
As if it were flying home.

From the first magical notes of the piano, we are transported into the serenity of the countryside at night, then the singer has to hit the notes on 'Es war . . .' dead centre, *piano*, and then summon up all his reserves of breath for the first long rising phrase, 'Es war, als hätt' der Himmel':

* Eichendorff's poem has 'nur' (only).

This is a modified strophic Lied which lies well for all the voices: the second verse has the identical melody with the same beautifully rhythmical turn on 'wogten' (swayed) as on 'still' in verse one. The voice and piano are wonderfully fused here – and when Schumann reacts to Eichendorff's change of mood in the third stanza, the effect is even more miraculous. In almost religious ecstasy, the poet pictures his soul reaching out its wings to fly up to heaven – the composer matches each word with telling accuracy: as the soul 'spreads its wings out wide', the music 'spreads' with it – 'und meine Seele spannte . . .':

a model of word-setting.

Schumann brings the vocal part to a peaceful and satisfying close on a descending phrase – 'als flöge sie nach Haus', (as if it were flying home) – to indicate the soul's arrival at its haven, but then he adds what was to become a characteristic of all his great settings – a piano postlude of great beauty which, as in this case, not only sums up the mood and atmosphere,but gives the accompaniment that importance which it was increasingly to have in the 19th century, until, eventually, composers felt that the piano was not enough and turned to the resources of the full orchestra.

Here however, the piano is more than enough, and those eight bars of epilogue hold singer and audience in their thrall till the last *pianissimo* notes and the song ends as it began, 'zart, heimlich' (gently, intimate).

[13] ROBERT SCHUMANN

Stille Tränen, Silent tears (op.35 no.10, 1840)

Du bist vom Schlaf erstanden	You have risen from your sleep
Und wandelst durch die Au.	and wander through the meadow.
Da liegt ob allen Landen	Over all the countryside
Der Himmel wunderblau.	lies the wonderfully blue sky.
So lang du ohne Sorgen	As you were sleeping free from care
Geschlummert schmerzenlos,	and without pain,
Der Himmel bis zum Morgen	Heaven was pouring down its
Viel Tränen niedergoss.	tears, till the morning.
In stillen Nächten weinet	In silent nights, many
Oft mancher aus den Schmerz,	a man weeps away his grief,
Und morgens dann ihr meinet	and then, in the morning, you all think
Stets fröhlich sei sein Herz.	that his heart is always happy.

THIS POEM by Justinus Kerner was one of twelve by him that Schumann set at the end of 1840. Considering that Schumann had just married his Clara at last, the choice of texts might be thought to be rather strange, since they are uniformly melancholy and the 'cycle' ends with two of the saddest, yet most remarkable settings that Schumann ever made: *Wer machte dich so krank?* (Who made you so ill?) and *Alte Laute* (Old sounds), both set to the same melody and ending the group of twelve songs on a remarkable whispered *pianissimo*.

Stille Tränen, however, No.10 of the group, is anything but *pianissimo*; it is a song for a singer with a 'big' voice, plenty of breath and opulent tone. So sung, and accompanied by an above-average accompanist, it becomes one of Schumann's most thrilling songs. It has been chosen here, firstly, because it is not performed much in recitals and should be heard more often, and, secondly, as we shall shortly see, it will reinforce the point made above about accompaniments becoming so 'orchestral' that they out-grew the piano.

The song is constructed like a piece of architecture, the huge phrases spanning the composition like church arches. Marked *Sehr langsam* (very slow), the song begins with exciting piano chords, above which the voice enters *piano* and climbs to the first climax on 'und wandelst durch die Au' (and wander through the meadow):

141

und wan___ delst durch _____ die Au,'_____

That top G is only the first of many such high notes, and the singer is well advised not to forget the Everests ahead! Although much of the score is, or should be, sung *piano*, these glorious top notes are rarely wasted by great performers, particularly when they are written so kindly by Schumann for words like 'Au' and 'blau'. (Later, in verse three, however, we find a top B flat on 'Schmerz' – which is a rather different matter!)

One would not choose this song to demonstrate the fusion of 'Wort' and 'Ton' – indeed, there is room for the opinion that Schumann came nowhere near to matching the music to the text. The poem, a very definite 'second-rate' production, has a rather maudlin theme – the 'you' of the poem is told that sleep has knit up the 'ravell'd sleave of care', but that his and other people's insouciant manner is seen to be but a brave face on one's real troubles.

These remarks are made merely to underline what has been already noted – that a great song can be made out of a mediocre poem. The 'other side of the coin' is that a great song can be made out of a great poem! Here, the melody and the structure of the song do not marry with the text and the accompaniment does not marry with the vocal line, yet both vocal line and accompaniment are in themselves superb. How thrilling is the trill in the piano part before the singer returns to repeat 'und morgens dann ihr meinet' (and then in the morning you all think) and how eloquent the eight-bar postlude!

The song is 'unisex' of course, but it needs a powerful baritone voice to make the most of the great climaxes on 'Au' and 'Schmerz' – once heard, this song will not be easily forgotten.

[14] ROBERT SCHUMANN

Die beiden Grenadiere, The two grenadiers (op.49 no.1, 1840)

SCHUMANN met Heinrich Heine briefly in Munich in 1828, when he was eighteen and the poet thirty-one, and the meeting seems to have had a lasting influence on him. Heine, of Jewish origins, fell out with his native country and went to live in Paris, where, after a dreadful illness, during which time he was confined to what he called his 'Matratzengruft' (literally, his mattress-tomb), he died in 1856, the same year as Schumann died in the mental home in Bonn. For Heine, French culture was infinitely superior to German; many of his poems praise the former at the expense of the latter, which he once pictured as a lumbering dancing bear. Heine's bitter attacks on his native land have still not been forgiven, it seems, and the town of Düsseldorf, where he was born, has been arguing for years about calling its University the 'Heinrich-Heine' University!

Some of Heinrich Heine's love of France is evident in this fine ballad – too long to print here – of the two soldiers returning from Russian captivity after Napoleon's ill-starred winter campaign in 1812, to learn that the Emperor had been captured and his valiant army decimated. Badly wounded, one of the grenadiers asks his companion to take his body back to France and bury him in French soil. The poem rises almost to ecstasy as the wounded warrior envisages the Emperor riding over his grave, from which he is sure that he will rise to guard his leader.

Schumann felt the affinity to Heine's poetry that I feel sure Schubert would have, had he been spared a few more years. Schumann set forty-one Heine poems, thirty in 1840 alone, and although critical opinions differ as to whether he ever really understood Heine's very sophisticated irony, he did manage to catch the lyricism of the most beautiful poems. One would really only need to cite the first song of *Dichterliebe*, 'Im wunderschönen Monat Mai' (In the wonderful month of May):

to prove the point. As with Schubert and Goethe's *Über allen Gipfeln*, a greater synthesis has been born.

In this ballad too, Schumann produced a miraculous marriage of words and music; he follows the progress of the poem in every

143

important detail – the slow, dragging, yet somehow march-like steps of the two tired soldiers at the beginning, marked *mässig* (moderate):

then the sudden stab of excitement as the one asks the other to do him the favour of burying him in France, should he die – 'Gewähr mir, Bruder, eine Bitt'' (Do me this favour, my brother) – up to the pulsating conclusion when the dying grenadier sees himself rising to defend his Emperor. The words 'a stroke of genius' must be applied here when we listen to Schumann's setting of the words 'So will ich liegen und horchen still' (So I shall lie there and listen):

Yes, the *Marseillaise*! How well Schumann makes the fine melody fit Heine's words, with only one or two dislocations – and how exciting it is to sing and to listen to! Schumann does not leave it there however – for the by now customary piano epilogue will describe the dying soldier's being gently laid on the ground after his paean of praise:

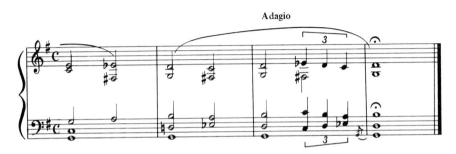

Although Dame Clara Butt in her *Land-of-Hope-and-Glory* manner might well have sung this ballad, it is a man's song – a ringing tenor or a weighty baritone is needed to give it the martial tone that it needs and deserves. An 'unashamed accompanist' is also a *sine qua non* to pound out the exciting bass octave quavers. What a conclusion this makes to a Schumann group!

[15] JOHANNES BRAHMS

Die Mainacht, The May night (op.43 no.2, 1866–8)

ALTHOUGH, purely chronologically, there is a case for regarding Brahms (born in 1833) as the lineal successor to Robert Schumann (born in 1810), there are many, including the author of a recent book on Brahms' songs, A. Craig Bell, who would rather see him as *Schubert's* successor, principally because of the importance he placed, firstly, on melody and, secondly, on the superiority of the strophic form of the Lied.* To be accurate, one would write the 'modified strophic' form, since Mr Bell and others have pointed out that Brahms wrote only about thirty-five or so *strophic* Lieder; there are sixty or so 'through-composed' songs, and the rest of his output is made up of modified strophic songs. If only because of his friendship with two of the finest Lieder singers of his generation, Julius Stockhausen and Frau Amalie Joachim, Brahms always maintained an intense interest in the German Lied – indeed, his first and last compositions were songs, although he never worried very much about what he called them – they appear variously as *Lieder, Gesänge, Romanzen*, or even just *Gedichte* (poems).

Die Mainacht is the second of the group of four Lieder which also contains *Von ewiger Liebe* (see above, p. 65). The poem is by Ludwig Hölty (1748–1776), a pre-*Sturm und Drang* poet, who had attracted Schubert as well. Schubert had set nine of Hölty's poems by 1815, including this one, *Die Mainacht* (D194). A comparison of the two settings – Schubert's artless strophic and Brahms' 'psychologically' more complex, modified strophic – tells us a good deal about the progress of the Lied in the 19th century.

---

* A. Craig Bell: *The Lieder of Brahms* (Darley, The Grian-Aig Press, 1979).

Wann der silberne Mond durch die
    Gesträuche blinkt,
Und sein schlummerndes Licht über
    den Rasen streut,
Und die Nachtigall flötet,
Wandl' ich traurig von Busch zu Busch.
	When the silvery moon gleams
	    through the bushes,
	And spreads its slumbering
	    light over the grass,
	And the nightingale flutes,
	I wander sadly from bush to bush.

Überhüllet von Laub girret ein
    Taubenpaar
Sein Entzücken mir vor; aber ich
    wende mich,
Suche dunklere Schatten,
Und die einsame Träne rinnt.
	Concealed by the foliage, a pair
	    of doves coo out
	their joy to me; but I turn
	    away,
	And seek darker shadows,
	And the solitary tear flows.

Wann, o lächelndes Bild, welches wie
    Morgenrot
Durch die Seele mir strahlt, find' ich
    auf Erden dich?
Und die einsame Träne
Bebt mir heisser die Wang' herab!
	When, o smiling image, which
	    illuminates my
	soul like the dawn, will I find
	    you on earth?
	And the solitary tear
	courses more hotly down my cheek!

Like Schubert, Brahms omitted the second verse of Hölty's poem ('Selig preis' ich dich dann, flötende Nachtigall') (I praise you as blessèd, fluting nightingale), which tells of the blissful love of the nightingale pair in their nest. Like Schubert too, in another way, Brahms loved to write long spacious melodies which are gifts to the singer with ample breath control and good resonance. The poem breathes an 18th century atmosphere of 'man-versus-nature'; Man is unhappy and restless, Nature is joyful and contented. Brahms' long opening line, marked *largo ed espressivo*, sets a scene of moonlit calm:

which is only slightly disturbed by the fourth line describing the poet's lonely walk. Here the superbly melancholic vowels of 'von Busch zu Busch', dark 'u' sounds, are wonderfully captured in the long two-bar phrase.

Although Brahms reproduced most carefully in verse one the metric form of Hölty's poem, the power of the musical idea proved too strong thereafter, and Brahms was carried away by his beautiful melodies from faithfulness to the original form. Singers however will scarcely worry about Brahms' 'faithlessness', when they are given a gloriously long and melodic phrase such as this to sing in the last verse:

Indeed, this is the crux of the great argument between the poetry-lover and the music-lover; in the above example, observe the false emphasis placed on the unimportant word 'und'. Yet what music-lover would really cavil at its position in this beautifully-constructed melodic pattern? Indeed, the greater the singer, the more flexibility he can give to such phrases – when this phrase is sung in one long glorious breath, the length of the note on 'und' is not noticed, particularly if the singer takes a short breath after it to enable him to sing the main phrase right through to the rest after 'bebt'.

The song ranks as one of Brahms' loveliest and is a fine challenge to singer and accompanist alike, since the latter – once again – is given the stern task of maintaining the rhythm in the quavers accompaniment, while the singer sets off on these long melodic phrases. As with No.1 of this group, *Von ewiger Liebe*, this fine song can be sung by either the male or the female voice.

Vergebliches Ständchen, A serenade in vain (op.84 no.4, 1881–2)

FOR whatever reason, British people are often unwilling to grant 'the Germans' a sense of humour; indeed, it is a cliché of film, TV serial or novel that the German is humourless, stolid and pedantic. Those who know Germany well can easily rebut this prejudice, but it does die hard; no doubt, the two wars of this century and the rather awesome reputation that some German philosophers, scientists and psychiatrists (and musicians) have earned over the last two hundred years has given Germany and the Germans this place in folk-myth.

Perhaps because of the portrayal of the composer in his advanced years as a heavily-bearded patriarch, although then only in his sixties, Brahms is often thought of as the 'type of a type' and since much of his music is predominantly of a autumnal, rather melancholic cast, the prejudice is strengthened. Yet a look through a collection of his songs might suggest to the unbiased reader that he *could* write in a light, almost Spring-like vein – not often, it is true, but sometimes.

Vergebliches Ständchen would be a case in point. Brahms originally believed that the poem was a genuine *Volkslied* and set it in that spirit:

'Guten Abend, mein Schatz, guten Abend, mein Kind!
Ich komm' aus Lieb zu dir,
Ach, mach' mir auf die Tür,
Mach' mir auf die Tür!'

'Good evening, my love, my child,
I come out of love for you
Oh, open your door,
Open your door!'

'Mein' Tür ist verschlossen, ich lass dich nicht ein,
Mutter, die rät mir klug,
Wärst du herein mit Fug,
Wärs mit mir vorbei'.

'My door is locked, I'll not let you in
Mother, who gives me good advice,
(says that) if you were let in,
It would be all up with me'.

'So kalt ist die Nacht, so eisig der Wind,
Dass mir das Herz erfriert,
Mein' Lieb' erlöschen wird,
Öffne mir, mein Kind'.

'The night is so cold, the wind so icy
that my heart is freezing
and my love will die.
Open up to me, my child'.

'Löschet dein' Lieb', lass sie löschen nur,
Löschet sie immerzu,
Geh' heim zu Bett, zur Ruh'.
Gute Nacht, mein Knab'!'

'If your love will die, let it die,
And if it keeps on dying,
Then go home to bed, to sleep!
Good night, my lad!'

Nothing could be more intoxicating than Brahms' opening music to this pseudo-*Volkslied*. (It was actually written by one A.W. Zuccalmaglio who put together a collection of *Volkslieder* which proved to be

148

tremendously popular in the 1880's.) Brahms was never to lose his love for *Volkslieder* – witness that superb collection for male and female voice published in 1894, *49 Deutsche Volkslieder* – and this is a perfect example of the ease with which he could fall into the style. (Those who would like to follow up Brahms as a composer of *Volkslieder* might like to sample the wonderful recording of these Lieder made by Elisabeth Schwarzkopf and Dietrich Fischer-Dieskau on Electrola SMA 91 487/8 in 1965, or in the recent (1983) DGG 'Brahms Edition' – 25 LP's of his Lieder sung by great artists like Jessye Norman, Lucia Popp, Brigitte Fassbaender, Edith Mathis, Peter Schreier, and Dietrich Fischer-Dieskau, accompanied by Barenboim, Engel, and Sawallisch.)

As we see, the four verses form a dialogue between the ardent (if physically freezing!) lover and an emotionally rather cold young girl. The *topos* is a familiar one; readers may know Schumann's setting of Reinick's *Ständchen* (Komm' in die stille Nacht) or Richard Strauss' more famous 'Mach' auf, mach' auf, doch leise, mein Kind', a setting of von Schack's *Ständchen* (see below, p.163) – in both cases, we can assume that the serenades were *not* in vain! Here however, the lover meets with an icy refusal.

The essence of this song is *rhythm*, and the accompanist must set the racy 3/4 going from the very first bar:

The singer (or singers q.v.) will no doubt want to inject a good deal of hearty masculinity into the first verse, since the lover has made his intentions fairly clear from the outset. The interesting fact about the technically very competent melody is how well it fits the girl's answer in the second verse, when it should be sung with quiet decisiveness. The accompanist too will note the change and play his graceful music more delicately.

The good singer will then obey the unwritten law for strophic songs – 'No two stanzas should be sung alike' – and adopt a more wistful, pleading tone for verse three – and slip back into the 'no-entry' voice for the fourth and final stanza. The marking for the song is *Lebhaft, gut gelaunt* (Lively and in a good mood), and the listener in the concert-hall or at home with his record player must be left with a feeling of fun. There is no great tragedy here – perhaps the boy will be luckier next time when the girl has not just washed her hair!

The song comes from a group titled 'Romanzen und Lieder für eine oder zwei Stimmen' (Romances and songs for one or two voices), so Brahms obviously foresaw the possibility of a tenor/soprano duet here. I prefer it in the high soprano register if only because the woman has the last word – we can safely assume from Brahms' closing musical phrase that she shuts the window pretty firmly!

In a letter to the noted and stern critic Eduard Hanslick, who had praised the song warmly, Brahms wrote: 'For this one song, I would sacrifice all the others . . .' Many might agree with him.

[17] JOHANNES BRAHMS

Feldeinsamkeit, Alone in the fields (op.86 no.2, 1877–8)

THE POET of these verses, Hermann Allmers, reputedly disliked Brahms' setting, which he felt did not do his poem justice. I wonder how many people nowadays would ever have heard of Herr Allmers but for Brahms?! In any group of Lieder chosen to present 'aspects of the seasons', *Feldeinsamkeit* would merit inclusion as one of the most tranquil descriptions of summer in music. Not even Delius bettered this magical evocation of the poet lying in the green grass watching the white cottonwool puffs of clouds drifting by and feeling that he himself is in another, better world:

Ich ruhe still im hohen grünen Gras	I rest peacefully in the tall green grass
Und sende lange meinen Blick nach oben,	And look upwards, long and steadily,
Von Grillen rings umschwirrt ohn' Unter-lass,	Surrounded by the unceasing whirring of crickets,
Von Himmelsbläue wundersam umwoben.	Wrapped in the magic blue of the sky.
Die schönen weissen Wolken ziehn dahin	The beautiful white clouds drift past
Durchs tiefe Blau, wie schöne stille Träume;	Thro' the deep blue, like lovely, still dreams.
Mir ist, als ob ich längst gestorben bin	I seem to be long since dead
Und ziehe selig mit durch ewge Räume.	And to be drifting blissfully with them thro' the eternal regions.

The music seems to start from the depths of the earth as the piano's bass octaves set the song in motion, but then the right hand takes the music skywards:

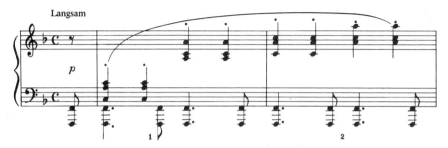

It is a song which cannot be sung too slowly and, as a result, is a severe test for any singer without the requisite breath-control. Most of the great singers take the first line (to 'Gras') in one majestic breath, but, after that, they vary considerably in where and when they draw breath. The problem is of course twofold: on the one hand the song must be sung *piano* throughout – there is a slight *crescendo* on 'meinen Blick nach oben' (look upwards, long and steadily) – and secondly, as has been said, it must be sung as slowly as possible. Those singers and listeners who understand German will be more sensitive to those breath pauses than those who have none. For example, the last line of the second verse demands a breath – but where? Some singers take it after 'selig' (blissfully) – but the German verb is '*mit*ziehen' and the breath should properly come after 'mit'!

The song is again a 'modified strophic' one; for the first verse, Brahms found a well-nigh perfect melody, both in structure and in shape. It matches the sentiment of the lines, the voice soars on 'nach oben' (upwards), and there is a magical turn to indicate the 'wrapped up' ('umwoben') of the last line in verse one, while the piano bass seems to keep us in touch with the solid earth.

The second verse takes on a slightly different shape; the key-change on the second line leading us into the strange dreaminess of 'Mir ist, als ob ich längst gestorben bin' (I seem to be long since dead), where the voice sinks down to a whisper on the bottom B, only to recover the spiral up to the 'eternal regions'. The magical moment in each verse is indeed at that semi-quaver turn on 'umwoben' and 'Räume' (regions); taken as slowly as the rest of the song with smooth *legato*, the effect is unforgettable – one of the great moments in the Lieder repertoire.

In many ways, *Feldeinsamkeit*, both as poem and as Lied, could be taken as a typical product of the Age. The Age of Universality, of the common man, is far away; the poet sits now alone in a field, communing not with his fellow-man, but with nature, thinking deep thoughts of this and the after-life, while the musician, released from the servility of being a mere 'valet de chambre' (see p. 33), now escapes into the countryside and paints scenes from Nature. The introspection which was to become so much a part of all our lives, what, at its worst, Germans derogatorily call *grübeln* (morbid contemplation), was here to stay.

[18] HUGO WOLF

Der Gärtner, The gardener (7 March 1888)

WITH HUGO WOLF, the 'Golden Age of the German Lied' may be said to have come to an end. Not that composers ceased to write Lieder – we have still to consider the songs of Strauss and Mahler, and there have been a considerable number written in our own century – but that tradition of the *Klavierlied* (song with piano), settings of 18th or 19th century poems, written for largely domestic performance, was never the same after Wolf's death in 1903.

We should not forget that Brahms had died only in 1897, although he was twenty-seven years older than Wolf, and that the two men had quarrelled about the importance of the up-and-coming musical figure of their day – Richard Wagner. Brahms, looking backwards as he was wont to do, saw little good in the pushing Saxon whom Wolf revered, and it might have been Wolf's support for Wagner's call to his 'disciples': 'Kinder, macht Neues!' (Children, do something new!) which both estranged him from Brahms and led him to stretch the Lied beyond its natural confines.

Der Gärtner, however, one of the settings of Eduard Mörike's poems (see p.68 above), written at white-heat in Wolf's 'year of miracles', 1888, has nothing 'new' about it; it is a beautiful example of the 'modified strophic' Lied, and if, at first sight, it may appear to be what Frank Walker calls it in his biography of the composer, viz. 'slight', not only has the song hidden depths, but it is also a charming song to sing for those who believe that Wolf's songs are only for the *cognoscenti*:

Auf ihrem Leibrösslein	On her favourite horse
So weiss wie der Schnee,	As white as the snow,
Die schönste Prinzessin	The loveliest princess
Reit't durch die Allee.	rides through the avenue of trees.
Der Weg, den das Rösslein	The path down which the horse
hintanzet so hold,	prances so divinely,
Der Sand, den ich streute,	The sand that I strewed
Er blinket wie Gold.	glistens like gold.
Du rosenfarb's Hütlein,	O, little pink-coloured hat,
Wohl auf und wohl ab,	bobbing up and down,
O wirf eine Feder	O, throw a feather
Verstohlen herab!	down to me in secret!
Und willst du dagegen	And if in return you
Eine Blüte von mir,	want a blossom from me,
Nimm tausend für eine,	Take a thousand for one –
Nimm alle dafür!	O, take them all!

Wolf set the first two stanzas to the same melody, accompanying it with a jaunty 'riding' motif in 6/8 time. The little masterpiece is over in a flash – it takes only about seventy-five seconds to perform – and one is left, as so often with Hugo Wolf, with an impression of fragile and ephemeral beauty. The rhythm is intoxicating, the melody bewitching.

It makes a wonderful encore number as can be imagined. The singer – it is a 'unisex' song – has a chance to make the song even more bewitching, if she or he will observe the slight *ritardando* on 'Eine Blüte von mir' (A blossom from me) – the effect is to express the yearning of the young besotted gardener and then to increase the intensity of his expansive gesture – 'Take a thousand for one . . .'

[19] HUGO WOLF

Anakreons Grab, Anacreon's grave (4 November 1888)

THIS SONG and No.20 share a fate which is probably unique in the history of German Lieder. *Anakreons Grab* and *Kennst du das Land. . .?* were two of five songs (in their orchestral versions) which Wolf left on a tramcar in Vienna when on his way to post them off to Berlin in 1893! This orchestral score of *Anakreons Grab* was never recovered, although the Mignon song did turn up many years later.

Opinions differ about Wolf's settings of Goethe's poems; many miss the sheer lyricism of the Schubert and Schumann settings, others believe that only Wolf got to the heart of, say, the great trilogy *Prometheus, Ganymed* and *Grenzen der Menschheit*, examples of what German scholars call *Gedankenlyrik* (philosophical poetry), because Wolf's settings are more intellectual than lyrical, as Frank Walker writes, and these poems need such music. There will always be supporters of either view. The fragile setting of *Anakreons Grab*, either in the piano or in the orchestral version of 1893 (after the 1890 one had been lost!), on the other hand, meets with general praise. The poem describes the resting place of Anacreon, the Greek lyric poet of the 6th century BC who died aged 83, and whose few remnants of poetry describe the gentle joys of the seasons:

Wo die Rose hier blüht, wo Reben um Lorbeer sich schlingen,	Here, where the rose blooms, where vines twine round the laurels,
Wo das Turtelchen lockt, wo sich das Grillchen ergötzt,	Where the turtle-dove calls, where the cricket delights,
Welch ein Grab ist hier, das alle Götter mit Leben	What grave is this, which all the gods have decorated and
Schön bepflanzt und geziert? Es ist Anakreons Ruh'.	planted with life? It is Anacreon's resting-place.
Frühling, Sommer und Herbst genoss der glückliche Dichter;	Spring, summer and autumn were enjoyed by the happy poet;
Vor dem Winter hat ihn endlich der Hügel geschützt.	From winter, finally, this grave mound has protected him.

These restrained classical lines were set by Wolf to twenty-one bars of austerely beautiful music. It is my favourite of the composer's fifty-one settings of Goethe poems, principally because of its so successful evocation of the classical scene. Wolf begins by matching the music perfectly to the metre:

'Wo die Rose hier blüht, wo Reben um Lorbeer sich schlingen', a quite

154

remarkable feat. But although the fusion of word and music is, on the whole, so successful – Wolf does not quite manage to retain the perfect fusion throughout the setting – it would be pedantic to claim that this is the reason for the popularity of the song, since not one singer in a hundred would be concerned with the faithfulness of the reproduction of the classical verse forms! No, its popularity lies in the sheer beauty of the vocal melody and the exquisite restraint of the piano accompaniment.

The setting breathes peace; it is true, it is the peace of the grave, but there is nothing morbid here; when, in the middle of the song, the singer murmurs the line, 'es ist Anakreons Ruh' (it is Anacreon's resting-place) to a *ppp* in the accompaniment:

the silence is the silence of utter contentment. The performers will pray that the audience will be moved in the same way and will hold their breaths – for nothing should destroy the peace of the scene. The beauty of the description of the poet's happy spring, summer and autumn is somehow deepened by the thought that, in death, he is now protected from winter by the grave-mound of classical times.

All voices can sing this song, but it is ruined when sung above anything louder than *piano*. Although there are a few *crescendi* in the song (cf. on 'das alle Götter mit Leben . . .'), Wolf scatters markings like *sehr zart* (very tenderly) throughout the score. The tempo is *sehr langsam und ruhig* (very slowly and peacefully) – as always the singer will depend on the accompanist to maintain this tempo and yet to allow the music (and the singer) to breathe. The problem is accentuated when the singer is accompanied by an orchestra; perhaps it is in such performances of gentle songs like these that the listener would most appreciate why I point to Wolf's songs as marking the close of the Golden Age of the Lied. A Lied with an orchestral accompaniment – particularly one with such intimate charm as this one – has become something intrinsically different from the domestic 19th century *Klavierlied* – even when these are performed in large 20th century concert-halls in front of several thousand people.

[20] HUGO WOLF

Mignon I: Kennst du das Land . . .?, Do you know the country . . .?
(17 December 1888)

THERE ARE grounds for agreeing with some critics that this is the finest song that Wolf ever wrote, although the adjective 'finest' might require a rather sharper definition. I believe that it is one of his finest songs for the performers, and also for the listeners in the concert hall; the student of the Lied, of the technicalities of setting words to music, might not agree, as we shall see.

In Goethe's novel *Wilhelm Meisters Lehrjahre* (Wilhelm Meister's Apprenticeship Years) published in 1795/96, Wilhelm, the 'hero', who, in the German fashion, is travelling round Europe to gain experience and knowledge of 'Life', meets up with a travelling theatre-company and a group of acrobats. He finds the latter maltreating a thirteen-year-old child called Mignon, and buys her from the acrobats to protect her. It is to this Mignon, 'the most ethereal of Goethe's characters', as a writer on Goethe once called her, that Goethe gives four of his finest poems. She is a mysterious, unworldly character, accompanied throughout by the even stranger figure of the *Harfner* (the Harper), who, at the end of the novel, turns out to be her guilt-laden father – to whom Goethe has likewise given three remarkable poems.

Some knowledge of Mignon's background is essential if one is to make a judgement on the quality of the musical settings of the poems, or, indeed, if one is to attempt to perform them. Some programme notes seem to suggest that Mignon is Wilhelm's mistress, a dark, southern beauty who is seducing him. She is, on the contrary, a little girl, a waif, and any setting and any performance should underline the puzzled naivety of a child who is pathetically grateful to Wilhelm, her benefactor, and, at the same time, confused and home-sick for her native Italy:

Kennst du das Land, wo die Zitronen blühn,	Do you know the country, where the lemon-fruit blossoms,
Im dunkeln Laub die Goldorangen glühn,	In the dark foliage, the golden oranges glow,
Ein sanfter Wind vom blauen Himmel weht,	A gentle breeze blows from the blue sky,
Die Myrte still und hoch der Lorbeer steht?	The myrtle stands silent and the laurel tall?
Kenst du es wohl?	Do you know it?
Dahin, dahin	There, there
Möcht' ich mit dir, o mein Geliebter, ziehn!	is where I want to go with you, my love!

156

Kennst du das Haus, auf Säulen ruht sein Dach,	Do you know the house? The roof rests on pillars,
Es glänzt der Saal, es schimmert das Gemach,	the hall gleams, the rooms shimmer,
Und Marmorbilder stehn und sehn mich an;	and marble statues stand gazing at me;
Was hat man dir, du armes Kind, getan?	What have they done to you, poor child?
Kennst du es wohl?	Do you know it?
Dahin, dahin	There, there
Möcht' ich mit dir, o mein Beschützer, ziehn!	is where I want to go with you, my protector.
	Do you know the mountain and its cloudy path?
Kennst du den Berg und seinen Wolken- steg?	The mule seeks its way in the mist,
Das Maultier sucht im Nebel seinen Weg,	the ancient brood of dragons dwells in caves,
In Höhlen wohnt der Drachen alte Brut,	The cliff plunges down and the waterfall
Es stürzt der Fels und über ihn die Flut;	over it;
Kennst du ihn wohl?	Do you know it?
Dahin, dahin	There, there
geht unser Weg; O Vater, lass uns ziehn!	is our way; oh father, let us go!

In the novel Mignon comes into Wilhelm's room and sings this song to a zither accompaniment: 'She began each verse solemnly, magnificently . . . at the third line, the song became darker and more sombre . . . she expressed the "Kennst du es wohl?" mysteriously and with deliberation . . . And when Wilhelm asked her where she had heard the song, she answered, 'Italy''.

Wolf's setting is of a quite overwhelmingly opulent magnificence; from the mysterious opening chords to the final dramatic, operatic-like D on the 'Flut' of 'und über ihn die Flut' (and the waterfall over it) in verse three, there is a progression of surprise and excitement. The singer needs a big voice and enormous reserves of strength to conquer these long and difficult phrases – and to make the notes tell against the crashing chords of the accompaniment:

And yet – is this not all rather far removed from Goethe's Mignon? She is, after all, thirteen years old, a waif. *This* Mignon of Wolf's is an Italian operatic singer who looks back with longing to her Italian homeland, while Wolf's setting really does not marry with Goethe's verses. Schubert's more modest version is nearer the simplicity that Goethe saw in Mignon – only *his* version is spoiled by those repetitions on 'dahin' which threaten to become comical – at one stage there are eleven! One is left to agree with Schumann who thought that, apart from Beethoven's setting, none could compare with the poem *without* the setting. (There had been quite a few settings even when Schumann wrote that in 1836.)

Wolf's setting is nevertheless always a great favourite in the concert hall, where those who have heard Elisabeth Schwarzkopf sing it, with all her magnificent power, will never forget the experience.

[21] RICHARD STRAUSS

Morgen, Tomorrow (op.27 no.4, 1893–4)

A WRITER once summed up the typical Straussian melody as being 'motionless ecstasy', and this setting is a fine example of the definition.

To begin with the rather curious name of the (German?) poet!: John Henry Mackay was born on 6th February 1864 in Greenock, Scotland, the only son of a Scottish father and a German mother. After the sudden death of the father, Mackay's mother returned to her native Germany with the two-year-old boy, who then, to all intents and purposes, became German – although he always insisted on his name being pronounced with the Scottish stress, i.e. on the second syllable! Just like Hermann Allmers, the poet of *Feldeinsamkeit* (see above, p.150), Mackay too is possibly remembered by the layman for the settings of his poems made by Strauss, *Morgen* and *Heimliche Aufforderung* (Secret Invitation) (op. 27 No. 3.).

The opus 27 songs proved to be Strauss' 'breakthrough' as a song-writer, and the four Lieder (the others are *Ruhe, meine Seele* (Rest, my soul) and *Cäcilie*) have remained among his most popular songs. They were dedicated to his wife, Pauline, on the day of their marriage, 10 September 1894. *Morgen* in particular is an established recital favourite; its placid, almost drugged-like tempo forms an excellent counterbalance in a Strauss recital group to songs like *Ständchen* (q.v.) *Morgen* tells of the hopes of two lovers that the morrow will see them united, lost to the world in each other's eyes:

Und morgen wird die Sonne wieder scheinen,	And tomorrow the sun will shine again,
Und auf dem Wege, den ich gehen werde,	and the path, that I shall take,
Wird uns, die Glücklichen, sie wieder einen	shall unite us, the happy pair, again
Inmitten dieser sonnenatmenden Erde . . .	Amidst this sun-drenched earth . . .

Und zu dem Strand, dem weiten, wogenblauen,	And down to the broad, blue-waved beach
Werden wir still und langsam niedersteigen,	We shall descend quietly, slowly,
Stumm werden wir uns in die Augen schauen,	Speechless, we shall look into each other's eyes,
Und auf uns sinkt des Glückes stummes Schweigen . . .	And a speechless, blissful silence will sink down upon us . . .

The song is 'through-composed' and needs the utmost concentration from singer, accompanist – and audience. (Here again, a misplaced, reckless cough can spoil the effect for all.) Gerald Moore has pointed out more than once that amateur (and some professional) accompanists are often very careless in their work with slow songs, since they seem to believe that all the technical problems are with the singer. Undoubtedly, most of them are, but an insensitive accompanist, one who moves about unnecessarily on his stool while playing these slow songs, or who fails to observe the carefully-planned markings, can ruin the song.

The peculiarity of the song – I think it may be unique – lies, in fact, in the prelude which, sixteen bars long, is almost half the total length of the song. The marking is *Langsam* (slowly) and at the beginning *Sehr getragen* (very broadly), and, above all, *piano*.

This is a great test for the singer too, who must find a comfortable position and a suitable expression during the minute or so that this introduction takes to play. The breathtaking moment is when the vocal part – ever so gradually and ever so naturally – grows out of this introduction:

It is a wonderful moment and it must not be hurried. The great singers sing the whole song absolutely evenly without *crescendi* and without undue stress on any single word. There are many temptations to do so – many singers (even the greatest!) lean just a little too heavily on 'weiten, wogenblauen' and again on the 'stumm' in the penultimate line – but these stresses are unnecessary. Strauss – and Mackay too, for that matter – was trying to present a picture of undisturbed bliss, of Nature in harmony with human love. The music seems to produce that effect, particularly at the conclusion, when, as the words describe the silence settling on the two lovers, Strauss gives us a beautiful descending phrase down to the A sharp and the F of 'Schweigen' (silence) – and then, as the singer lets his breath go and the audience holds *its* breath –

the pianist must allow the music to murmur away into the five bars of *his* silence, 'leaving not a rack behind':

All the various voices have sung this song. The text allows both male and female interpreters, the music sounds well in any register. The singer must however have the requisite firmness of tone and breath control to keep a steady *legato* and to manage Strauss' 'long line'. Everything must be calm here – singer, accompanist and audience. When all play their part, the result is one of the most life-enhancing experiences to be had in the concert-hall.

[22] RICHARD STRAUSS

Freundliche Vision, Friendly vision (op.48 no.1, 1900)

Nicht im Schlafe hab' ich das geträumt,	I did not dream this in my sleep.
Hell am Tage sah ich's schön vor mir.	I saw it quite clearly in the light of day.
Eine Wiese voller Margeriten;	A meadow, full of daisies,
tief ein weisses Haus in grünen Büschen;	A white house, deep down in the green bushes
Götterbilder leuchten aus dem Laube,	Statues of gods gleaming through the foliage;
Und ich geh' mit Einer, die mich lieb hat,	And I am walking with a girl who loves me,
ruhigen Gemütes in die Kühle	Calm in heart, into the coolness
dieses weissen Hauses, in den Frieden,	Of this white house, into the peace,
der voll Schönheit wartet, dass wir kommen.	full of beauty, which awaits our coming.

ALTHOUGH often, indeed usually, sung by women, the poem indicates quite clearly that this is a man walking hand in hand with his girl ('mit Ein*er* . . .' i.e. the feminine dative ending) into some imaginary haven of love and peace. But, it *could* be seen from the point of view of the woman, and the music sounds most beautiful in the upper register, although Strauss was not very enamoured of the tenor voice. His penchant was for sopranos; in his Lieder, one can always hear the music of his operatic heroines, Sophie in *Der Rosenkavalier* or Arabella in the opera of that name, since he was, after all, the only great operatic composer to make a name as a writer of Lieder.

The poem is by Otto Julius Bierbaum, whose *Traum durch die Dämmerung* (Dream in the twilight) was set by Strauss as his opus 29 No.1, and, with *Morgen*, is the third setting of this type: songs to be sung extremely slowly, with a simple but important piano accompaniment, and a long *cantabile* melody. The music evokes wonderfully the tranquil scene – never rising above *piano*, it seems to paint the colours of the environment – the meadow full of white and yellow daisies, the white house, the green bushes. For some critics, this and songs like it are mere 'salon music', pretty trifles written without the honest sincerity of the great Lieder composers. That may be. It is undoubtedly true that Strauss was not a 'natural' song-composer; like Mahler's, many of his bigger songs are over-orchestrated, and need, and eventually received, a full orchestral accompaniment. These are the two major contrasting criticisms of his Lieder. I can only hear a beautiful melody in *Freundliche Vision*, a song which lies gratefully for the voice and which conveys the atmosphere of peace that Bierbaum's poem was seeking to give.

To maintain this atmosphere of perfect peace, the singer has to remember once again the secret of good Lieder singing – the 'sense of long phrases' as it has been called, here *a fortiori*. The song begins with a typical phrase to illustrate this:

and the next line is no less difficult to sing, especially the lovely turn on the word 'sah' which, perhaps fancifully, one might take as the joy of seeing the beautiful scene spread out in front of the pair.

The poem itself is of good quality and competently structured; the very structure presents a composer with a difficult problem: what does one do with that long final section beginning 'Und ich geh' mit Einer . . .' to '. . . dass wir kommen'? Strauss solved the problem in a clever way: he set the whole phrase twice – or, at least, practically the whole phrase. The first time, the phrase is set to what might be called a continuous melody, starting with an ascending phrase which has a touch of expectancy about it:

Und ich geh' mit Ei - ner, die mich lieb hat

Strauss ends on a descending phrase on 'dass wir kommen'. Then he re-thinks the material, as it were, and sets the words as the gentle and spiritual conclusion to the song by subtly altering the melody and the timing to 'Und ich geh' mit Einer . . .' by interjecting pauses which give the impression of a 'stammering lover', overcome by the beauty both of his beloved and of the peace stretched out in front of them:

immer ruhiger

Und ich geh' mit Ei - ner, die mich lieb hat in den

ritard

Frie - den voll Schön - - - - heit!

The effect is magical and allows an ineffable peace to settle on the listener. All words in German which begin with *Sch-* are difficult to pronounce, both in conversation and in singing. '*Schön*heit' has to be given the least ugly stress possible – one way is to take a tiny breath before singing the word and then to sing it out on the breath. Dietrich Fischer-Dieskau's performance on his recording with Gerald Moore (ALP 1487) of January 1956 might serve as a model.

[23] RICHARD STRAUSS

Ständchen, Serenade (op.17 no.2, 1885–6).

LISTING composers in a seemingly chronological order has its grave dangers. The perceptive reader will have noticed that, although Hugo Wolf died in *1903* and Richard Strauss in *1949*, this song, *Ständchen*, arguably one of Strauss' most famous and most popular, was actually written *before* Hugo Wolf's famous 'year of song', 1888, when he composed his Mörike settings. Strauss has been such a dominating figure in 20th century music, mainly because of the importance of his great operas, from *Salome* (1905) to *Capriccio* (1942), that we sometimes forget that he is another representative of what Harold C. Schonberg so memorably called 'Romanticism's long coda'.

Ständchen is one of six settings of poems by Count Adolf Friedrich von Schack; the title is common to many Lieder – one thinks of Schubert's *Ständchen* (a setting of Shakespeare's *Hark, hark, the lark*), Schumann's *Ständchen* (*Komm in die stille Nacht* – Come into the still night), and that of Brahms' *Ständchen* (*Der Mond steht über dem Berge* – The moon hangs over the mountain). The word itself goes back to a 17th century German student's word for a 'song sung underneath a (girl's) window'.

For those who collect records, and have been collecting them for some years, this song will always be associated with the ethereal voice of Elisabeth Schumann, although, in truth, the orchestral accompaniment to her famous version made in January 1927 is not entirely satisfactory, and I agree with Desmond Shawe-Taylor that the recording with Karl Alwin's piano accompaniment (of 14 November 1927) is too hurried to be acceptable either. Strauss was only twenty-one when he wrote the song and he often accompanied Elisabeth Schumann in performances in the early 1920's.

The setting is a complete success, a superb fusion of words and music. There is indeed an 'elfin'-like lightness about the many *arpeggios* in the accompaniment and a buoyancy of spirit about the vocal part which decorates von Schack's pleasant lines:

Mach' auf, mach' auf, doch leise, mein Kind, | Open up, open up, but softly, my child,
um keinen vom Schlummer zu wecken. | so as not to waken anyone,
Kaum murmelt der Bach, kaum zittert im Wind | The brook hardly murmurs, the wind hardly
Ein Blatt an den Büschen und Hecken. | makes the leaves tremble in bush and hedge.
Drum leise, mein Mädchen, dass nichts sich regt, | So softly, my girl, so that nothing stirs
Nur leise die Hand auf die Klinke gelegt. | as your hand lifts up the latch.

163

Mit Tritten, wie Tritte der Elfen so sacht,	With steps as soft as elfin treads,
Um über die Blumen zu hüpfen,	to jump over the flowers.
Flieg leicht hinaus in die Mondscheinnacht,	Come out into the moonlit night,
Zu mir in den Garten zu schlüpfen.	Out to me here in the garden.
Rings schlummern die Blüten am rieselnden Bach	All around, the flowers slumber by the rippling brook,
Und duften im Schlaf, nur die Liebe ist wach.	They scent us as they sleep – only Love is awake.
Sitz nieder, hier dämmert's geheimnisvoll	Sit down, the twilight is dark and mysterious
Unter den Lindenbäumen.	Under the linden trees.
Die Nachtigall uns zu Häupten soll	The nightingale above will
Von uns'ren Küssen träumen,	dream of our kisses,
Und die Rose, wenn sie am Morgen erwacht,	And the rose, when she awakes in the morning,
Hoch glühn von den Wonneschauern der Nacht.	shall glow from the blissful ecstasy of the night.

The first two verses are set strophically to the same melody, although, again, interpretation of the melody must each time vary according to the sentiments of the verse. Verse two describing the girl's 'elfin treads' as she leaps over the garden flowers to join her lover, must have much more 'spring' in the singing than in verse one, where the atmosphere is quieter and more secretive. The genius of the melody is best seen indeed at the end of each verse, in its suitability both for the conspiratorial 'auf die Klinke gelegt' (lifts up the latch) and 'nur die Liebe ist wach' (only Love is awake), a quite different category of statement, yet, when whispered, perfectly allied to the music:

— auf die Klinke ge - legt.

— nur die Lie - be ist wach,

Some writers have felt that the music must have been originally written for verse two since it matches so perfectly the elfin-like steps. That may well be, but it is also a perfect example of how difficult it is to write a melody that matches more than one stanza – more difficult, many believe, than to write a 'complicated' 'through-composed' setting.

(To be absolutely fair here, there *is* a tiny change in bar seven of verse two of the setting, but it is barely noticeable to the listener.)

The music changes dramatically at the beginning of verse three, at the command 'Sitz nieder' (Sit down), set to a downwards-plunging phrase. The *arpeggios* of the rippling accompaniment never cease however – and when the singer repeats the phrase 'hoch glühn' the second time on that never-to-be-forgotten high A sharp:

the piano epilogue hurries on to an exciting conclusion. Elisabeth Schumann liked to tell the story of how, rehearsing *Ständchen* for the first time with the composer, Strauss asked her if she wanted him to play the lovely piano postlude. When she expressed surprise that he should even *ask* such a question, he pointed out that his wife Pauline, also a distinguished soprano, would never allow him to play it, lest it spoil her beautiful last phrase on 'Wonneschauern der Nacht' (the blissful ecstasy of the night)!

Perhaps because of Elisabeth Schumann's close involvement with this song, it is truly difficult for any but the narrowest pedant to imagine anyone other than a high soprano singing it. Dietrich Fischer-Dieskau, among other great singers, has recorded it, and, of course, the text clearly indicates that a *man* is talking to his girl – but so much of the fragile loveliness of the song vanishes in the lower register, that it is one of the few exceptions to my rule about male and female songs!

[24] GUSTAV MAHLER

Ich ging mit Lust durch einen grünen Wald, On a delightful walk through a green forest (1887–90)

FOR THOSE who would like to sing or hear one of Mahler's songs set in the tradition of the German *Volkslied*, there could be no better example than this song taken from the *Gesänge* out of the collection *Lieder und Gesänge aus der Jugendzeit* (not Mahler's own title, by the way). These 'Songs from His Youth' were settings of poems which Mahler found in that seminal collection made by Achim von Arnim and his brother-in-law Clemens von Brentano in the early 1800's and known as *Des Knaben Wunderhorn* (The Youth's Magic Horn) (see p.36 above). Like Brahms with his settings of 'folk-poetry', Mahler was aware that many of these poems were hardly authentic; the important point for him was that they *sounded* authentic, and he set them in this spirit for voice and piano between 1887 and 1890. *Ich ging mit Lust. . .* is in the true *Volkslied* tradition, four regular stanzas with an immediately appealing melody:

It tells the familiar tale of the illicit nocturnal activities of a pair of lovers:

Ich ging mit Lust durch einen grünen Wald,
Ich hört' die Vöglein singen;
Sie sangen so jung, sie sangen so alt,
Die kleinen Waldvögelein im grünen Wald!
Wie gern hört' ich sie singen, ja singen!

On a delightful walk through a green forest
I heard the little birds singing.
They all sang, young ones, old ones,
These little woodland birds in the green forest
How nice to hear them sing, yes, sing.

Nun sing', nun sing', Frau Nachtigall!
Sing' du's bei meinem Feinsliebchen:
'Komm schier, wenn's finster ist,
Wenn niemand auf der Gasse ist,
Dann komm' zu mir,
Herein will ich dich lassen, ja lassen!'

Now sing to me, dear nightingale,
Sing to my beloved,
'Come to me quickly, come quickly, as soon
as it is dark and no one is in the street.
Then come to me,
I'll let you in, yes, let you in!'

Der Tag verging, die Nacht brach an,
Er kam zu Feinsliebchen gegangen,
Er klopft so leis' wohl an den Ring:
'Ei, schläfst du oder wachst, mein Kind?
Ich hab' so lang gestanden!'

Day passed, the night arrived.
He came to his beloved's house.
He knocked so quietly at the door:
'Are you asleep or awake, my child?
I've been standing out here so long!'

Es schaut der Mond durch's Fensterlein
Zum holden, süssen Lieben.
Die Nachtigall sang die ganze Nacht.
Du schlafselig' Mägdelein, nimm dich in Acht!
Wo ist dein Herzliebster geblieben?

The moon shone through the little window
on the innocent, sweet love-making.
The nightingale sang throughout the night.
You sleepy girl, beware,
Where is your beloved?

The charm of the song lies in the rather 'jaunty', cheeky music to which it has been set, and for the German speaker, in the archaic familiar language of the old *Volkslieder* ('Frau Nachtigall', 'Feinsliebchen', 'schier', 'Fensterlein' etc) which is almost impossible to reproduce

166

in translation, since the English language has really no equivalent words to match the feelings aroused in a German-speaker by those words – or by the use of the many diminutives in *-lein* or *-chen*, which do not just mean 'little', but are rather symbolical of the warmth and intimacy of the folk-songs associated with their childhood and school-days. The composer has his tongue firmly in his cheek here – Mahler was not always 'searching his soul' – and the setting relates the little story with good humour and reticence. For the singer, the main problem is, as always with the strophic song, to vary the interpretation of each stanza so as to bring out the progress of the tale. In verse one, he has to adopt a rather jaunty tone to illustrate the young man's walk through the forest alive with bird song. The second verse must be sung more softly, more secretively, as the girl bids the nightingale carry her invitation to her lover. The AABA *Volkslied* setting then gives a different, though related, melody to verse three – the sense demands it too, since this is the intermediate step between the 'invitation' and the 'deed'! The link between the stanzas is however retained by the 'cheeky' little bird-call figure in the accompaniment:

which then leads us back to the original melody for the fourth and last stanza.

What voice would one choose to sing this song? In a sense, the text is 'unisex' – verses one and four are narration, while the 'woman' speaks in verse two and the 'man' in verse three. The soaring phrases in lines two and four lie well for the high or the low voice, too – thus, it is a song for everyone – and could even be sung as a duet, of course!

[25] GUSTAV MAHLER

Um Mitternacht, At midnight (1901–2)

FRIEDRICH RÜCKERT'S poem was set, with four others, 'for voice and orchestra', although singers often choose it for recitals with piano accompaniment only. The Rückert poems, written some eighty years previously, mirror the loneliness of the Romantic soul – indeed Mahler's third song, *Ich bin der Welt abhanden gekommen* (I am lost to the world), has been called the 'quintessential Mahler Lied of farewell and withdrawal from the world' (Charles Osborne). *Um Mitternacht* is in the same vein:

Um Mitternacht	At midnight
hab' ich gewacht	I awoke
Und aufgeblickt zum Himmel;	and looked up to Heaven.
Kein Stern vom Sterngewimmel	None of the stars of the constellation
hat mir gelacht	smiled on me
Um Mitternacht.	at midnight.
Um Mitternacht	At midnight
hab' ich gedacht	my thoughts
hinaus in dunkle Schranken.	went out to the darkest limits;
Es hat kein Lichtgedanken	No ray of thought
mir Trost gebracht	brought me comfort
um Mitternacht.	at midnight.
Um Mitternacht	At midnight
nahm ich in acht	I listened to
die Schläge meines Herzens.	the beating of my heart.
Ein einziger Puls des Schmerzens	One single pulse of pain
war angefacht	was stirred
um Mitternacht.	at midnight.
Um Mitternacht	At midnight
kämpft' ich die Schlacht,	I fought the battle
o Menschheit, deiner Leiden;	of your sorrows, o Mankind,
nicht konnt' ich sie entscheiden	but I could not decide it
mit meiner Macht	with my strength
um Mitternacht.	at midnight.
Um Mitternacht	At midnight
hab' ich die Macht	I gave my powers
in deine Hand gegeben;	up into Your hands:
Herr über Tod und Leben,	Lord over life and death,
du hältst die Wacht	You keep watch
um Mitternacht.	at midnight.

Mahler scored this song for the full woodwind, brass and horns, with timpani, harp and piano – but he stipulated that there should be no strings. (Each of the five songs mentioned above is written for a different composition of instruments, which makes the piano transcriptions a more useful measure of comparison.)

Um Mitternacht is one of the best songs for judging the effect of the move away from the *Klavierlied* to the quasi-symphonic treatment of song-texts by these later 19th century composers. In the orchestral version the music follows the 'thought' of the five verses; the lonely man (*Der Einsame* in German, a term of which Mahler was fond), is keeping watch at midnight, accompanied in the music by an equally lonely oboe d'amore, and the next three verses depict his inner struggle with his sorrow, which the poet then takes to be a Christ-like taking of the burdens of the world on his own shoulders, until, in verse five, he gives the burden over to God. (The song is 'durchkomponiert', in essence, but the little three-note figure in the accompaniment:

m.s.

and the repetition of the four-note figure at the end of each stanza give the song an inner, almost strophic unity.)

The handing-over is apostrophised in the orchestral version by thrilling calls in the brass. The singer (man or woman) has an opportunity to display all the operatic splendour he or she possesses by soaring up to the E on the repetition of the word 'du' at 'du hältst die Wacht' (You keep watch), Man's acknowledgement of God's omnipotence:

169

It is here more than anywhere else in the song that the difference between the orchestral and the piano versions is made apparent – and the listener will make his own decision as to which is preferable. Those whose tastes are more operatic, who are excited by the splendour of an opulent voice supported by and contrasted with majestic brass, will probably choose the orchestral version; those who prefer the more domestic, intimate, chamber-music atmosphere of the early 19th century Lied will find the piano version more appealing! There are excellent recordings of both to be heard, by both male and female singers – and both are worth listening to.

These two examples of Mahler's Lieder-writing represent the two ends of his spectrum. The singer or listener seeking simple Schubert-like Lieder with interesting piano accompaniments will not be disappointed in Mahler – and will be delighted to find the melodies of many of his songs recurring in his symphonies – while those who expect 'something different' from a composer writing as late as 1900 will no doubt turn to the orchestral versions for sounds recognizably of the future.

PART FOUR

Lieder on Record

COLLECTORS of gramophone records will be well aware of the history of that most remarkable invention which has revolutionised the world of music and given to the man and woman in the street the opportunity of hearing, in the comfort of their own home, not only the great musicians of today but also the luminaries of the past, some of whom were dead before the record-collectors were even born.

Serious record-making began in the early years of this century; what had been for the early *aficionados* a rather esoteric hobby, viz. the collecting of those massively heavy shellac records, made between, say 1900 and 1950, has become a possibility for Everyman, since many of these recordings now exist on long-playing transfers. Of course, the warning that Alan Blyth had to give in the introduction to his splendid book *Opera on Record* (Hutchinson 1979) viz. that 'the speed 78 (r.p.m.) seems to have been regarded in a haphazard manner', and that many of the transferred performances are therefore being played at the incorrect speed, and, consequently, are distorting the singer's true timbre, holds good for the Lieder recordings as well.

It is not my intention in this final part to give a full 'discography' of Lieder, but rather to mention some of the outstanding performances on record which have given me such pleasure over many years, and which will also perhaps illustrate some of the remarks made in earlier sections. I am only too well aware of the short life enjoyed by many recordings – they may vanish from the catalogues within a few months of issue – but I have relied on the excellent *Gramophone Classical Catalogue* (issued quarterly by the periodical *The Gramophone*) for some indication of records at present available.

If anyone has been surprised by the regularity with which the name of Dietrich Fischer-Dieskau has appeared in this book, the reason is simply that no artist, past or present, has so dominated any one field of music as this German baritone. In a career which began in 1947, he has studied, performed and recorded more Lieder of more composers (and with more accompanists) than any other singer. But more than that: by

173

general consent, his performances have rarely fallen below the highest standards, and since he stands unique in his chosen profession, many of his recordings have been taken as model, although, of course, not as *definitive* performances, since there are many other great artists who offer fascinating alternative renderings.

[1] THE YEARS 1900 TO 1945

IF WE LIVED in an ideal world, I might say that full enjoyment of this art form, the Lied, depends on a competent knowledge of the German language, an appreciation of developments in music, and, of slightly less importance, some awareness of movements in German literature since, say, 1800. But I have been trying to demonstrate the attraction of Lieder for *all* people – and the main attraction is undoubtedly the proliferation of beautiful melodies. This is, above all, what German songs offer to the listener, and who is to say that this is not the most important aspect of 'Song'?

To be sure, the first and third of the above conditions were certainly not fulfilled in the Anglo-Saxon countries in the early years of this century. And the events leading up to the First World War – and that War itself – did not produce a climate conducive to the support of German-language cultural activities. In the First World War, the music of German composers was often banned, and there was only the short respite of the 20's and early 30's before the Second World War was upon us.

In addition, the German language has never been widely taught in Anglo-Saxon schools; for many, some obvious, reasons, French has remained the first foreign language of most British and American children, which meant that the inhabitants of these countries had not only little general knowledge of German, but also, in consequence, of German 'culture', so that even where the populace was musically cultured, the background knowledge of German literature and, in particular, of German poetry, was lacking. Translations are a help, but only a substitute and sometimes an inaccurate one, not only because of actual *mistakes* in the translation, but also because of the transmission of the wrong 'register', which seems to be less acceptable to modern Anglo-Saxon audiences than does the original German to German speakers, that is, talk of 'bowers', 'maidens', 'flowrets' and 'dewy eves'.

Just before, and naturally too just after the Second World War, the influx of immigrants from Central Europe into the Anglo-Saxon countries brought a wealth of cultured German speakers who had been brought up on the great Lieder singers of the past. Their influence on the music scene in these countries was immense; their presence in the great musical centres in the United States, in London, at Glyndebourne and the Edinburgh Festival in Britain, ensured the preservation and (in some cases) the attainment of the highest musical standards. How much the growth of interest in the German *Kunstlied* is due to them is obviously impossible to assess, but the number of voices speaking German, or English with a recognizable German or Austrian accent, at the Edinburgh Festival or in London's Royal Festival Hall, is always striking. They provided the main clientèle for recitals and records before and after the Second World War.

It is probably true to say that the pre-war Lieder recital which had been known to the people that I have just been describing was a rather esoteric event; dress was usually formal, and the singer, if a lady, would normally be addressed as 'Madame Gerhardt' or 'Madame Schumann'. Pre-war BBC recitals were often introduced in hushed and reverent tones by announcers who were themselves often dressed in black tie and dinner jacket! The pronunciation of the titles of the Lieder was, alas, not so distinguished and must have raised many a smile among the members of the German-speaking community – as did the *gaffe* of a post-war BBC announcer who told us that 'Elisabeth Schwarzkopf had just sung Schubert's Wanderers Na*ck*tlied', i.e. The Wanderer's *Naked* Song instead of the Wanderer's Night Song (= Na*ch*tlied)! (It was the same singer who had had to suffer an early Edinburgh Festival headline 'Schwarzkopf sings leider' – which means 'Schwarzkopf sings *unfortunately*'!)

The great names of the pre-Second World War era were possibly: Elena Gerhardt, Elisabeth Schumann, Lotte Lehmann, Heinrich Schlusnus, Herbert Janssen and Gerhard Hüsch – but there were many others, of course – Tiana Lemnitz, Meta Seinmeyer, Frida Leider, and until he 'changed course', Richard Tauber. But recordings of the first six names would be fairly representative, not only of the standards of these years, but also of the Lieder-singing traditions of the age. Theirs are certainly the records which have given me the most pleasure over many years.

Nevertheless it is extremely difficult to draw valid comparisons between the singers of today and those of yesterday. So many circumstances have changed; recording techniques of the years 1900–1926, the so-called 'acoustic recordings', as well as those of 1926–1950, the era of 'electrical recordings', look and sound so primitive beside those of our moon-landing age; demands on present-day singers are now so enormous – no longer could a singer afford the luxury of a ship's cruise from Australia to sing in London; nowadays, a singer must rise early the morning after a concert in New York to fly off to appear the next evening, or at most the evening after, at a recital in Munich or London.

And do these pre-war records tell us the 'truth' about the *singer*? They may well tell us something about the *voice* – but what about the personality? Desmond Shawe-Taylor, the British music critic, wrote an essay at the end of Elena Gerhardt's memoirs *Recital* (op.cit.), in which he suggested that her recordings of twelve Lieder from Schubert's *Winterreise* (accompanied by Coenraad Valentyn Bos and issued for the Schubert Anniversary Year 1928) would convey to young listeners only 'something of the excitement' which he had experienced at her *Winterreise* recitals, which surpassed anything that he had heard before – or since.

MY PURPOSE here is not to draw comparisons, but to suggest a few recordings which are well worth seeking out and which might help to support some of my earlier remarks.

Elena Gerhardt's legacy can be sampled on a record *Gerhardt and Nikisch Recital* (Delta TQD 3024), where we can hear those Lieder recorded with the famous conductor Arthur Nikisch in 1907 and 1911, when she was twenty-four and twenty-eight respectively. They give some idea of the majesty of her mezzo-soprano voice and the depth of her interpretations. Like so many singers of the period – in opera and in Lieder – she had her own way with *tempi* and some of the songs *do* drag – Schubert's *An die Musik* (To music) would be a case in point – but others (*Du bist die Ruh*) are quite simply magnificent. The record ends with an out-of-context performance of *Ich grolle nicht* (No.7 of Schumann's *Dichterliebe*) which is certainly exciting, if rather typical of a cavalier attitude to the cycles no longer allowed or appreciated nowadays. Only if one has no feeling for the poetic values of these great cycles could one appreciate a song torn out of musical and literary context; few great pianists would think of playing one movement of a three-movement piano sonata at a recital, surely?

Her *Winterreise* records mentioned above (D1262–1264 and E460), where she is accompanied by Coenraad V. Bos, are also very interesting, although they too lose for being out of context. My favourite is D1263 (No.6, *Wasserflut* and No.11, *Frühlingstraum*) which must give the true flavour of her greatness. She caresses the words in the latter song in the true fashion of a great interpreter.

What I do not like, however, is her treatment of Schubert's *Erlkönig*, backed by Schumann's *Der Nussbaum* on the 1923 Vocalion A-0215 and accompanied by Ivor Newton. She fails completely to differentiate the four voices (see p.87) and consequently loses the drama of the song.

Her Wolf recordings are also famous and are now to be found again on the Hugo Wolf Society's collection of seven records, the first of which is devoted to Elena Gerhardt. (These were re-issued in March 1981 on RLS 759.) The recordings were made between 1931 and 1938 and give as splendid a measure as one could have of the standard of Lieder singing between the wars. (Elena Gerhardt died in 1961 and is remembered with affection, above all in London, which was her home from 1934.)

All record collectors owe a great debt to the enlightened policy of those record companies who take the trouble to re-issue these treasures of the past. In September 1982, the hearts of all Schubertians were gladdened by the appearance of a box entitled *Schubert Lieder on Record, 1898–1952* (RLS 760), an anthology of recordings by sixty-four artists of the past and present. The recordings range from the very first recorded performance of a Schubert Lied – the London soprano Edith Clegg singing (a rather rushed) *Ave Maria* (D839) with a 'piano accompaniment', recorded in Maiden Lane, London, by the legendary Fred Gaisberg on 11 October 1898 – up to Kirsten Flagstad's magisterial, if unidiomatic recordings with Gerald Moore in 1952. There are eight records in the box.

One will have to live some time with the records, but my early judgement was that these recordings confirmed Alan Blyth's warning above (p.173). Not only has one to remember the uncertainty of the recording speed, but also that the sheer unfamiliarity with the technique of recording would make many great artists hurry over their interpretation for fear of transgressing the 12-inch format – even to the extent of omitting – conveniently or inadvertently – words, lines and verses of the Lieder.

I found the careless intonation of many of the artists rather disturbing – many simply 'sing' the words – but many of these artists were towards the end of their musical careers, in some cases towards the end of their lives, when recording began – like Gustav Walter, born in Bohemia in 1834, who had studied with Schubert's Michael Vogl in Prague! Yet, as with the Hugo Wolf anthology, this is a record of 'what was', and the true lover of the Lied now has the opportunity to hear what the older critics are constantly championing. The performances range from the 'exquisite' (such as Lotte Schöne's 1929 *Der Hirt auf dem Felsen* or Karl Erb's *An die Laute* of 1937), through the 'so-so' to the 'frankly appalling' (Hans Duhan's *Pause* from *Die schöne Müllerin*). Listening carefully to the earliest artists, those who recorded before, say, 1914, one has the feeling that only the purblind would claim that a recording like Lilli Lehmann's *Erlkönig*, recorded in 1906 when the singer was (only) 58, is in any way 'artistic'; the tone is poor, the breathing imperfect and the melodrama embarrassing.*

Elisabeth Schumann (1885–1952), a high soprano easily contrasted with Gerhardt's more dramatic mezzo-soprano, was a singer whose stage charm made an audience overlook her many vocal imperfections. Her vitality and sense of fun in a Lieder recital covered up the annoyance felt at her exaggerated 'scoops' and sometimes mere 'vocalising' on the higher notes; these are, alas, very obvious in recordings. The best examples of her art as a Lieder-singer are on the records in the HMV *Great Recordings of the Century* series (COLH 102, 154 and 130/131), Lieder by Strauss and Wolf, and also in the EMI *Golden Voice* series (No.15, HQM 1187), on which she sings *inter alia* Schubert's *Der Hirt auf dem Felsen* (D965), for me, the most magical of all her performances. The way in which she phrases the reprise of the line *Der Frühling will kommen* (Spring is coming) has already been mentioned – and has never been surpassed. (Strauss' *Ständchen*, which she recorded on COLH 102, was mentioned above, too (see p.000).

Lotte Lehmann (1888–1976) was a more majestic figure than the diminutive Elisabeth Schumann, although she too could be charming in opera. The difference between them is perfectly summed up by the different rôles that they played in Strauss operas – where Schumann was the soubrette, Lehmann was one of the most distinguished *Feld-marschallins*. As a Lieder singer she had all the qualities of greatness, and even seemed to combine the insouciance and grace of a Schumann with the dramatic power and grandeur of a Gerhardt. Her career lasted a full forty years (1910–1951), and she died as late as 1976, aged eighty-eight. An interesting example of her art can be heard on the HMV Treasury record *The Grand Tradition* (HLM 7026) where she sings Schumann's *Aufträge* (Messages) with a terrible violin and piano accompaniment, a pre-1928 recording. A better recording to look out for is of two Strauss songs, *Ständchen* and *Traum durch die Dämmerung* (Dream through the twilight) (Odeon RO 20096, a 10-inch record), recorded at 80 r.p.m. The second Lied is beautifully floated and gives some idea of the highest pre-Second World War standards. The *Ständchen* is more 'operatic' than Elisabeth Schumann's and taken more slowly, which means that the final high A sharp lacks the ecstasy of the lighter and more vital voice.

The two most famous German male singers of the pre-war period were the baritones *Heinrich Schlusnus* and *Herbert Janssen*, in some ways the complement to the Fischer-Dieskau/Prey duo of today. *Heinrich*

* In January, 1984, HMV released *Brahms and Schumann: Historical recordings of Lieder* (1901–1952) (8 records) RLS 1547003

Schlusnus (1888–1952) had a very beautiful voice, capable of both heroic and lyrical singing; his art is preserved on many collections, *inter alia* on a German series *Heinrich Schlusnus* (*Grosse Stimmen des Jahrhunderts*) (Great Voices of the Century), on Europa Exquisit 1230, where, particularly in those Lieder recorded in his later years, the problems of intonation which always plagued him show up more clearly – in Schubert's *Über allen Gipfeln*, for example. The DGG selection (LPEM 19265) has a lovely performance of Liszt's *Es muss ein Wunderbares sein* which displays the beautiful lyrical quality of his baritone voice.

Herbert Janssen (1895–1965) was a much more versatile singer than Schlusnus and had a great career in opera, particularly at Covent Garden. He, too, had problems of intonation. Many of his best recordings are of operatic arias; for me, his finest were *Wie aus der Ferne* from Act II of Wagner's *Der fliegende Holländer* and those from the 1930 Bayreuth season. In Lieder, my favourite recording is of Brahms' *Wie bist du, meine Königin*, accompanied by Gerald Moore (DB 3941), which makes such an interesting comparison with versions from present-day singers and accompanists. Although I find his tone much less appealing than some of the present-day baritones, he has a wonderful way with words, particularly with that magical word 'wonnevoll' (blissful) at the very end of the song. Nevertheless, I find his artistry at its greatest in that Hugo Wolf collection mentioned above, on which he sings the Goethe Harper's songs from *Wilhelm Meister* (I–III), on the second record of the seven. Accompanied by Coenraad V. Bos, his artistic phrasing is outstanding – as it is on the seventh and last record where he sings four late songs of Wolf, including the very beautiful and very rarely recorded *Keine gleicht von allen Schönen*, a translation of Byron's *There be none of Beauty's daughters*. It is a little-known song, but Janssen's performance, with a wonderful *legato*, could hardly be bettered and makes one long to hear the song more often in the concert-hall.

The last of this small group of pre-Second World War singers, *Gerhard Hüsch* was also, like the first two male artists mentioned, a distinguished operatic baritone – a fine Papageno, for example – and who, like them, used a great deal of his histrionic talent in the interpretation of Lieder – some think a little too much and too often. Hüsch's many records are a most valuable and indispensable contribution to the repertoire of recorded Lieder – my favourite performance remains the warm and lyrical recording of Beethoven's *An die ferne Geliebte* (originally on DB 4496–4497). Hüsch's is an exciting performance, beautifully enunciated, and if one misses the significant pointing of words and phrases that one has come to expect from post-war singers, then we are certain that some readers and listeners will feel that that is no great loss! For a big voice,

Hüsch's could demonstrate a remarkable smiling quality which he also displayed in a BBC interview on his 80th birthday in 1981.

[2] THE YEARS 1945 TO THE
PRESENT DAY

IT MUST be again stressed that the singers mentioned earlier were not, of course, the only, nor indeed necessarily 'the best', of the pre-1945 period; they happened to be my own particular favourites but I would hazard the guess that they would figure among the 'Top Ten' of most people's choices. With the enormous increase in the numbers of people interested in classical music, mainly because of their experiences gained in the War – men who had served in Italy, for example, and who had had first-hand experience of Italian opera in Milan and Rome, or who had been in Germany during the re-establishment of German musical life after 1945–1949 – and in the numbers of recordings available since the invention of the Long Playing record, it has become almost impossible to keep track of, or even sample, the riches of this period. The aim of this section is to give *some* guidance to the reader seeking to build up a collection of Lieder recordings by mentioning some of the most distinguished and popular performers and their work.

At the head of a distinguished company would surely stand the name of *Dietrich Fischer-Dieskau*, who was born in Berlin in 1925. It would be impracticable, if not impossible, to mention Fischer-Dieskau's finest recordings. Suffice perhaps to say that, with his fine, warm, lyrical baritone voice, the intensity of his deeply thought-out interpretations, his insistence on singing *what the composer wrote* and, last but not least, and especially for the foreign listener, the clarity and purity of his diction, Fischer-Dieskau has come to be regarded as the model by which other singers have been measured over the last thirty years or so.

As has been mentioned, he has recorded almost everything in the Lied repertoire – boxes of the Lieder of Haydn, Mozart, Schumann, Brahms, Mendelssohn, Loewe, Liszt, Mahler and Strauss – but I know that he would like to think that his 'testament' would be the twenty-nine L.P.'s of those Lieder of Franz Schubert which he felt were most suited to the male voice and singer. These Deutsche Grammophon recordings (Vol.1: 2720 006, Vol.2: 2720 022 and Vol.3: 2720 059), over five hundred

Lieder in all, accompanied by the indefatigable Gerald Moore, then approaching seventy, give us an unparalleled opportunity to admire and appreciate Schubert's (and Fischer-Dieskau's) genius. From the early songs of 1814 to the great *Winterreise* of 1828, there is set out in front of us a map of Schubertiana; to live with these records is to realise what treasures the Lied-form has to offer.

For those whose budget will hardly run to the outlay required for twenty-nine L.P.'s, I suggest one record of Fischer-Dieskau which would serve as a substitute until the collector can afford what he or she one day *must* buy! – that would be a recording of Schubert's Goethe Lieder where, accompanied by Gerald Moore (on DG 2530 229), Fischer-Dieskau sings fifteen beautiful examples of the magical synthesis of word and music that is Goethe and Schubert, including wonderful performances of *Heidenröslein* and, of course, *Erlkönig*.

Dietrich Fischer-Dieskau's appearances all over the world – America, Europe, Israel and Japan – and particularly at the Edinburgh Festival, gave a great impetus to the popularity of the Lieder recital, but it would be grossly unfair to suggest that he and he alone was responsible. What he *did* do was to act as an 'ambassador' for the new Germany which had been created out of the physical and moral ruins of Hitler's Third Reich, and to remind those who had fought against that monstrosity that Germany had also brought good and beauty into the world.*

One of the finest singers who had also helped Federal Germany to bridge that gap between the pre-war and the post-war periods was the soprano *Elisabeth Schwarzkopf*. Born in 1915, she had made a name in opera shortly before the War, and, after her marriage to the dynamic British impresario Walter Legge – the man who was behind the pre-war Hugo Wolf Society's recordings already mentioned – she contributed greatly to the spread of popularity of the Lied, particularly in Britain. Schwarzkopf's voice and stage presence radiated a rare distinction and beauty; there were some critics who found her too 'coy' and 'pert', particularly in those sometimes embarrassing 'little girl' songs of Wolf, and, to a lesser extent, of Schubert, but to listen to those 1951 recordings of Wolf Lieder recorded at the Salzburg Festival with the great conductor Wilhelm Furtwängler as accompanist, and now available on Discocorp 1G1–382, is to experience Lieder singing at its most radiant. She too has recorded a vast number of Lieder by all the famous composers – one might mention her Mozart Lieder (on ASD 3858) accompanied by Walter

---

* For the reader who is interested in the career of Dietrich Fischer-Dieskau, and in his recordings, there is a full discography in my book *Dietrich Fischer-Dieskau, Mastersinger*: (Oswald Wolff, London/Holmes and Meier, New York, 1981).

Gieseking, and a superb Wolf record (SLS 197), accompanied by Gerald Moore, which contains the winsome *Epiphanias*. She and Fischer-Dieskau with Gerald Moore recorded a fine version of Wolf's *Italienisches Liederbuch* in 1969 (on HMV Angel San 210–211), which was very highly praised and is well worth looking out for. At her best, Schwarzkopf has no equal among the post-war group of soprano Lieder singers and, like Dietrich Fischer-Dieskau, she became a model for the new generation of artists.

Supreme among the post-war singers in Great Britain is *Dame Janet Baker*, born in 1933. A mezzo-soprano with an astounding range, Janet Baker has built up an enormous reputation as the leading British Lieder singer; she has conquered audiences in opera and oratorio as well and has gained *entrée* into the world of Lieder as few British singers have managed to do – she is as popular and as accepted in Munich as in Manchester.

If I had to choose only one record to illustrate Dame Janet's talents as a Lieder singer it would have to be – if this does not sound too Irish! – the two-record set *A Schubert Evening* (1971), an 'enchanted evening' indeed, on which she is accompanied by her great friend Gerald Moore (EMI SLS 812). The set is a constant delight, particularly their riveting perform-ance of Schubert's *Gretchen am Spinnrade*, one of the finest on record. Of particular interest too are the rarely-performed songs from Sir Walter Scott's *Lady of the Lake* (*Ellens Gesänge I, II* and *III* – the last, the famous *Ave Maria* – D 837–839), and her beautiful version of *Die junge Nonne* (D828), where her skill as an actress is combined with her unmatched vocal technique to present a gripping scena.

But Janet Baker has contributed much more than Schubert Lieder in her promotion of Lieder recitals in Britain and elsewhere. The perform-ance of Liszt's songs (ASD 3908), with Geoffrey Parsons at the piano, complemented Fischer-Dieskau's recordings with Daniel Barenboim, while her *Frauenliebe und -leben*, recorded with Martin Isepp on SAGA 5277, must be one of the most enjoyable that we have. Dame Janet has a thrilling voice which she can pare down to the finest *pianissimo*; although I find a woman's personality and voice generally unsuited to Mahler's *Lieder eines fahrenden Gesellen*, Janet Baker's enunciation of that heart-rending final section 'Auf der Strasse steht ein Lindenbaum' (A linden tree stands by the roadside) is extremely moving. (She is accompanied by the Hallé Orchestra conducted by Sir John Barbirolli on ASD 2338.)

When I was writing my book on Dietrich Fischer-Dieskau, Dame Janet wrote to say how fortunate all singers were 'to be working in his time'; I am sure that many young singers would wish that remark to apply to her own massive contribution to vocal music of the 20th century.

A good-natured witticism current in the early post-war years was: 'Has Benjamin Britten over-written? Not for the ears of Peter Pears'! The duo Pears-Britten also made an enormous contribution to popularising the Lied during the period 1950–1975. *Sir Peter Pears* had one of the most distinctive tenor voices of his time – a voice which was certainly not to everybody's liking, with its faint memories of the English choir-boy's 'hoot', but, at its best, possessed of a rare, haunting quality. In his book on Schubert, Dietrich Fischer-Dieskau makes especial mention of the Pears-Britten recording of Schubert's *Winterreise* in the original tenor keys; of all the tenor versions, Pears' has certainly led the field. The mournful, at times, almost wailing, timbre seems to be exactly right for Müller's sorrowing verses and Schubert's tragic music, while Britten never played better than when playing for Pears. Their *Winterreise* is on three sides and the fourth side is taken up with Schumann's *Dichterliebe*; the record (SET 270–1) is a wonderful tribute to their artistry and to English Lieder singing. Sir Peter's German (like Dame Janet Baker's too) is almost 'akzentfrei', free of English accent, which allows them to sing the music as it was intended to be sung – by which I mean that the notes match the vowels! The examples set by these superb artists were eagerly followed by younger British singers like Ian Partridge, Benjamin Luxon, Felicity Lott and many others.

I HAVE discussed in detail only a few of the many Lieder singers who have made their name in the post-war years and have given so much pleasure in the concert hall and on record. Many people will be dismayed that their own favourites have been omitted: Victoria de los Angeles, Kathleen Ferrier, Elly Ameling, Christa Ludwig, Peter Schreier, Hans Hotter, Gérard Souzay, Hermann Prey – and many others, proof, if proof were demanded, of the 'strength-in-depth' that exists nowadays in Lieder singing. It would be idle to pretend however that Lieder recitals will ever have the popular appeal of operatic evenings with their wealth of colour and pageantry, with tenors hitting those exciting 'High C's', and sopranos going mad in cabaletta form! The Lieder recital is a much less exhibitionist affair, but, to my mind, all the more dramatic for that.

This book has attempted to show the enormous attraction of the world of the Lied, a world that *can* be explained if the seeker will equip him- or herself with a few basic items for the exploration: some knowledge of the German language – if only the pronunciation! – some knowledge of the background to the poem, some insight into the problems of the composer who set the poem to music. Lieder evenings are meant to be enjoyed, and it is difficult to enjoy what is not understood. That Lieder evenings can also be *fun* has been amply demonstrated time and time again by that extraordinary group formed by the enthusiasm of Gerald Moore, *The Songmakers' Almanac*. The original group, Felicity Lott (soprano), Ann Murray (mezzo-soprano), Anthony Rolfe-Johnson (tenor), Richard Jackson (baritone), and Graham Johnson (piano), have carved a niche for themselves in the English music world by presenting unified evenings of Lieder which when introduced, sometimes wittily, sometimes facetiously, lose a great deal of their strangeness and appear to the audience as what they really are: simple songs composed for domestic enjoyment. Once entered into, this is a world never to be left.

APPENDICES

APPENDIX 1

TWO TYPICAL LIEDER RECITAL PROGRAMMES

For Soprano

W. A. Mozart	Abendempfindung (K 523)
	Das Veilchen (K 476)
	Warnung (K 433)
Franz Schubert	Gretchen am Spinnrade (D 118)
	An die Musik (D 547)
	An Sylvia (D 891)
Robert Schumann	Der Nussbaum (op. 25 no. 3)
	Die Kartenlegerin (op. 31 no. 2)
Johannes Brahms	Vergebliches Ständchen (op. 84 no. 4)

INTERVAL

Robert Schumann	Die Lotosblume (op. 25 no. 7)
	Meine Liebe ist grün (op. 63 no. 5)
Johannes Brahms	Feldeinsamkeit (op. 86 no. 2)
Richard Strauss	Ruhe, meine Seele (op. 27 no. 1)
	Freundliche Vision (op. 48 no. 1)
	Hat gesagt, bleibt's nicht dabei (op. 36 no. 3)
Hugo Wolf	Philine
	Das verlassene Mägdlein
	Ich hab' in Penna einen Liebsten wohnen

For Baritone

FRANZ SCHUBERT
1. *Six Lieder from 'Schwanengesang' (D 957)*
   To poems by Heinrich Heine
   No. 8   Der Atlas
   No. 9   Ihr Bild
   No. 10   Das Fischermädchen
   No. 11   Die Stadt
   No. 12   Am Meer
   No. 13   Der Doppelgänger

2.

Der Wanderer (D 493)
Über Wildemann (D 884)
Das Zügenglöcklein (D 871)
Der Strom (D 565)
Memnon (D 541)
Der Einsame (D 800)

INTERVAL

3. *Seven Lieder to poems by Johann Wolfgang von Goethe*
   An den Mond (D 296)
   Geheimes (D 719)
   Erster Verlust (D 226)
   An Schwager Kronos (D 369)
   Meeres Stille (D 216)
   Prometheus (D 674)
   Der Musensohn (D 764)

187

APPENDIX 2

BIBLIOGRAPHY

Some Books on the German Lied

BARFORD, PHILIP: *Mahler: Symphonies and Songs* (BBC Music Guides, 1970)

BELL, A. CRAIG: *The Lieder of Brahms* (Barley, The Grian-Aig Press, 1979)

BROWN, MAURICE: *Schubert's Songs* (BBC Music Guides, 1967)

CAPELL, RICHARD: *Schubert's Songs* (Macmillan, Duckworth, 1928, revised by Martin Cooper, 1957)

CARNER, MOSCO: *Hugo Wolf's Songs* (BBC Music Guides, new edn., 1982)

DESMOND, ASTRA: *Schumann's Songs* (BBC Music Guides, 1972)

FISCHER-DIESKAU, DIETRICH: *Schubert: A Biographical Study of His Songs* (translated by Kenneth S. Whitton; Cassell, 1976; Knopf, USA, 1977) – *The Fischer-Dieskau Book of Lieder* (translated by George Bird and Richard Stokes; Gollancz/Pan Books, 1976)

GÁL, HANS: *Johannes Brahms* (translated by Joseph Stein; Weidenfeld and Nicholson, 1963)

GERHARDT, ELENA: *Recital* (Methuen, 1953)

LEHMANN, LOTTE: *Eighteen Song-Cycles* (Cassell, 1971)

MOORE, GERALD: *Singer and Accompanist* (Methuen, 1953, new edn., Hamish Hamilton, 1982) – *The Schubert Song-Cycles* (Hamish Hamilton, 1975) – *Poet's Love: The Songs and Cycles of Schumann* (Hamish Hamilton, 1981)

PLUNKET GREENE, HARRY: *Interpretation in Song* (Macmillan, 1913)

PORTER, ERNEST: *Schubert's Song Technique* (Dobson, 1961)

PRAWER, SIEGBERT: *The Penguin Book of Lieder* (Penguin, 1964)

SAMS, ERIC: *The Songs of Robert Schumann* (Methuen, 1969) – *Brahms' Songs* (BBC Music Guides) (1972) – *The Songs of Hugo Wolf* (1961)

SCHIØTZ, AKSEL: *The Singer and His Art* (Hamish Hamilton, 1970)

STEIN, JACK: *Poem and Music in the German Lied* (Harvard University Press, 1971)

INDEX OF TITLES

Books, Lieder, operas, records, poems etc.

199

201

Index of Titles